Foundation Coldfusion for Flash

Fiaz Khan
Bryan Mahoney

friendsof

DESIGNER TO DESIGNER™

Foundation Coldfusion
for Flash

© 2001 friends of ED

Trademark Acknowledgements

friends of ED has endeavored to provide trademark information about all the companies and products mentioned in this book by the appropriate use of capitals. However, friends of ED cannot guarantee the accuracy of this information.

Published by friends of ED

30 Lincoln Road, Olton, Birmingham.
B27 6PA. UK.
Printed in USA

ISBN 1-903450-40-3

Foundation Coldfusion for Flash

Credits

Authors	Fiaz Khan, Bryan Mahoney
Additional Material	Danny Bishop, Jon Bounds, Dan Britton, Paul Doyle
Content Architect	Keith Small
Editors	John Bounds, Dan Britton, Andy Corsham, Adam Dutton, Keith Small
Graphic Editors	Tom Bartlett, William Fallon, Katy Freer, Deb Murray, David Spurgeon
Production Manager	Tom Bartlett
Technical Reviewers	Danny Bishop, Gahlord Dewald, Shiela Farrell, Fiaz Khan, Vicki Loader, Phil Sherry
Index	Simon Collins
Cover Design	Katy Freer
Proof Readers	Jon Bounds, Dan Britton, Simon Collins, Libby Hayward, Richard O'Donnell, Mel Orgee, Lumbotharan Thevathasan, Gavin Wray
Team Leader	Mel Orgee

Fiaz Khan

Having gained a degree in Chemistry then thrown onto the job market I found myself being offered very exciting career opportunities,

"like cement testing around the UK (true story).. :("

Then I took a career turn and studied for an MSC in real time systems. Now... several years later, I have experience in back end web site development using languages such as ColdFusion, ASP and PHP with various other technologies / databases. Not only developing back-end systems but front-end websites in different client side languages for many blue chip companies.

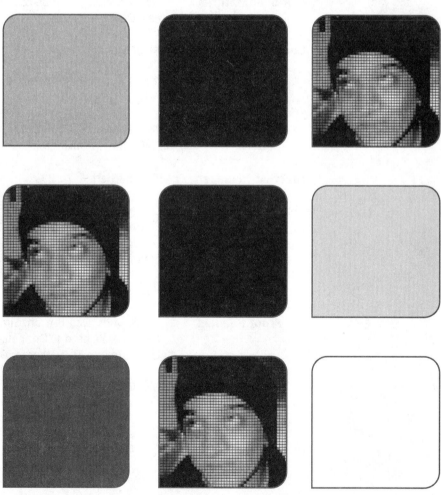

Bryan Mahoney   www.GoDynamo.com

Having graduated from McGill University in Montreal, Canada, where he majored in finance and entrepreneurship major,

Bryan promptly founded Dynamo e-Media Inc. with fellow McGill graduate Alex Nemeroff, and turned his focus to developing dynamic and innovative web applications. Today, the Dynamo team continues to experiment with Flash's ability to interact with server-side scripting languages like ColdFusion.

Table of Contents

Table of Contents

Table of Contents

▶▶|

Introduction

Welcome to Foundation ColdFusion for Flash

"Data, we've got lots of it and we want it on the web".

That's a cry that you, as a web designer constantly hear, and that's OK, but then you're asked to "make this data-driven web site look cool, exciting, whizzy and dynamic". Words not easily associated with data; and on top of all that, the data on the web page has to update as soon as the database changes, not when the Webmaster has time to update the HTML page.

So how can we make it happen? One solution is available using a combination of Macromedia products, **ColdFusion & Flash.** Flash you already know but ColdFusion?

ColdFusion is one of those **middleware** technologies called a **web application server** that sit between the client PC and the web server doing nothing until a ColdFusion page request comes its way, but when called into action it carries out its task quickly and efficiently, so much so that you'll hardly know it's there.

Why have it then you may ask? Remember earlier when we are asked to design a site that displayed the data dynamically, that's exactly what ColdFusion does best: talking to databases via ODBC, pulling out the latest data, and displaying it, and where necessary putting data back.

With its own tag-based programming language CFML (ColdFusion Markup Language) creating ColdFusion pages can be quick and easy, or complex depending on how much you like to get your hands dirty with code, or not, and is certainly much more accessible than other languages like PHP or ASP.

How does Flash fit in? Fantastically well, as you'll see. The ability of Flash to deal with variables makes it perfect for passing data to and from the database via ColdFusion, allowing you to create web sites that are functional yet funky.

At friends of ED we realise that designers are always looking out for ideas and solutions that will give their web sites maximum impact so, here we offer ColdFusion for the solution and Flash for the ideas.

▶

The aim of this book

This book is designed to:

- Give you a foundation in ColdFusion programming with CFML.

- Take you step-by-step through the techniques needed to build dynamic web applications.

- Introduce you to databases, and SQL, at least enough to enable you to use then in ColdFusion applications.

Throughout the book you will find examples of CFML code, and an appendix with descriptions of the ColdFusion tags used in this book.

By the end of the book you will have built a Flash Forum like the one below, as part of a case study.

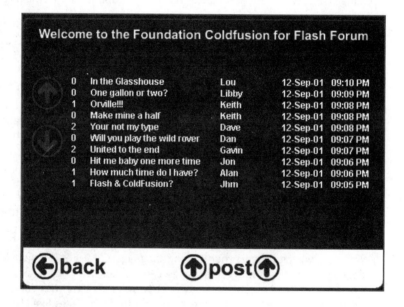

So where's the ColdFusion? Exactly where it should be, out of sight of course.

No Macs

Unfortunately Macs are not able to run any of the ColdFusion programs.

ColdFusion Server will only run on Windows NT/2000 or Unix/Linux platforms, ColdFusion Studio only runs on Windows 95/98/2000

What you'll need to know

You should, ideally:

- Know your way around Windows and be comfortable with creating folders, renaming files and so on.

- You will have read Foundation Flash 5 or another basic Flash tutorial.

- Have some HTML experience.

Conventions

We've tried to keep this book as clear and easy to follow as possible, so we've only used a few layout styles:

- When you come across an important word or phrase, it will be in **bold** type.

- We'll use a different font to emphasize phrases that appear on the screen, code and filenames.

- Menu commands are written in the form Menu > Sub-menu > Sub-menu.

- When there's some information we think is really important, we'll highlight it like this:

> *This is very important stuff - don't skip it!*

- Worked exercises are laid out like this:

1. Open up Studio

2. Save your file as spencer.asp

    and so on.

- When the code we're showing you is too long to fit onto one line, we've used a code continuation character like this ➥ to show you that the code is still on the same line in Studio. If you see an ➥, don't go hitting that enter key.

- All CFML and HTML code is lowercase with uppercase used for some variable names and all SQL commands

- ColdFusion tags are enclosed in angle braces like so `<cfoutput>`

Download Files

We've included all source files and the fully completed files for every exercise for you to download chapter by chapter from friendsofed.com . Do whatever you like to them, but when things go wrong with your version, take advantage of the potential to compare your file with the finished file before giving up – it often helps.

Trial versions of ColdFusion Server 5 & ColdFusion Studio 4.5 are available from the Macromedia download site at www.macromedia.com/downloads

MDAC (Microsoft Data Access Components) contains all of Microsoft's software components for database access; it's a collection of little programs that tell your computer how to connect to all kinds of databases. As long as you have the latest release they'll look after themselves, so it's worth downloading the current version from: www.microsoft.com/data/download.

Support:

If you have any questions about the book or about friends of ED, check out our web site www.friendsofed.com. There's a range of contact addresses there, or you can just use feedback@friendsofed.com.

There's a host of other features on the site: interviews with top designers, samples from our other books, and a message board where you can post your own questions, discussions and answers, or just take a back seat and look at what other designers are talking about. If you have any comments or problems, please write to us - we'd love to hear from you.

1 About ColdFusion

What We'll Cover in this Chapter

- *The structure of ColdFusion and what it can do for our applications,*

- *Why ColdFusion is ideal for intergrating with your Flash movies*

- *Server-side technologies and how they're used on the Internet*

- *The basics of CFML the ColdFusion tag-based language*

Some anecdotal bits & pieces, to flesh out this multi-dimensional technology:

ColdFusion

ColdFusion is a sly old animal. It lived in the shadows for some time, was used by hard-core CF evangelists and was softly promoted by Allaire, the owners up until this year. Before we knew it, it was a mainstream web scripting language with a large following, a GUI (Graphical User Interface) design environment, and a rugged multi-platform web server. All in one!

Web Scripting Language? seb server? What does it all mean, and which is it? Is ColdFusion not a Web editor like Dreamweaver or GoLive? Or is it a Web Server like IIS or Apache. What about HTML and ASP – is ColdFusion an alternative to those scripting languages? Exactly which one of these things is ColdFusion?

Dear friends, we will explain all. ColdFusion is many things, all at the same time and all good. Read on now for a little light history:

Macromedia

Macromedia seem to control a lot of the new media market these days, don't they. Within the shadow of Microsoft's rival ASP technology and Sun's JSP (Java Server Pages) technology, Macromedia has certainly waited and have obviously wanted to promote their own server-side web scripting platform for a long time.

Enter ColdFusion: Macromedia merged with Allaire out early in 2001, paving the way for a one-vendor approach to almost all aspects of dynamic web development. This clear strategy takes advantage of the currently less-than-solid Microsoft framework to wean ASP users away from a Microsoft-centric approach, to give the Macromedia-faithful a viable alternative, and to drive the hugely popular Flash technology forward into the database area while keeping all the supporting technologies in-house and in-control.

The future...

And so, while Flash and ColdFusion continue to grow and the competition between Microsoft, Netscape and Sun continues, we can only watch with great interest how today and tomorrows Macromedia-based Web Developers and Flash Designers choose their tools for practicality and interoperability. Jakob Nielsen may preach death-by-Flash to e-commerce, but the database-enabled Flash site is here to make a statement - and its delivey platform is increasingly likely to be ColdFusion.

The many faces of ColdFusion

The CF (as we will now start to refer to it as) technology is in 3 main parts: the CFML markup language itself; the Server software that interprets the markup languages' special **cf tag**; and the CF Studio's design environment that helps us put the pages together with syntax checking, prompts and wizards. Lets look at these three in a little more detail:

ColdFusion Markup Language (CFML)

The **ColdFusion Markup Language** is based on a set of custom-built tags. These tags strongly resemble the regular HTML tags in terms of syntax (structure) and semantics (meaning), but they are instantly distinguishable by the ubiquitous cf preceding every tag name: `<cfform>`, `<cfoutput>`, `<cfset>`,`<cfparam>`

The tags obey the rules of HTML such as the forward-slash in the closing tag element, and the need for strict nesting with no overlapping. The tags surround and control text elements, and the tags contain their own special name-value pairs. There are roughly an equivalent number of HTML tags as there are **CFML** tags, and - true to form - a great deal can be accomplished with just a small subset of these CFML tags.

Probably the biggest advantage is that CFML tags do not try to recreate the layout elements of HTML. In fact, CFML is designed to coexist with and complement HTML. CF tags give us the ability to form logic statements in dynamic web pages – something beyond the bounds of HTML.

If you are at all familiar with the if logic of Flash and JavaScript, and have a smattering of HTML, then you will find the following tags somewhat familiar and pleasingly all-encompassing:

```
<cfif myname IS "thisvalue">
        do this...
        <cfelse>
        do that...
        </cfif>
```

Have a look at how it is clearly a set of tags, but has the if...else logic that we are used to seeing in logic-based scripting languages.

The structure of this logic-enabling CFML itself remains comfortingly similar to HTML. We are not required to interpret or apply nested Scripts as we do with Server-side VBScript, Jscript or JavaScript. And if we want to work with client-side JavaScript, we can still do so within the page structure.

ColdFusion Markup Language pages can be written with any text editor. Notepad will do fine. HTML can be interwoven with CFML, or CFML could be the only language present. The pages are always referred to as templates and the file extension is always .cfm

In the Internet Explorer and Netscape Navigator DOM's (Document Object Models) we might be used to seeing the document structure expressed with dots. In ColdFusion, it is a little similar. We refer to scopes instead, and may point to a value in a form like this:

```
FORM.myvalue
```

Where form is the scope and myvalue is the value within that scope. This leaves the variable name myvalue free to exist in other scopes without fear of confusion.

ColdFusion Server 5

A powerful proprietary scripting language like CFML needs a powerful Server to interpret its commands, and ColdFusion Server 5 is that Server. Currently at version 5, the server software will run on all mainstream platforms and co-exist with other more fundamental web-server software, such as a Mail Server or a Database Server.

Macromedia ColdFusion Server 5 was recently known as Allaire ColdFusion Server 4.5. As you will see in chapter two, the installation is a breeze and setup is via a relatively simple browser-based Administrator. If you already have an earlier version of ColdFusion Server installed, the upgrade is automatic and painless.

On my development machine, CF Server 5 runs alongside SQL Server, MS Access and IIS4 quite happily. As I perform a local test, CF Server quietly intercepts any pages with the .cfm extension and re-interprets them, publishing the result in my browser. If you look at the source file you won't see any CMFL code.

ColdFusion Studio 4.5.2

Now, with just the markup language and the server itself, you could be away for a song. Knock the pages up in Notepad and publish them via CF Server, all done!

But this smacks of the text-editor-only days of early web development, and these days we prefer to use an **Integrated Development Environment (IDE)** - like the very useful ColdFusion Studio 4.5.2. This Web Design software package is a boon to writing and testing CFML code. It prompts, checks syntax, auto-completes and generally makes life easier. We'll have a word with Macromedia about a tea-maker on the side, but they may draw a line there. So, while not an absolute requisite for CF development, the Studio is nonetheless well worth considering.

Fusion time...

Lets get into a bit of CFML and get a grip on what we're dealing with here. These examples are designed to show what CFML can do with very little effort. In later chapters, we'll explain these concepts in more detail, however for now you may just find this a little more intuitive than you had perhaps expected. I certainly hope so!

Example code: templates & HTML

A quick reminder: CF pages are always referred to as templates and always carry the `.cfm` extension. Here is an example of an extremely simple `.cfm` page. The CFML tag is easily distinguishable from the HTML document structure tags. In this case, its purpose is to output the text it encompasses (hardly world-shattering, granted!):

When saved as a text file with the extension `.cfm`, this page is picked up by the CF Server and processed into plain old html, like so:

```
<html>
<head>
</head>
    <body>    hello
    </body>
</html>
```

in our browser, we simply see the single word `"hello"`

Example code: setting & outputting page elements

Let's have a look at some simple but still practical uses for cf tags, using just two: the `<cfset>` tag to set a variable and the `<cfoutput>` tag to write it to the page:

```
<html>
<head>
</head>
    <body>
        <cfset myvalue="101">
      <cfoutput>
                Read this book for some #myvalue#
      </cfoutput>
      </body>
    </html>
```

The `<cfset>` tag sets the variable `<myvalue>` and the `<cfoutput>` tag-pair picks the value up later. We used the # # signs to say what variable we wanted to pick up – there could have been several to hand, you see.

Example code: expressions & variables

Once it is plain how to set a variable, as we did above, we can start to use a couple of variables to create an expression. In this example, `<cfset>` is used to create three variables, gravity, power and altitude

```
<!DOCTYPE HTML PUBLIC "-//W3C//DTD HTML 4.0 Transitional//EN">
<html>
<head>
    <title>
        Untitled
    </title>
</head>
    <body>
        <cfset gravity=10>
        <cfset power=12>
        <cfset altitude=power - gravity>
          <cfoutput>
                The altitude of the rocketship is #altitude#
          </cfoutput>
      </body>
    </html>
```

Notice how very algebraic it is. If you have experience with ActionScript in Flash then this should be really familiar. Even if you have not, the equations possibly are not difficult to write at all.

Example Code: conditional Logic with If...Elseif

Now let's try something with some Boolean logic – in other words, some "if...else" thinking. We are going to use the cf tags <cfif>, <cfelseif>, <cfelse> and </cfif> to create a short and sweet sniffer: We are expecting either Harry or Jane to stop by our site, and want to greet them individually. However anyone else could also stop by, and we want a more formal greeting in that case.

```
<!DOCTYPE HTML PUBLIC "-//W3C//DTD HTML 4.0
Transitional//EN">
<html>
<head>
    <title>
        Untitled
    </title>
</head>
    <body>
    <cfif visitorname is "harry">
            <cfoutput>
                    Hello #visitorname#, been
expecting you today
            </cfoutput>
            <cfelseif visitorname is "jane">
            <cfoutput>
                    Hello #visitorname#, thanks for
the flowers
            </cfoutput>
    <cfelse>
            <cfoutput>
                    Welcome to our site,
#visitorname#
            </cfoutput>
    </body>
</html>
```

Notice how very straightforward and logical that was? This is covered in much greater detail in later chapters, but so far this should have given a basic idea of what CF tags look like and how they function.

Flash & ColdFusion integration

Flash communicates with other web services via the HTTP protocol. In other words, it strings the information up inside the HTTP header in URL-encoded format, or attaches the information in URL-encoded format to the end of the URL. URL-encoded means that the special characters are all expressed with ASCII key codes - for example the space is expressed as %20 and the dash comes up as %22.

Reading data into Flash

Data is read into Flash in the form of name-value pairs. So long as the name exists in Flash on the targeted timeline (as a variable name or as a dynamic text field), the association will be made fairly easily. Flash does not like reading in data that is not URL-encoded, and Flash has trouble reading HTML 4.0 into a text box. Flash will read very simple HTML into a text box. Values tend to come in as strings, and must usually be turned back into values in Flash.

Writing data from Flash

As Flash reads data in as name-value pairs in URL-encoded format, so too does Flash export or "pass" data to a web page. The data is sent using the GET or POST method, and along with it is sent a small trigger to cause the receiving page to then continue and submit that information into a database. Flash cannot make the database connection, so is reliant on a ColdFusion template to act as a "medium". When the data is sent to the page, an additional command is sent from Flash to the page which commands the page to "insert" the data into the database via the page's database connection.

Internet architectures & concepts

Vint Cerf helped invent a set of rules called **TCP**, merged it with the US Defence's Internet Protocol, and **TCP/IP** was born.

Back here in Europe, Tim Berners-Lee bemoaned the inaccessibility of the data on the net and invented the World Wide Web, HTML, the URL and HTTP. Today, Cerf is the head of one huge Web governing body (ICANN), and Berners-Lee is the head of the other (the W3C).

The architectures that were put in place then are still predominant. They govern, enable and sometimes frustrate our efforts at web development. Lets have a look at them – we are going to have to work with Internet and Web Architectures a fair amount in future chapters, and a little knowledge now may go a fair way.

Web servers

At the centre of it all, it seems, are the web hosts – the big rooms full of racks of humming servers that house our websites and publish to the masses. Always-connected, web servers range from server farms to little single-CPU's in a bedroom somewhere.

Client/Server relationships

Those servers serve our digital offerings to clients. In this sense, clients are the computers accessing the net and requesting information. A lot happens between Client and Server, most of it completely transparent to us.

Static web pages

There must be in excess of 2 billion pages out there, online. The huge majority are static web pages. Even a so-called **dynamic HTML** web page (One which uses dynamic HTML to achieve glossy or animated effects) is probably "static" in precise terms.

A static page is one that does not update itself, regenerate itself from the Server based on new information received, or intelligently change itself according to an update to a database somewhere. And so most Web Servers serve static web pages. This is precisely what we try to avoid with ColdFusion: We want our pages to be updated almost instantly – we want them to be served with dynamic information!

Server platforms

Each Server will be probably run on a Linux, Unix, Mac or Windows operating system. This runs the basic box, and becomes the operating system platform.

ColdFusion Server is designed to run on top of all the mainstream Operating Systems, on Unix boxes and Microsoft boxes. It is known to be stable under a wide variety of conditions – in the trade, ColdFusion Server would be called "robust" and would be known as a multi-platform solution.

The server software

On top of the operating system that runs the box, there will run some kind of Web Server software. On Windows this is likely to be IIS (Internet Information Server) or IBM's WebSphere. On Unix or Linux it would probably be the world's favourite, Apache. WebSphere also works in this environment, as do dozens of other alternatives.

This is actually where ColdFusion Server slots in – it rides on top of the basic operating system and works with (where it has to) the other web server software.

A good example would be email: ColdFusion Server is not a Mail Server, so it would work with another Mail Server instead.

Internet Protocols

We do not need to get too technical. Like me, you are unlikely to be a Network Engineer. This introduction to ColdFusion is simply meant to convey some basic principles to make later chapters go that bit smoother.

One very key issue would have to be the way information is passed from page to page, and from ColdFusion pages to Flash .swf files living within or externally. The big player in this case is HTTP - lets look at it briefly:

HTTP – the Hypertext Transfer Protocol

Tim Berners-Lee invented this set of rules about the transfer of data, and we have two common ways of using it to pass information between pages: One is the POST method, the other is the GET method – both of which we'll cover in chapter 5. Using POST, we slot the information inside the HTTP header and pick it up later with a CFML tag designed for the purpose.

With GET, we string the information onto the end of the URL and intercept it (again with CFML) later on. For the GET method, think of the way a Search Engine makes a long URL in the address bar. That's GET in action.

TCP/IP – Transmission Control Protocol/Internet Protocol

The only time you are likely to be affected by this fundamental set of internet rules, even as you develop with ColdFusion, is when you are asked for an IP address for testing purposes. Every Web Host has an Internet Protocol (IP) address, written as a four-part number. When testing some CF websites locally on your own (non-web-host) machine, you will need to know that every machine has a standard IP address that identifies itself to itself. That number is 127.0.0.1, and you'll come across it in chapter 9.

Mailto – the mail protocol

Mail is not part of the web infrastructure. Mail pre-existed the Web by a couple of decades or so. You might say it has been the original killer app!

ColdFusion server does not handle mail directly, as we mentioned earlier. Some mainstream Web Server systems have built-in mail handling, like Microsoft's IIS which runs on WinNT and Win2k. If you are developing ColdFusion Applications on a Win95 or Win98 machine, finding Mail Server software to complement ColdFusion is going to be a little challenging.

That said, once given a third-party Mail Server, ColdFusion Markup Language has a full set of tags to handle mail, and ColdFusion Server is geared to accept mail settings for the third-party Mail Server.

FTP – File Transfer Protocol

File Transfer Protocol is going to affect you mostly when it comes time to upload that CF website. It is a fast means of transferring chunks of data, without actually viewing that data while in transit – unlike HTML pages sent by HTTP rules.

Application servers

Lets start to bring it home now. We've explained the basic parts of ColdFusion and demonstrated a few simple pages – although until you get to chapter two and setup your own ColdFusion server, you are simply taking our word for it!

We have also seen that there are Web Hosts out there running static pages, and tiers of software running on those web hosts to keep the PC box, the varieties of Web Server, the Mail Server and a million other services running.

Web applications – the core concept

ColdFusion is starting to get very relevant now: A web application is a set of pages that work together, passing information and updating/reflecting changes, reading and writing to a database, and so forth. In fact it is just like a desktop application like MS Word, when you think about all the DLL'S and other shrapnel.

ColdFusion helps build this framework, ties the pages together, links into a database, and otherwise turns a set of web pages into a dynamic web application.

Platforms, vendors & server–side scripting languages

Lets look at the competition: ASP (Active Server Pages) by Microsoft is much-hyped, but run almost exclusively on the Windows platform. The pages contain VBScript or JavaScript (or both) that provides the logic, while regular HTML provides the layout. The scripts are interpreted by the server at run-time (when the page is requested by the client) and ASP is replaced with current data and standard HTML.

So too with JSP (Java Server Pages). Peculiar to Unix or Linux, these pages form a web application driven by the Java language. At run-time, everything is turned into regular static web code and uploaded to the client.

And, of course, ColdFusion is the third player in this field. Later in this chapter, in the very next section in fact, we will explain exactly how the ColdFusion Server interprets and publishes those CFML pages with judicious use of JavaScript.
ColdFusion Web Application Framework

The parts of ColdFusion are established briefly, as are the core concepts of the web and web publishing. Now for the sequence of events that ColdFusion is so central to: the .cfm web template request from the client's browser, and the subsequent run-time re-processing of that template by the Web Host's copy of ColdFusion Server 5.

The network architecture will look something like this

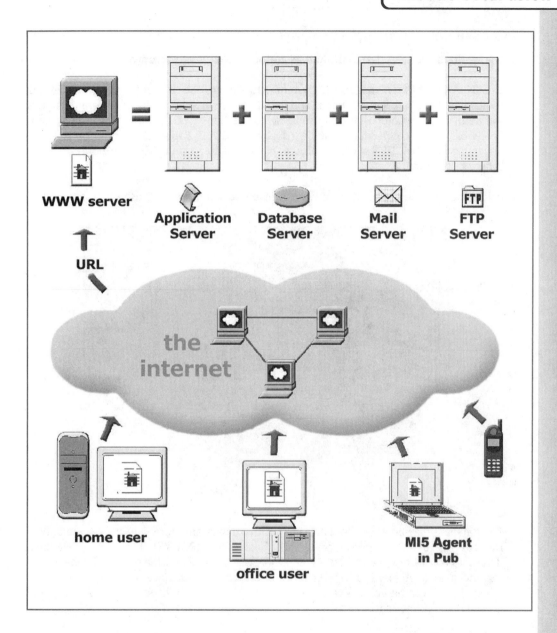

WWW server

Application Server

Database Server

Mail Server

FTP Server

URL

the internet

home user

office user

MI5 Agent in Pub

Database servers

The database is central to the dynamic web application. Not all web applications need access to a database, but they are unlikely to go far without one. As early as chapter 3, we connect to a database and pop the information into our template as it is published to the client browser.

Database core concepts

The world of the DBA (Database Administrator) is awash with acronyms:

Usually a Database Management System (DBMS) will be a front end to something fundamental like SQL Server, Oracle, and mySQL or similar. Connections to these databases will be made, and ColdFusion will use these connections to access the data itself when it needs to. These connections will be usually via ODBC (Open Database Connectivity) drivers, consist of DSN's (Data Source Names) and accept SQL (Structured Query Language) queries.

below shows some of the ODBC drivers available to Windows 2000 users

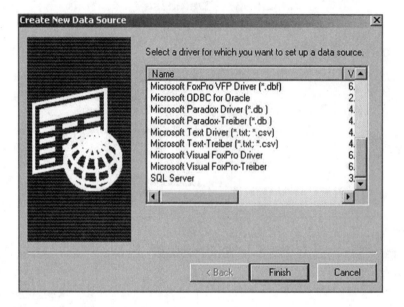

The database may be a flat file database, but these days are more likely to be a relational Database (RDB), which introduces a Relational DBMS (RDBMS) if you like. Relational databases consist of linked tables. Often a DBA will speak of "normalising" a database, and this means that otherwise often-repeated information is put once and once only into a table where it can be accessed many times. This is an efficient process in most cases, and is usually the prime reason for making a database relational.

Each row in the table is a record, and several columns (fields) will make up the details of that record. By pointing to a given range of fields in a given range of rows in a given table in a given database, we are able to generate a recordset of information for use in our web application at that moment in time.

Database vendors

The Databases you are most likely to come across are Microsoft Access and SQL Server. On Unix or Linux, mySQL is probably a favourite. In this book, we will use Access 2000 as our main database. Access is ubiquitous and the basic workings are not far removed from SQL Server. Access is not a true Database Server, unlike SQL Server. Access is a file-based system, and subsequently is slow and not suited to more than a very few concurrent users. It does come with some practice databases like the Northwind set of tables.

At a push, ColdFusion can hook into the simplest of spreadsheets. Excel, even comma-separated-value `.csv` files are able to be connected to via ODBC and DSN, and are therefore accessible to a ColdFusion Web Application.

Dynamic web applications with ColdFusion & Flash

As promised in the previous section, a much, much closer look at the parts of ColdFusion now: CFML, ColdFusion Server 5, and ColdFusion Studio 4.5.2

ColdFusion Markup Language

Almost all of the "intelligence" in the markup language is in the tags themselves. This may sound obvious, but a simpler markup language like HTML will be heavily dependant on name-value pairs and small nested JavaScripts. ColdFusion puts as much of the focus on the element name as it can, making the tag itself the true centrepiece.

The tags

CF tags number about 60. We have looked briefly at a small handful in the earlier examples. CF tags were designed with their current job in mind, and will perform a huge range of operations - such as:

Conditions:

<cfloop>, <cfif>, <cfelse>, <cfelseif>

- these tags are used for building conditional, logic-based templates. Nested conditions are possible, as are iteration loops based on incrementing variables

Databases:

<cfquery>, <cfupdate>, <cfinsert>

- these are the main tags are used for database access. You'll read more on this in chapter 4

Interaction:

<cfform>, <cfcookie>, <cfparam>

- these tags are a few that may be used for client feedback and session data. See chapter 7 for more on Form handling.

There are cf tags that redirect the browser, cf tags that perform an "include"-type function to slot data into the top every new page in the folder, and tags that insert data into the bottom of every new page in the folder. In fact, whatever you are thinking of, there is probably a tag already that you could use.

It is even possible to build your own tags, using the <cfmodule> tag. But that is for another day, and beyond the scope of this foundational book.

Writing CFML

Most of the same rules of HTML apply. Names used must not contain spaces, words may contain alpha characters, underscores and numbers but must begin with an alpha character. White space is not an issue in CFML, although this can pose a problem for data being read into Flash (Flash cannot tolerate white spaces and unusual non-URL-encoded characters).

Fortunately – and yup, you guessed it yourself – there is even a CF tag for URL-encoding output for Flash consumption!

ColdFusion Studio 4.5.2

Although it's not required, using ColdFusion Studio 4.5.2 will greatly help the development process. As an Allaire product, this was at version 4.5. too. Now a Macromedia product at version 4.5.2, you can probably guess that not much has changed – the interface is identical, the workings are the same.

The IDE contains a syntax checker, cf tag prompts, wizards, and my personal favourite: automatic completion of code writing. Although an irritant in Word (how can Word really predict what I am trying to say?), in CFML it is much more useful and a real timesaver. It also is the best way to get to grips with CFML quickly.

Various tabbed panels provide specialised text-based "environments" for coding features such as Forms, Tables, Lists and so forth. On the left is a very-dominant help screen and index, and current .cfm documents are arranged Excel-worksheet-like with tabs across the bottom of the window. The interface is highly accessible and uncluttered

Macromedia ColdFusion Studio 5

On the horizon is version 5 – the Macromedia rebuild, I guess. At the time of press this is still in Beta. I'm sure we'd like to see the ColdFusion Studio Interface look less Adobe-GoLive-like and yet keep its uncluttered appearance. One thing we are sure to see is of course, an IDE that leans towards the easier integration of Fireworks and Flash.

Allaire Express

Allaire, before being taken over by Macromedia, did offer a free lite version of ColdFusion Studio called "Express". Better than a basic text editor, this may lurk in dark recesses of the Net still, and provide a free temporary IDE for those who are not up to purchasing the full Macromedia ColdFusion Studio version. Especially if you are holding out for the full-version upgrade to 5!

ColdFusion Server 5

The heart of ColdFusion is, of course, the Server. In chapter two you will learn to install it, which should prove a relatively painless process. The Server exists as a download on Macromedia's site, as well as being distributed by several magazines on CD-ROM. The Server will run on Windows, Linux and Unix, but is not available for Macintosh.

ColdFusion Server 5 on Windows or Unix

Let us assume that, as a developer primarily, you are running ColdFusion Server on your development PC for testing purposes. As the PC's operating systems loads, the Server will start automatically and should run without any interruption to your working style. The server is "started" by default – a tray icon in Win95/98/NT/2k will allow you to stop the Server quickly.

On Windows, ColdFusion Server 4.5.2 or 5 are going to run well. Win95 and Win98 run PWS (Personal Web Server) instead of IIS (Internet Information Server). ColdFusion Server is quite happy to work within these confines – if the web directory is mapped correctly (see chapter two for details on this!) then the HTTP URL request will be passed to ColdFusion correctly and the data processed. Looking overleaf you can see the flow of events once the .cfm template is called

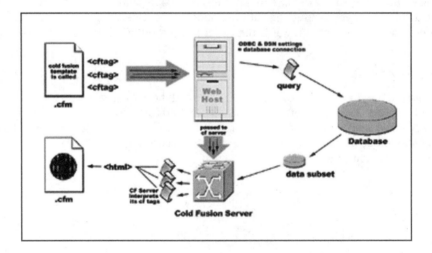

ColdFusion Administrator

ColdFusion Server is controlled by the Administrator – a web-based interface comprising an extensive indexing and help system, many flavours of online support and a neat set of configuration panels for your attention. Once again, this is accessed in Windows through a tray icon, or via the usual Start menu.

The Administrator – the door to the Server – is protected always by your password. This must be entered at the installation stage, so take note: think of a memorable name now, so that you don't have to scramble for one in the next chapter! That password must be entered absolutely every time you launch the Administrator

A small Help button conceals a large contextual help section with indexing, search area and contents.

Remote Development Services

A less-visible aspect of ColdFusion Server is the RDS (Remote Development Services) component. This provides both ColdFusion Studio and ColdFusion Server's Administrator with Database access and HTTP access to other files. HTTP access is important because it is the HTTP header which often carries the data that ColdFusion needs to work with.

A technology of three parts

And there we have all the parts of ColdFusion: the CFML, the Studio and the Server. CFML and the Server are inseparable, Studio is recommended but not required. Now lets see how, out there on the Net, other companies have put this all together with a sprinkling of Flash.

Examples of ColdFusion Applications:

Jaguar Australia (www.jaguar.com.au)

This site looks very slick indeed, as do many car manufacturers sites these days. It is a little surprising to see the use of frames in a high-profile commercial site. But what is of interest is the use of database-driven ColdFusion pages together with a very pretty Flash front end. Of course, a non-Flash version is also offered.

Take a moment to browse this site, and observe the way the web application passes data around the site. Instead of a usual page URL (address) for each hyperlink, the site passes specific page information to a central template called `control.cfm`. Try a search, and remember what you searched on. Later, as you move from page to page, you'll notice that your search result is being passed to every page. So you might notice that the URL reads something like `control.cfm?page=club&phrase=fast%20cars`. This means that Cold Fusion is passing a page reference to itself, (page=club), as well as some useful

information about your browsing process so far, (phrase=fast%20cars). The name-value pairs are separated by an ampersand (&) and any spaces are replaced by special keycodes (the space becomes %20).

My Switerland.com (www.myswitzerland.com)

This is another site using both Flash and database-driven ColdFusion.
Unlike the Jaguar example, this site is not frames-based and does not pass page information in quite the same way. Normal links in the site behave mostly as we expect, passing a request to the server for another specific .cfm page template. A click on the "reservations" link will take you to a page full of yet more links. Try rolling your mouse over some links, and notice (looking now at your status bar at the bottom of the window) that a little bit of JavaScript can be seen in the link. This shows that, although driven by ColdFusion, this site also employs standard client-side JavaScript for some of its interaction. Actually, this is more often the case with ColdFusion in the real world. Mix and match your approach to suit your audience as well as your preferred technology infrastructure.

Looking to the right, to the NavPage, notice that the link now does pass a name-value pair to the ColdFusion Server: try one of the links under "Switzerland vacations" to see the variable "category" be equated with a value like "family", and so forth. This is passed to the Server, the appropriate information is slotted into a template page and it is served up, pronto!

MTV2 (www.mtv2.co.uk)

This is well worth a look, but if you are on a standard modem then this is also a time to grab a coffee while it all loads! I do recommend you have a look though, especially for the (reminiscent of soulbath) Flash effects. And here's a hint for the navigation - click on the big blocks of color, not the labels.

How's that coffee? You'll be having another before this finishes loading the second screen, but stay with it...

Now, not a lot to say about how this site does its stuff - and that in itself is a great thing. It is all tucked away inside the Flash movie, handled by ColdFusion in the background. Flash movie after Flash movie (or are they one? Who can tell!) are passed variables from the database, pass variables back to the database, and maintain a non-html facade all the while.

And that is what is refreshing about this site. The price we pay in time for sitting through the long downloads is rewarded by a non-PC experience. Even MTV2 themselves keep it up by referring to, and I quote them directly, "the email 'thingy' that is (officially) working again"

This is a site that well illustrates the potential of a database-driven ColdFusion engine with a committed Flash interface.

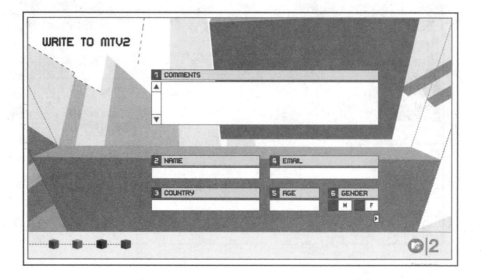

Databases, ColdFusion & Flash

Database-driven advantages

Have we sold you on the concept of a dynamic database-driven ColdFusion/Flash web application yet? If not, then follow through these advantages (and disadvantages – let's be fair!) of the ColdFusion development framework

Template-based design

Every page in ColdFusion is referred to as a template – for obvious reasons! Once the template is created, it can take on as many subtle changes as the nuances of the database can provide. With such a strong focus on template-based reusable design, we can expect to spend less time in repeat tasks and more time designing databases and front-ends.

Flash & ODBC

A major disadvantage of Flash is the inability to connect to an ODBC database. Flash has some fast-evolving XML objects which means that most all things are possible really, but simple database connectivity straight into Flash escapes us for now. Techniques exist for database read-write capabilities via ASP, CGI and JSP, and of course we can do so via a ColdFusion web application that has a connection to a database.

Connecting to databases

Focusing now on those database issues in more detail, especially having seen that Flash relies on the core web application to make the connection to the database, read from and write to the database:

Connection strings

In the simplest terms, a connection string can be set up to point directly at the database. This is the most fundamental and most difficult method of making a connection. On a Windows machine especially, you will want to employ the existing tools for database connectivity – ODBC and DSN.
A connection string is used when the database is of an unusual type, is accessed across platforms, or is otherwise difficult to connect to normally.

ODBC - Open Database Connectivity

ODBC-compliant databases are much easier to work with, these days, all the major databases are ODBC-compliant. ODBC-compliance means access to databases on platforms alien to ColdFusion Server, even – for example on a Macintosh running Filemaker Pro5.

The ODBC component that makes the connection possible is in fact a driver – a database driver that standardises the database interface so that disparate applications can interact according to a common set of rules.

DSN's – Data Source Names

Once an ODBC database driver has been configured to point to a given database, that database is given a new name. This becomes its DSN (data source name), which we use later on in ColdFusion to again identify that database.

The ColdFusion Server Administrator has a section devoted to picking up the names of databases that have been set up previously in the operating system's ODBC control panel.

Recordsets

The whole point of the connection to the database is to generate a recordset – a subset of data that is used in the web application, as we mentioned earlier. In the next section, we will look more closely at how and why we generate such a recordset.

Querying databases

Flash cannot access a database directly, and so neither can it query a database directly. To truly enable our Flash movie within its Web Application framework, the Flash movie must have easy access to data – and so the query process becomes important to Flash/ColdFusion integration.

The need for a query method

A classic example of a query might be something like: Select all records from the table `customers` where `lastname` begins with "B". This becomes the structured question we put to the database.

To pass this query to Flash would be pointless – Flash could not carry out the query. So instead the query is handled by ColdFusion (using CF tags designed for the purpose) and the results are then passed across to Flash. And so too in reverse – if Flash wants to query the database, it must ask the web application to run the query on its behalf. This all necessitates a practical means of communication between the Flash movie and the host ColdFusion application

Structured Query Language

SQL, the Structured Query Language, is used as standard within CF tags to run queries across the database. Pronounced "see-quel" by some and "ess-q-el" by others, this interrogation method is standard across most mid-level databases like Access, mySQL and SQL Server.

Complex queries

Massively attractive are the advantages of running complex queries to generate some really clever answers sometimes. An example might be to run a query-within-a-query that asks a database "call up all the flash movie paths that begin with `.swf3**`" and then to query that result with the question "list all the movies that are numbered above `.swf398`" to filter out the single movie whose name fits both criteria (`.swf399`)

Another thing we can do with a database is store queries in the record fields, and then do a query that results in a query which then results in something concrete. The database is as versatile as your creative and structured approach to SQL, and that versatility can be passed to Flash via ColdFusion templates.

Store it all in the database!

Databases store things – that we know. The databases used most often in business do not store binary data – that is, they do not store pictures. That does not stop anyone from storing the picture somewhere else and then putting the path to the image inside the database. This can be done with sound files, with `.swfs`, with variables and with strings of text. Anything that can drive your Flash movie and/or ColdFusion web application can be stored somehow in a database and recalled with precision.

Summary

So, what is the case for ColdFusion and Flash as a development partnership within the ColdFusion framework? Is this a viable alternative to ASP and VBScript, ASP and JavaScript, JSP, HTML with CGI? Can this marriage of cf tags and vector-based animation actually do anything worthwhile? The chapters to follow will speak volumes on all this, but for now a summary will suffice.

Ease of learning

In terms of a scripting learning curve, the special cf tags replace a lot of potential scripting with something far more familiar – the HTML-style syntax. The logic is there, so conditional statements are much easier, and the whole bang-shoot lives comfortably within standard HTML layout tags. ColdFusion's syntax remains essentially the same as HTML's:

```
<tagname name=value name=value> </tagname>
```

Ease of database access

Making a connection to the database is much easier in ColdFusion than in some rival technologies – the ColdFusion Administrator has a friendly ODBC/DSN interface, the CF tags are relatively simple to remember, and the whole thing is mostly tag-based.

Ease of integration

Information is written back and forth with a few specially designed tags and some variables. Once again integrating the movie itself is exactly the same as in HTML, because for the most part it is HTML. Within the HTTP protocol, moving data back and forth is made relatively simple by the customised tags.

Total design & development environment

Macromedia are keeping it in the family, and we can expect to see a ColdFusion suite that gets even stronger. Even smoother integration with Flash is bound to be on the cards – look forward to a 100% Macromedia IDE that works for you. Roll on the chapters, let's build something!

Case study

At the end of each of the first six chapters of this book you'll find a case study section. In this we're going to build up a project that integrates ColdFusion and Flash to make a fully functional and eye-pleasing message board system. By the time we've finished, you'll be able to view a list of postings, view an entire thread, make posts and make replies – all within a neat Flash interface.

In each chapter we'll be building up the necessary components of this forum. These are the Flash interface, the ColdFusion templates, and the database that stores all the messages and information.

The skills we learn along the way will be transferable to many other types of application. For example, the message board with just the post form and no reply function would make the perfect guestbook application, or a book review page. The principles behind the post form can be adopted by any application that requires data to be sent by the user.

All the files used to create this forum can be downloaded from the friends of ED web site, so there's a handy reference point if you encounter any difficulties along the way. I know I'm always making typing errors when I enter my code, and I'm sure you will too.

One word of warning. If ColdFusion outputs an error message when you're testing an application, the error often lies elsewhere, so don't waste too much time if you're sure your code matches the sample files.

Enjoy a truly interactive ColdFusion and Flash experience.

2 Installation and Interface

What we'll cover in this chapter:

- *The hardware and software required to run ColdFusion and ColdFusion Studio.*

- *The installation process.*

- *The ColdFusion Studio interface, and how it can help you code.*

- *Creating a very basic ColdFusion application.*

▶

Before you begin

You will need to check your hardware and operating system to make sure they are suitable. ColdFusion can run on two different hardware platforms:

- Pentium Compatible

- Sun SPARC

Chances are you will have Intel hardware, if you are running Windows software then you will definitely have an Intel compatible machine. ColdFusion can be installed on a sun SPARC machine but for the sake of this chapter we will be installing on an Intel machine with Windows 2000.

Choosing an operating system

If you have an Intel machine then you will probably have either Windows 98, 2000 or NT, if you have a Sun SPARC machine then you will have Solaris.

Windows 98 is a practical operating system for development for various reasons. Cost is always an issue with web development and with Windows 98 you get a comparatively low cost operating system which is suitable for most software you might require. Another reason is its low level of maintenance and ease of installation/configuration of both operating system and development software. More often than not you just want to install software and get building sites. With Windows 98 you can.

Windows NT and 2000 Server are best for live sites or sites that will have a heavy load.

Do I have enough disk space and memory?

For a successful installation, ColdFusion Server requires 200MB of space along with ColdFusion Studio, which requires 35MB of space. When ColdFusion server is up and running for it to perform at a suitable pace you will need at least 128MB of memory, 32MB for ColdFusion Studio.

Software requirements

Most importantly you will need a web server. There are several web servers that support ColdFusion, examples are:

- Microsoft Personal Web Server (PWS) www.microsoft.com

- Microsoft Internet Information Server (IIS) www.microsoft.com/iis

- Apache www.apache.org

- Netscape Enterprise Server www.netscape.com

In most instances choosing a web server shouldn't be an issue as operating systems normally come with one, either installed or available on their install CD.

With Windows 98 the web server you will have will be PWS. This will probably need to be installed separately off the Windows 98 CD. Refer to your manual for instructions on how to do this. Unfortunately there is no ColdFusion Server available for Windows ME, though there is a version of ColdFusion Studio available.

On Windows NT/2000 you will require IIS (Internet Information Server). This comes installed with Windows NT/2000. To verify that IIS is installed look for Internet Service Manager in the Programs menu or under Administrative Tools in the Control Panel. If it is not installed, you will need to install off the CD, ask your systems administrator for instructions on how to do this.

If you wish to install other web servers then refer to their web site for further information. You can change your web server after install, to do this you will have to manually configure all settings, and instructions are available for this in the ColdFusion manual.

Connections

You should ensure that you have the most recent version of **MDAC**, or Microsoft Data Access Components, installed. These are updated database drivers, and will required by ColdFusion Server for database functionality. It is found on the CD and when installed can be found within the ColdFusion directory. If the ColdFusion install detects you haven't got MDAC it will attempt to install it for you.

One other requirement would be to check you have **TCP/IP** protocol installed on your machine. TCP/IP is a type of connection used by two machines to transmit data over a network. By default it should already be installed, but to be sure we'll perform a check.

> *Each machine on a network has with it a unique number that identifies it to other machines, this is called an* **IP Address**. *To connect to other machines you connect by using this unique number. All machines have a special internal number which is the same, if this number is entered into a browser it doesn't go looking for the machine with that number it instead loops back on itself. This number is* **127.0.0.1** *(also known as localhost). So to test* test.html *developed on the same machine you can enter* http://127.0.0.1/test.html *as the URL in a browser.*

Testing for TCP/IP

1. Open an MS-Dos or Command Prompt by selecting it from the Start > Programs > Accessories menu.

Depending on the version of Windows you are running, or your own Start menu customization, this may be in a different position.

2. At the command prompt type the following:

```
ping 127.0.0.1
```

> **Ping** *is a tool found on most systems which tests for the existence of IP Addresses.*

You should now see a series of responses:

```
Command Prompt

Microsoft Windows 2000 [Version 5.00.2195]
(C) Copyright 1985-1999 Microsoft Corp.

C:\>ping 127.0.0.1

Pinging 127.0.0.1 with 32 bytes of data:

Reply from 127.0.0.1: bytes=32 time<10ms TTL=128
Reply from 127.0.0.1: bytes=32 time<10ms TTL=128
Reply from 127.0.0.1: bytes=32 time<10ms TTL=128
Reply from 127.0.0.1: bytes=32 time<10ms TTL=128

Ping statistics for 127.0.0.1:
    Packets: Sent = 4, Received = 4, Lost = 0 (0% loss),
Approximate round trip times in milli-seconds:
    Minimum = 0ms, Maximum = 0ms, Average = 0ms

C:\>
```

This means that you have TCP/IP installed, so you are now ready to begin installing ColdFusion Server.

If the response is more like this:

```
Pinging 127.0.0.1 with 32 bytes of data:

Destination host unreachable.

Ping statistics for 127.0.0.1:
     Packets: Sent = 4, Received = 0, Lost = 4
(100% loss),
Approximate round trip times in milli-seconds:
     Minimum = 0ms, Maximum = 0ms, Average = 0ms
```

Then you don't have TCP/IP installed. You mustn't proceed with the installation until you have installed TCP/IP. Please refer to your System Manual for instructions on how to do this.

To recap

Before you begin to install ColdFusion you should check the following:

- That the hardware you are to install on is suitable.

- There is enough free disk space and memory.

- You have a suitable operating system.

- That the web server installed supports ColdFusion.

- You have TCP/IP installed.

- You have MDAC installed.

If everything is okay then you are ready to install.

Installing ColdFusion Server

Installation of ColdFusion Server is a simple task, fortunately the install does a lot of the configuration of your web server for you.

1. Before you begin close down all applications.

2. Insert the CD and browse to the CD and double-click on demo32.exe. If you have downloaded the software then double click on the file.

   The installer will then test your system to make sure it is suitable and meets all the requirements outlined above.

If you have a previous installation of ColdFusion Server you may be asked to stop the service from running before the installation can begin. If you do then, from the services window, stop all ColdFusion services in the Services window. This is found under Start>Control Panel>Administrative Tools *in the Control Panel.*

When all is okay you will be taken to the introductory screen.

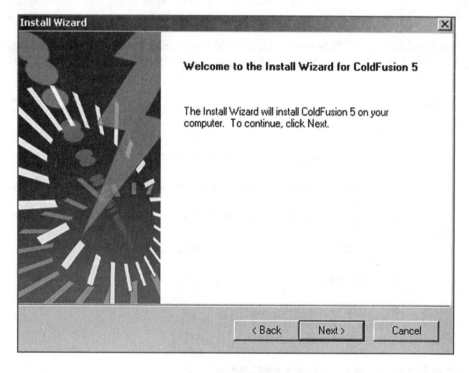

Click on Next to proceed to the licensing screen.

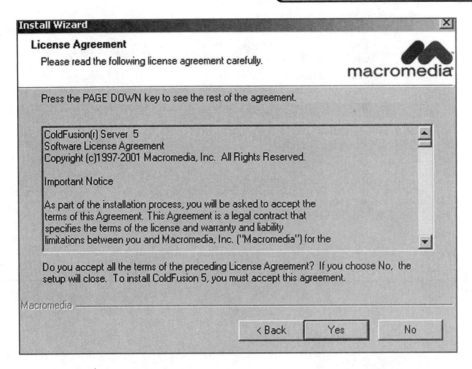

4. Clicking on Yes will now take you to the Customer Information Screen, here you will need to enter your details and serial number. Leave this box blank for the evaluation version.

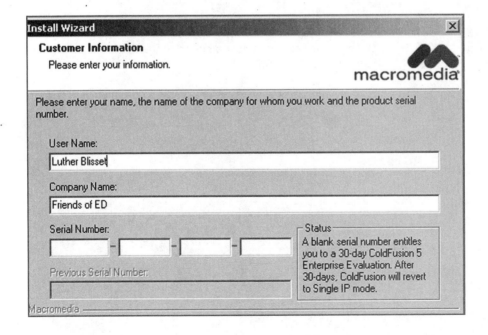

5. Once you have completed the form, click on Next to be taken to the Web Server Selection Screen, here you must choose your web server. If your web server is not listed you may need to cancel installation and re-install your web server.

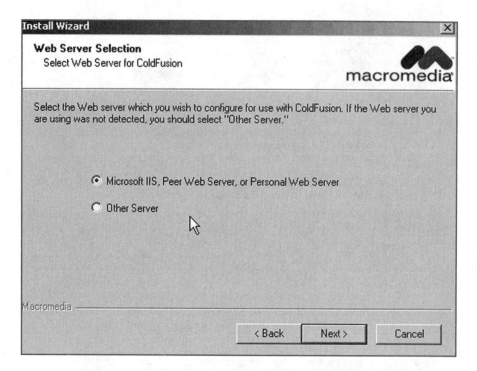

6. Once you have made your selection then click Next to begin selecting components to install.

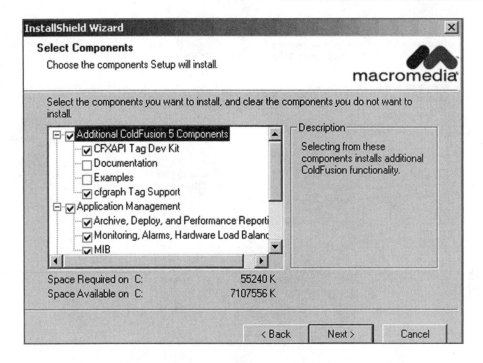

The following table explains each component (components found will differ between versions of ColdFusion Server 5).

Component	Description
CFXAPI Tag Dev Kit	Microsoft C++ Add-on for developing ColdFusion Extension Tags in C++.
Documentation	Complete online documentation.
Examples	Examples of all code found in the documentation.
cfgraph Support	Support for the graphing tag, this tag allows the output of graphs from data values passed in.
Advanced Security	Installs Advanced Security Options found in the Administrator.
ClusterCATS	Server Load Balancing Facility
ClusterCATS and Application Management	Application Threshold Management

If you don't select a component now you can install at a later date.

7. Once you have selected your components click Next.

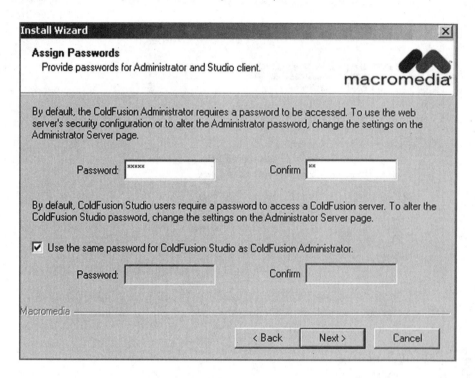

This screen allows you to enter passwords for the Administrative (Browser-based Server Administration) and Remote development (Remote file management) part of the server. You can either use the same passwords for both Server and Studio or specify different ones.

As always when selecting passwords, take as many security precautions as you think necessary. But make sure you can remember them!

When you have entered your passwords you can now proceed to the Confirm Selections window.

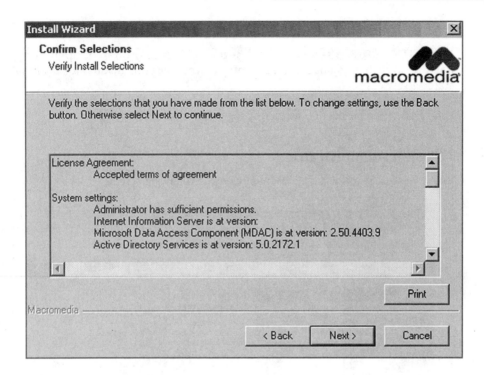

8. If you wish to change any settings, you can do so now otherwise click Next to continue.

   When install is complete you'll need to reboot your machine.

9. To test the installation open up Start>Programs>Macromedia ColdFusion Sever5>ColdFusion Administrator. You should be taken to a browser-based password prompt.

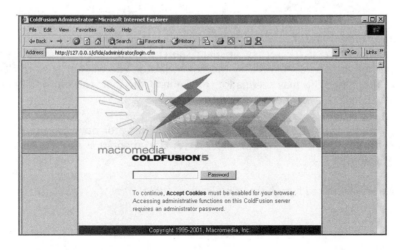

If installation is incomplete then you will get tips on possible problems and solutions.

Normally, ColdFusion services should begin automatically on boot up. If not you may need to start them manually. Please refer to your systems manual for information on starting services.

You can test the installation further by logging in.

ColdFusion Administrator

When you log in you will be presented with the following screen.

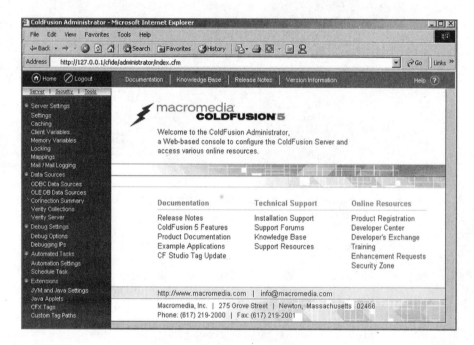

The **Administrator** is where Server administrative tasks are carried out. In particular you will soon use it for setting up data sources, or for creating scheduled tasks. Security settings are also configured by the Administrator, you will not need to alter these settings at this stage. This may seem a lot to take in at the moment, but don't panic, we'll explain everything as and when we need to.

If you do wish to learn more about the Administrator now, then refer to the manual or consult your systems administrator. Server Documentation can also be accessed at the top of the page.

Now you are ready to install ColdFusion Studio.

Installing ColdFusion Studio

ColdFusion Studio (referred to as Studio) is an application which works alongside ColdFusion Server creating a complete development environment. Installing Studio is a quick and painless task.

    1. To begin, insert the CD and again double-click on `demo32.exe`. If the file has been downloaded from the internet, locate it, using Windows Explorer and click on the filename.

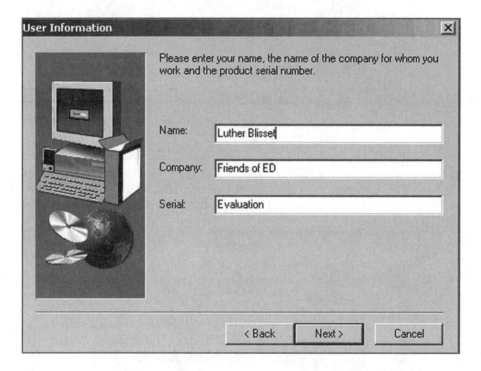

    Enter your details, if you have a serial number then enter it here, you can use the evaluation version by leaving "Evaluation" in the Serial box.

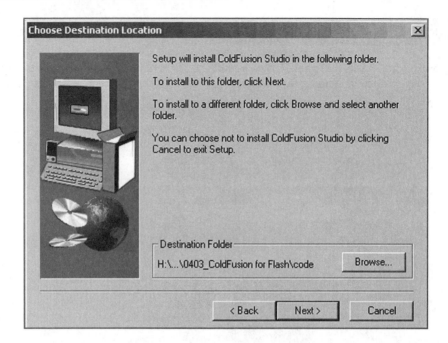

2. Select where you would like to install Studio, if you wish to install under a different directory then click Browse and select a different directory.

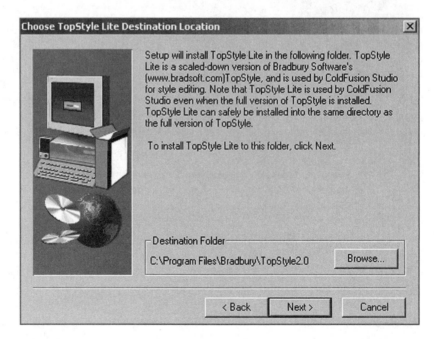

3.　You may get asked about installing TopStyle. TopStyle is a **CSS** editor which is integrated into Studio. Again if you wish to install it under another directory then click browse and select another directory.

CSS, or Cascading Style Sheets, is a way of changing the design of a site from one place. For example you may have a font tag which after time needs the color and size changing to fit the new style. Normally you would have to change each tag individually, with CSS you can change the style of the font tag in one place, this change would then be reflected throughout the site.

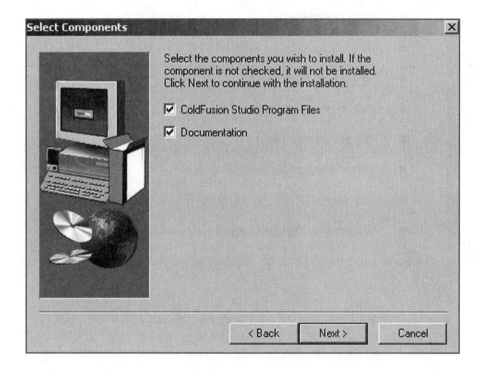

4.　Select both components then click Next.

When installation is complete you will be asked to reboot your machine. After doing so you may begin using Studio to develop ColdFusion applications.

ColdFusion Studio

ColdFusion Studio (referred to as Studio) is an editor. It allows you, the web developer, to create code at a more hands on level. This editor is not a WYSIWYG editor but it gives you more control over the application and its code.

How ColdFusion Studio can help development

Web development is a can be a complicated job so it is handy to have a development studio which can do most tasks. A discussion of all of Studio's features is beyond the scope of this chapter but we will attempt to introduce you to some of the options you will probably use the most. Some of the more common features are:

- Color coded syntax

- Shortcut toolbars for CFML and HTML

- Multiple document interface

- Built in project management

- Remote development

- Built in Browser for previewing

- Debugging

- Support for other languages besides CFML and HTML

We will introduce you here to enough of Studio to get you building sites with ease.

To begin, click on ColdFusion Studio in the programs menu. Let's start with the interface itself:

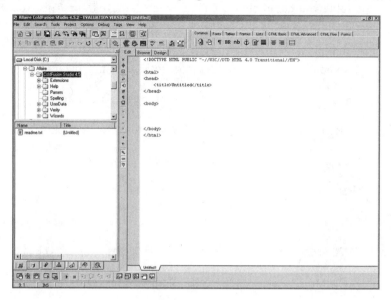

The main interface is broken up into various areas. There are toolbars that give you quick access to a majority of features.

To the left is the resources window. Here you can access features which don't affect your code directly, they are:

Resource Tab	Description
Files	Provides access to all file types in an explorer type window. Also allows you to manage remote servers for remote file editing.
Database	Allows access to databases currently set up on your system.
Projects	Displays all projects being managed by Studio.
Site View	A graphical representation of all links within a project.
Snippets	A place for accessing code snippets, for re-use.
Help	Displays all help documentation for all aspects of Server and Studio.
Tag Inspector	A hierarchical view of all tags.

The Tag Toolbar provides an interface way of writing code. For example if you needed to create a table you could click on Tables then Table Wizard. This would give you a wizard, which allows you to enter all the settings you need for the table you require.

Tag Toolbar	Description
Common	All frequently or commonly used HTML tags.
Fonts	HTML Font tag and attributes
Tables	Table Wizard for creating basic tables.
Frames	HTML frames tag wizard.
Lists	Creates all HTML lists.
CFML Basic	Basic CFML tags including <cfquery> and <cfoutput>.
CFML Advanced	Advanced CFML tags including <cfmail> and <cfpop>.
CFFORM	ColdFusion form tags and all Java controls.
CFML Flow	All conditional and error catching tags.
Debug	Debugging interface.
ASP	Basic ASP implementation.
Form	HTML form tag.
JSP	Basic Java Server Pages implementation.
Linkbot	Quick link to Linkbot. Linkbot is a link checking software that needs to be installed separately and is available from www.watchfire.com.
Script	Quick access to client side scripting languages.

The remaining right side part of the interface is the Editor Window. This is where most of the work is done.. You can view, edit and manage your code files.

To the left of the editor window is a vertical list of buttons, which give access to some useful features. For example you can close files, indent code and turn word wrap on/off.

There are various ways of opening, saving and closing files. You can do this from the toolbar, resource window or file menu. Once a file is opened you will notice straight away the color coding of the text.

Color coding makes it easy to spot different code within a page. It, for example, distinguishes between HTML and ColdFusion very easily. Color coding also highlights code errors, incorrect color on a piece of code would suggest an error. Colors can be changed at any time.

As well as the editor there are two other views for files. They are Browse and Design views. If you have Internet Explorer installed Browse view allows you to view HTML.

Using Studio features to build a template

1. Open Studio

2. In the Editor Window enter the following code.

```
<!DOCTYPE HTML PUBLIC "-//W3C//DTD HTML 4.0
Transitional//EN">

<html>
<head>
     <title>Untitled</title>
</head>

<body>

This is just HTML you know.

</body>
</html>
```

By default much of this should be inserted for you, that's one of the beauties of Studio-based development.

3. Click on browse and you should see your page in **Browse View**.

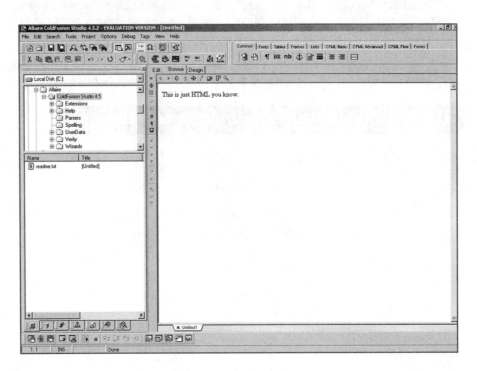

The Browse View works simply enough for HTML pages, but won't work alone for templates containing ColdFusion. Browse View is nothing but an embedded browser, and to view ColdFusion pages you will require ColdFusion Server. To be able to view ColdFusion pages in Browse View you will need to create a Development Mapping, we'll explain this later. This is a way of letting the editor know about the web server and ColdFusion server to allow it to display ColdFusion templates.

There is also another way of accessing a lot of Studio's more frequently used features. This is done by right clicking in the editor window. Here you can edit tags, carry out basic editing functions like copy and paste and insert new tags.

4. Go back to our example, by selecting **Edit view**, and place the cursor on the opening <body> tag. Right click and select Edit Tag. A dialog box will appear giving you the ability to edit all of the <body> tag's attributes like so:

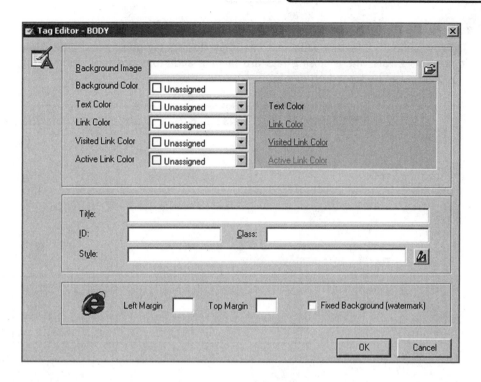

By entering details into the text boxes, code will be generated applying your details. There are dialog boxes for HTML and CFML tags. To find out if there is a dialog box for a tag place the cursor on a tag and right click. If Edit Tag is available then there will be help for you. Using this helps you in getting syntax correct first time and also is a good way of learning the tags.

There are numerous ways of accessing help from within Studio. This is a strong feature which shouldn't be overlooked. With web sites having to combine various languages it is handy to have an editor which helps you when you are writing code.

Tag completion

Tag completion is a feature which automatically closes a tag pair for you. This is useful as it prevents errors where closing tags are missing and stops possible typos in tags. Tag completion can be turned on or off.

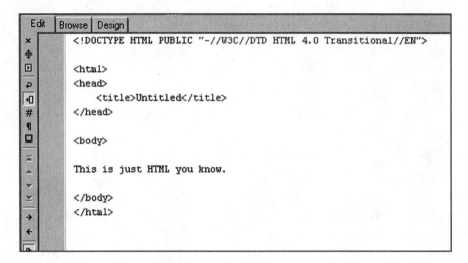

Try this:

5. In the body of the example type the following...

```
<b>
```

as soon as you type the closing > the editor will finish the tag for you so you will end up with:

```
<b> </b>
```

Tag insight

Tag insight gives you tag specific help as you type. It provides a list of all attributes for you to then select the one you want, then by pressing enter it will appear as part of your line of code.

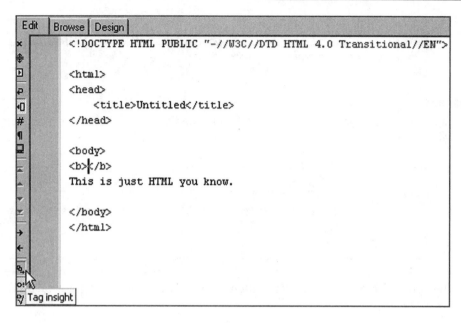

Try the following:

6. In your delete example type the following:

```
<font
```

Add a space, and a drop-down list will appear with all the attributes allowed in a font tag like so:

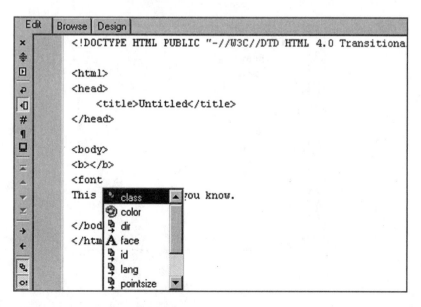

The menu offers all the attributes supported by HTML and CFML tags, this is a great way of learning all your options.

Tag tips

Tag tips are pop-up boxes which can be accessed by pressing F2 while your cursor is within a tag.

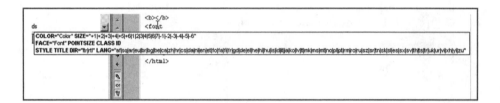

They provide more detailed information, showing which arguments are valid for each tag attribute.

Tag validation

You may get red warnings appearing at the base of your Studio window, informing you the future of tags. This particular warning appears when <FONT> is entered with **tag validation** enabled. The information is only a warning not an error in code, and as such can either be ignored or acted upon. Tag depreciation, which warns that the particular tag you have typed may not be supported in future ColdFusion updates, is a good reason to use CSS or Cascading Style Sheets.

The button enabling or disabling tag validation conventionally appears to the left of your edit window.

Edit Dialog box

Yet another way of accessing help is through using **Edit Dialog** boxes. To access these you must right click on a tag and select Edit Tag from the pop-up menu. As well as being presented with a tag dialog box you can also access its help page by clicking on Help button.

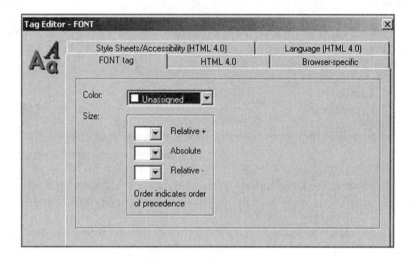

By selecting Edit Tag on a <font> tag you will be presented with the Font dialog box. In the bottom right-hand corner there is a help button which will, when pressed, open out the tag Help box.

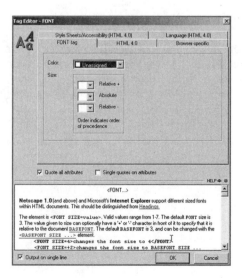

Online help

Another way of finding help is through the online help system. This is a searchable database of ColdFusion, HTML and JavaScript documentation which provides a great wealth of help with all tags and syntax.

To access this system you can either select Help > Open Help References Window from the menu bar or place the cursor within a tag and by pressing F1 its associated help page will appear.

This is only a snippet of what Studio is capable of. To get full use of all its features you will have to explore and experiment for yourselves, find out what works best for you. Spend time investigating some of the other editing options:

Feature	Description
Tag Chooser	A drill down tree interface to HTML, CFML tags.
Expression Builder	An interface, which allows you to use ColdFusion functions, variables and operators to create expressions.
Remote Site Development	Allows a PC anywhere to develop a site either through *RDS (Remote Development Service)* or *FTP*.
Access Datasources	Allows you to interact with a database either local or remote.
CSS Editor	Creates CSS code and places it in your template.
CodeSweeper	Analyses and tidies up both HTML and CFML code.

RDS, or Remote Development Service, is a service that allows HTTP access to files and databases on a server hosting ColdFusion. It is a service that needs to be configured through the Administrator.
FTP, or File Transfer Protocol, is a type of connection between two computers which allow the transfer of files.

Creating some basic ColdFusion code

Now that you know the basics of ColdFusion Studio, you may as well get down to some actual coding.

We will begin with writing a basic site which consists of a simple form. You enter your name, the site says hello, and tells you the date and time.

1. Open Studio and create a new file. Using the Default Template asks ColdFusion Studio to produce the bare bones of the template for you.

2. Creating forms is simple in ColdFusion Studio. In the editor window select forms from the tag toolbar. You may find that there is no Forms on the tag toolbar. To add it simply right-click on the toolbar and select Forms from the list. Then click the Form icon, and enter the details as shown, your Action will be `displayname.cfm`, which is the name of the template that the form's data will be submitted to:

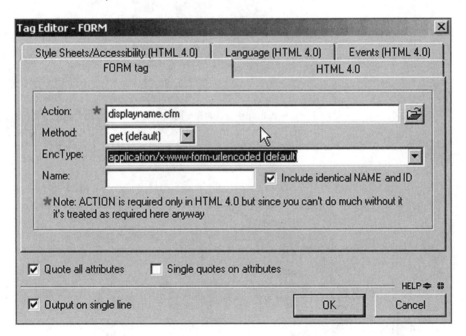

3. Click OK and you will have the opening and closing `<form>` tags. Next place the cursor between the opening and closing form tags, right-click and select Insert Tag.

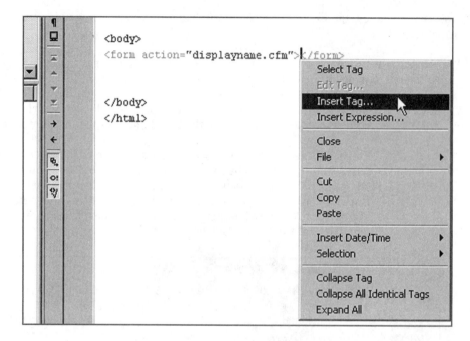

4. The Tag Chooser will appear with a list of tags in various scripting languages. Expand the HTML folder then Forms folder then click on General. In the right-hand window will be a list of all `<form>` HTML elements.

5. Select:

```
INPUT TYPE="Text"
```

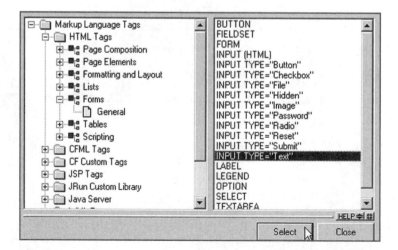

6. And click select. In the Tag Editor for INPUT enter myName like so and click OK.

7. Next, in the Tag Chooser select:

```
INPUT TYPE="Submit"
```

8. Enter Send in the value box like so, then click OK.

9. Close the Tag Chooser and you should end up with your code containing the following tags. They may not appear laid out exactly as shown, but the functionality will be identical. Running CodeSweeper, Tools > CodeSweeper > Default CodeSweeper should clean up the layout.

```
<!DOCTYPE HTML PUBLIC "-//W3C//DTD HTML 4.0
Transitional//EN">
<html>
<head>
    <title>
        Untitled
    </title>
</head>
    <body>
        <form action="displayname.cfm"
method="post">
            <input type="text" name="myName">
            <input type="submit" value="Send">
        </form>
    </body>
</html>
```

In order to run our ColdFusion templates they must be stored on our server. In some cases this will be on your development machine, but often it will not. In any case the templates will be stored in a directory known as your **Web Root**.

> When a user requests web pages they are to be found within a directory on a web server. The directory they are in is a special directory used by the web server. This special directory is commonly known as the web root. On a Windows machine this is normally c:\inetpub\wwwroot.

10. Create a directory called cfExample within your particular web root and save the file within it, as entername.cfm. If you are working on a remote server then you will need to upload it to your web space.

11. Next, create a new file and enter the following code.

```
<!DOCTYPE HTML PUBLIC "-//W3C//DTD HTML 4.0
Transitional//EN">
<html>
<head>
    <title>
        Untitled
    </title>
</head>
    <body bgcolor="Black">
      <cfoutput>
            <!--Randomnly selects a color from a
list of colors-->
          <cfset
➡fontColor=listGetAt("red,green,blue,teal,pink",ran
➡drange(1,5))>
          <font size="4" color="#fontColor#">Hello
➡#form.myName#, The time is
➡#timeformat(now())# and the date is
➡#dateformat(now(),"dd/mm/yyyy")#</font>
        </cfoutput>
      </body>
</html>
```

12. Save the file as `displayname.cfm` in the directory you created earlier.

Don't worry about the syntax, it will be explained later (if you wish to learn the syntax place the cursor within the word and press F1 to see if there is any help).

Now you have both your files saved in a directory off the web root called `cfExample` you will want to test them.

13. Open a browser and enter the appropriate URL, if your machine is your server it will be:

> `http://127.0.0.1/cfExample/entername.cfm`

If not the URL will take the form *YOURSERVER*/cfExample/ `entername.cfm`.. Where YOURSERVER represents the address of your particular web root directory. Your server can be referred to as `coldf`, as you will see in our screen shot. You will be presented with a page like this:

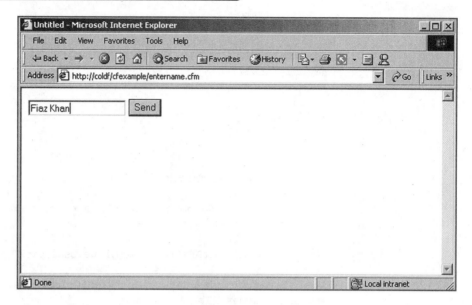

14. Enter your name, or whatever pseudonym takes your fancy, and click Send. Your browser should be sent to displayname.cfm:

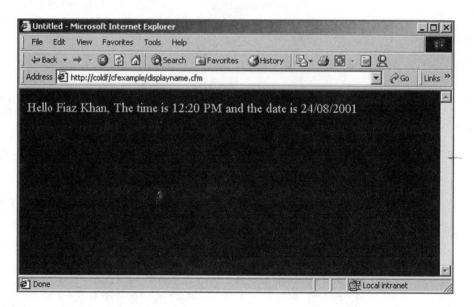

15. Refresh the page and you should see the color of the text change, due to it being set randomly by our template. You may be presented with a pop-up box like so:

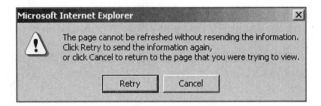

This is simply informing you that the information you sent from `entername.cfm` needs to be resent for `displayname.cfm` to work.

16. Click Retry to continue.

You can also test the page in **Browse view**. To do this you will have to create a **Development Mapping**.

> *Development Mappings are the way of letting ColdFusion Studio know the URL and file paths for use in Browse view (and for Debugging). Studio relies on these mappings to communicate the correct file paths of all files with the browser in Browse view.*

Creating a Development Mapping

1. Choose Debug > Development Mappings to open the **Mappings panel** of the Remote Development Settings dialog box.

2. In the ColdFusion Server list box at the top of the dialog box, choose localhost **or the name of your particular server.**

3. In the Studio Path box, enter the file path ColdFusion Studio uses for the page you're viewing (e.g. `C:\Inetpub\wwwroot\cfExample` or in our case `\\Coldf\cdrive\Inetpub\wwwroot`). Click Add.

4. If you're viewing against a local server, the Studio and ColdFusion Server paths are the same. If you're viewing against a remote server, enter the CF Server Path.

5. In the Browser Path enter `http://127.0.0.1` or the IP address or your server and click Add.

6. Click OK.

7. Click on Browse and you will be able to test in Browse View.

Congratulations, you have just created your first ColdFusion site.

Case study

At the end of the last chapter we outlined the case study project that we're going to build throughout the book. In this chapter we're going to start the building. We're going to ease into the task by refreshing our skills on building buttons and in Flash. We'll also be building a preloader movie clip. These symbols will be an integral part of our completed forum.

Building the back button

1. Open up Flash and save the new movie as `forum.fla` in a new case study folder. It doesn't matter where you create the folder, as we'll need to move the SWF file to a web folder when we integrate the ColdFusion in later chapters. Open up the Movie Properties box (Modify>Movie) and ensure the Frame Rate is set to 12fps and the stage dimensions to 550px by 400px. We'll leave the background color as white for the moment.

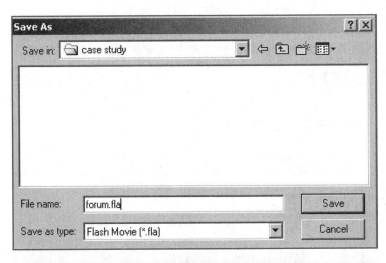

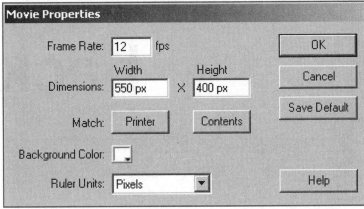

2. Create a button symbol (Insert>New Symbol...) and name it bnback. We all have our own naming conventions and the importance of consistency can't be stressed enough. The naming convention we'll use throughout this case study will have buttons with a bn prefix, graphic symbols with a gr prefix and movie clips with a mc prefix.

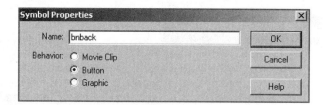

3. Next, open the Character panel from the Text menu and change the font to Arial, the color to black and the character size to 28. Also select the bold icon. Using the Text Tool type back on the stage.

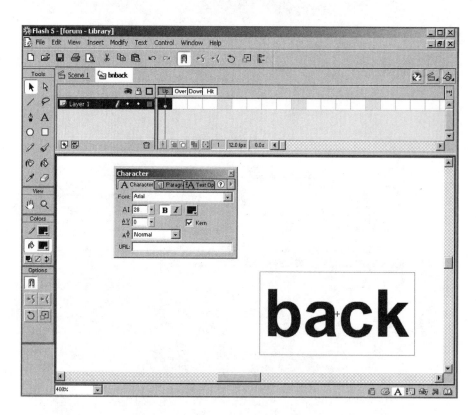

4. Find a blank area of the stage and open up the Stroke panel. Set the stroke to 2.5 and keep the color black. We'll now use the Oval Tool to draw a circle that measures 32 pixels across. We don't want the circle to be filled so draw it with no fill or delete the fill after you've drawn it. To ensure we get the size right it's best to open up the Info panel and set the w and h values to 32, making sure that we have the circle selected.

5. Our next step is to make an arrow that points to the left within the circle. To do this, increase the stroke width to 7 and draw a horizontal line within the circle. We then reuse the line tool to add the wings of the arrow.

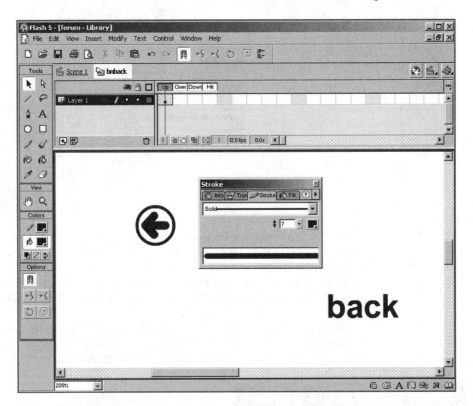

6. Position the arrow to the left of back and group the two together (Modify>Group). We'll align the group to the center of the stage now We've now created the basis of the back button. We'll make a slight modification on the Over state of the button so the user can see that the button is meant to be pressed. Create keyframes on the Over and Hit states of the timeline. On the Hit state click on the lines of the arrow until the lines become selected, either individually or as one, and change the stroke color of the arrow to red. When the user moves their cursor over the button the color of the arrow will change to red, so they'll realize that it's a button.

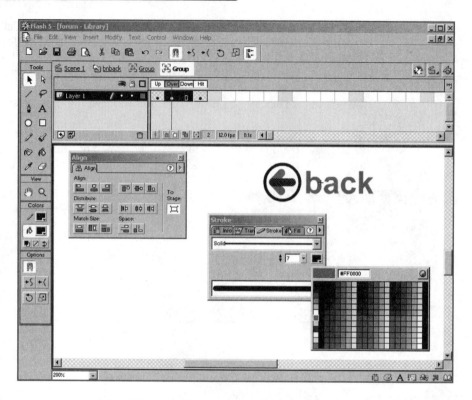

7. On the Hit state draw a rectangle of any color over the text and the arrow. This rectangle won't be visible when the button is used, but ensures that the whole symbol acts as a 'hot spot' and not just the lines of the text and image. We want the white space between the arrow and its circle, and the area between letters to be active so this rectangle is vital.

There we go! The back button is now complete and ready for use. The next button we're going to create is the reply button. This button will be used when a user wishes to respond to a message in our forum.

Creating the reply button

1. We can use the foundations of the back button to create our reply button. Open the library and select bnback. From the library's Options menu select Duplicate.... This will make a copy of the back button, which we'll name as bnreply.

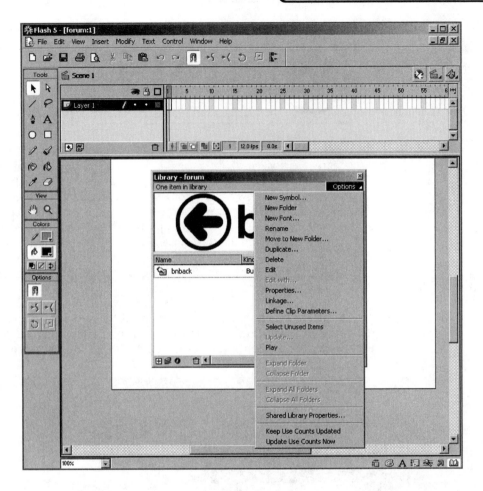

2. Open up our new button in edit mode. Delete the Over, Down and Hit
states of the button from the timeline. It's quicker for us to duplicate the
Up state once we've done it than editing all four states in turn. Click on
the back text until it becomes editable, and type reply instead.

3. Our next move is to select the arrow symbol and its circle and rotate the 90 degrees clockwise so the arrow now points upwards (Modify>Transform>Rotate 90° CW). With the arrow and its circle still selected copy them. Now paste a copy onto the stage and position it to the right of reply. We now have an arrow pointing upwards on either side of the word. Using the arrow tool group the arrows and text together and then center them on the stage. Insert keyframes on the Over and Hit states again. The reply text and arrows should now be on the center of all four states. If not, copy them from the Up state and Paste in Place on the Over and Hit states.

4. As with the back button, we want the color of the arrows to change to red in the Over and Down states. Use the same technique as we did for the back button to change the stoke color of the two arrows to red.

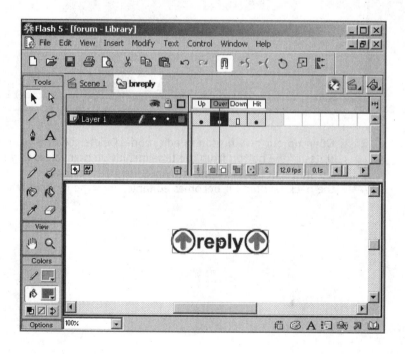

5. The last step in completing this button is to once again draw a rectangle over the buttons content on the Hit state. Once this is done we've finished our second button. The next button is an exact replica of the reply button, but has post instead of reply. The post button will be pressed when a forum user wants to make a new post on the forum.

6. To make the post button, once again duplicate bnback and then follow the exact steps we've used above to make the reply button – only remember to change the text to post and not reply this time! Name the new post button bnpost.

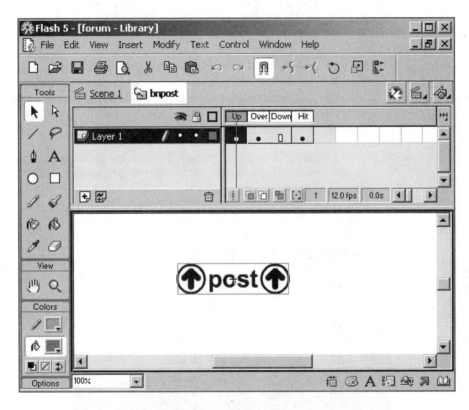

We've now created three of the five buttons we're going to make in this chapter. Before we move on the last two, let's make the movie clip that will be show while the user waits for sections of the site to load.

The preloader movie clip

1. From the Insert menu choose New Symbol.... This time we want to select the Movie Clip behavior and we'll name the clip mcpreloader.

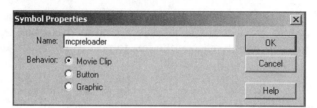

2. Start by drawing a large black rectangle that covers the stage on the default layer and make this layer 20 frames long. This layer is only temporary so we can see white text on the stage, its dimensions are therefore not important. Lock this layer so we don't accidentally put any content on it.

3. Create a second layer above Layer 1 and call it text symbol. Open up the Character panel and choose the Arial font, set the font size to 25 and choose white as the text color. Click the Text Tool on the stage to create a text box and type Loading. By not purposefully inserting a keyframe on frame one our text should span all 20 frames of the clip.

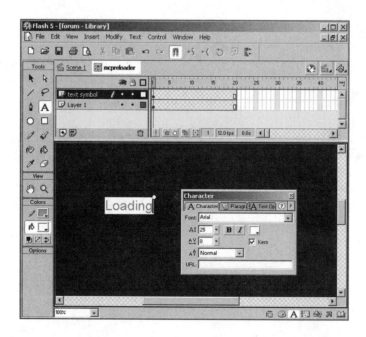

4. Next, select the Arrow Tool and click on the text box we've just made. Center this on the stage using the Align panel. With the text box still selected covert it into a graphic symbol called grloading (Insert>Convert to Symbol). We're doing this so we can easily create a tween with the text.

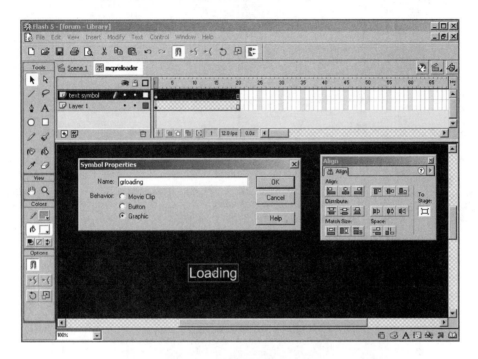

5. Create a keyframe at frame 10, and then insert a motion tween between frames 1 and 10. By inserting a further keyframe at frame 20 we should be left with two motion tweens.

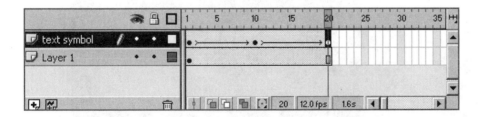

Select frame 10 on the timeline and open up the Effects panel. Choose the Alpha option and reduce it to 0%. Press Enter and watch the screen. You'll see the text fade out and then fade in again. We want this to run as a constant loop so we'll add a gotoAndPlay action to frame 20 to loop the movie back to frame 1:

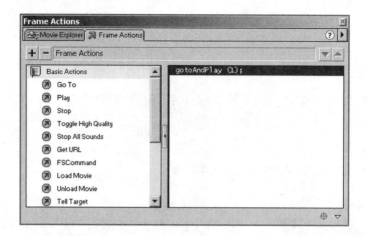

6.   Create a new layer and name it spinner. Let's start this layer by opening up the Stroke panel. Select red and a stroke width of 2. Using the Oval Tool draw a circle with this stroke and no fill that measures 200px across – remember we can make the measurements exact by using the Info panel. Center the circle on the stage so it's over the loading graphic.

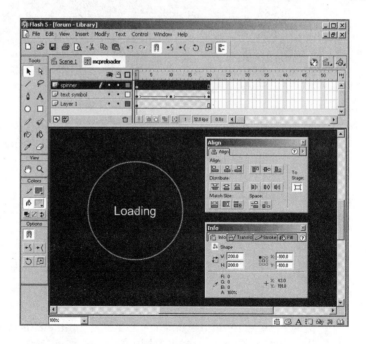

7. Select the Eraser Tool and erase the top portion of the circle. We'll now use the Line Tool to make an arrow on the left side of the broken circle.

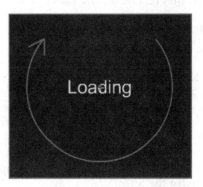

8. Create a motion tween between frames 1 and 20 and then insert a keyframe at frame 20 to complete the tween. With frame 1 selected, open up the frame panel and change Rotate from Auto to CW (clockwise). Set the number of rotation times to 4. If you press ENTER now and watch the movie you'll see our circle spinning round. However, it doesn't spin in a perfect circle. That's because we chopped the top of the circle off so the rotation shape is no longer square. We can sort this slight problem out by changing the point around which the circle rotates. Select our circle on the screen and you'll see the center point is below the center point of the stage. Choose Modify>Transform>Edit Center and move the circle's center so it is above the stages center cross. Our spinner should now rotate in a near perfect circle.

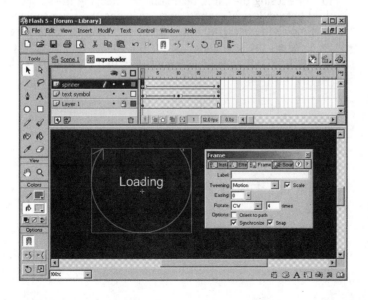

Our preloader movie clip is now completed and we can delete the temporary Layer 1 from the stage. We've just got two small buttons left to create, and the good news is that they're virtually the same!

The up and down buttons

1. Create a new button symbol and call it bnup. In the Stroke panel and set the width to 2.5 and the color to red. Using the Oval Tool draw a circle with no fill using this stroke. Make the circle 40.5px in diameter, using the Info panel to make sure we get the sizes right. Center this circle on the stage.

2. We're going to make an arrow in this circle, just as we did with the back button. This time the arrow will be pointing upwards. We'll use a 7pt red stroke to make the arrow.

3. As with all our other buttons, we want keyframes on the Over and Hit states, so do this now. On the Over state change the color of the arrow to white, using the same technique of changing the stroke color that we used before. It may seem strange changing the color to white, but in the final movie the background will be black so we'll be able to see the arrows then. When the user passes over this button they'll see the arrow color change from red to white and will realize that the button can be activated.

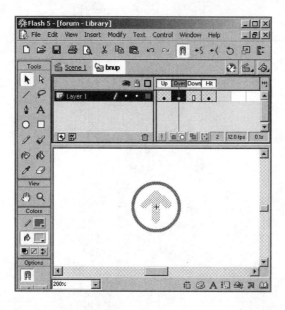

4. We complete the up button by drawing a rectangle over the arrow and its circle on the Hit state. Once again the purpose of this rectangle is to make the entire button active and not just the lines (remember that this rectangle will not be viewable in the published movie).

5. So, we've just got one button left to do now: the down button. As I mentioned earlier, this is almost exactly the same as the up button, except that it points down. From the library make a duplicate copy of the up button, naming it bndown. Open the new button in edit mode. All we need to do to finish this button is flip the arrow so it points downwards on the Up and Over states. We achieve this by selecting the arrow and its circle and using Flip Vertical from the Modify>Transform menu.

That's it! All the major buttons that will appear in our forum have now been created. In the case study section of our next chapter we'll start putting these symbols to use as we build the basis of the Flash movie that will house our forum.

Summary

Installing ColdFusion Server and Studio is a simple task, the main bulk of the work is finding your way round the Administrator and Studio features. It may seem daunting now, but once you are aware of all the ways in which ColdFusion Studio can help you write your code you'll be able to progress quickly, saving your effort for the really meaty issue - learning CFML and integrating with your Flash movies..

3 CFML Concepts

What We'll Cover in this Chapter

- *CFML syntax*

- *Creating ColdFusion templates with CFML*

- *Using variables*

- *Linking ColdFusion templates to a Flash Movie*

What is CFML?

CFML is a tag-based language which allows you to write feature-rich, dynamic, database-driven websites. What we mean by tag-based is that it is similar to HTML (note the similarity in names) in that it has tags which tell the server what to do. So, for example, in HTML you have a form tag which takes the format of an opening tag:

```
<form action="somepage.html" method="post">
```

and then a closing tag

```
</form>
```

Similarly in CFML...

```
<cfform action="somepage.cfm" method="post">

</cfform>
```

For some of you this will make learning CFML a breeze. For those without much HTML experience don't worry, neither of these languages are that hard to grasp and we will, of course, explain absolutely everything as we go along. So let's go!

Starting to write CFML

Firstly you have a Web Server and ColdFusion Server installed and running, we did all this in Chapter 2. There are several text editors on the market which make the job of writing code easy and if you're of a masochistic bent you can even use Notepad, but to be honest, there isn't anything better than ColdFusion Studio for writing CFML. Along with its text editing capabilities, and all the tag help we saw in Chapter 2, there is also excellent documentation covering pretty much all of CFML.

Have you got the time?

Let's create a simple example which will further demonstrate what is required when creating ColdFusion templates.

1. Open up ColdFusion Studio and begin by inserting the following line of code into the editor window, within the default <body> HTML tags.

```
<cfset timeNow = #timeformat(now())#>
```

The `<cfset>` tag is used to define variables, `timeNow` is set here to become the current time. `now` being a CFML function that returns the current time, and `timeformat` a function to format the data in differing ways. We're using its default setting here.

2. Now we've set the variable, we need to tell ColdFusion to output it to our browser, start by adding an opening `<cfoutput>` tag.

```
<cfoutput><!- - - opening CFML tag - - ->
```

3. Within our `<cfoutput>` tags we can add HTML code if we so wish, add this line which sets the font style and size:

```
<font face="Arial" size="2"><!- - - opening HTML
tag - - ->
```

4. Now we add the actual text to be output, and enclosed in # pound signs, (hashes for the English) the variable name:

```
The Time is #timeNow#
```

5. Finally we close the CFML and HTML tags, with the lines:

```
</font><!- - - closing HTML tag - - ->

</cfoutput><!- - - closing CFML tag - - ->
```

Which leaves our template looking like this:

```
<!DOCTYPE HTML PUBLIC "-//W3C//DTD HTML 4.0
Transitional//EN">

<html>
<head>
     <title>Untitled</title>
</head>

<body>

<cfset timeNow = #timeformat(now())#>

<cfoutput><!- - - opening CFML tag - - ->

<font face="Arial" size="2"><!- - - opening HTML
tag - - ->
```

```
The Time is #timeNow#
</font><!- - - closing HTML tag - - ->

</cfoutput><!- - - closing CFML tag - - ->

</body>
</html>
```

> *All ColdFusion template files must end with a* .cfm *extension. This instructs the web server to pass the template onto the ColdFusion server for processing.*

6. If you save this within your web root directory and then open it in a browser you'll see what the current time is.

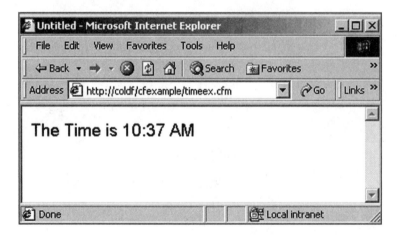

This is a simple example but does highlight the similarities between CFML and HTML and how they sit together in the template. But what goes on when someone views a CFML template? It's time we found out.

Behind the scenes

Go back and view our time example in a browser, then view the source code of the web page (View > Source in Internet Explorer, View > Page Source if you're using Netscape). We get to see the following.

```
<!DOCTYPE HTML PUBLIC "-//W3C//DTD HTML 4.0
Transitional//EN">

<html>
<head>
      <title>Untitled</title>
</head>

<body>

<!- - - opening CFML tag - - ->

<font face="Arial" size="2"><!- - - opening HTML
tag - - ->
The Time is 12:17 PM
</font><!- - - closing HTML tag - - ->

<!- - - closing CFML tag - - ->

</body>
</html>
```

As you can see all the CFML has disappeared from the code. This is because ColdFusion server processes and removes all CFML and returns HTML to the browser.

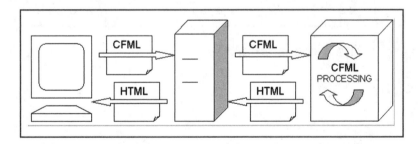

- The client requests a page that contains CFML tags.

- The web server passes the files to ColdFusion Server if the file has a `cfm` extension.

- ColdFusion Server scans the page and processes all CFML tags.

- ColdFusion Server passes back only HTML and other client-side web technologies back to the web server.

- The web server passes the page back to the browser.

As you can see in our time example there are # symbols around pieces of code. This tells the Sever that this is not a piece of text but an expression that needs evaluating.

7. Try this, open the file back up in Studio and remove the pound signs.

```
The Time is #timeNow#
```

becomes

The Time is timeNow

8. Save the file and view it in your browser.

What's happened here is that ColdFusion Server no longer recognizes that `timeNow` is an expression, and is treating it as a piece of plain text.

9. To get ColdFusion Server to look for and evaluate `timeNow` it needs to be surrounded by the # sign. Go and put them back now!

    But the # symbol isn't the only requirement for displaying expressions. If you look back at the CFML code you can see that around the font tag we used the `<cfoutput>` tag. This tag tells the server to find any expression between the opening and closing tag and try and evaluate any that are found. In this case it found `#timeNow#` and evaluated it into the current time.

10. Try removing the opening and closing `<cfoutput>` tags and display it in a browser, and you will see:

This time ColdFusion Server has ignored the # symbol because it has not been instructed to evaluate an expression which is the function of the `<cfoutput>` tag. As well as outputting content `<cfoutput>` also outputs recordsets from database queries, but we're getting ahead of ourselves here and this will be explained later in the book, when we learn about using databases.

> *Use pound signs (#) to distinguish expressions from plain text. When expressions are evaluated, the resulting value is substituted for the expression text. An expression or a database query needs to be within `<cfoutput> </cfoutput>` to be evaluated.*

CFML building blocks

As with all programming languages CFML code is divided into sections based on functionality, in the same kind of way that natural language is categorized into verbs, nouns and the like. Before we get into any deep coding we should discuss this and how it'll impact upon our work:

Variables

A **variable** is simply a temporary storage place for data within a web page. The most basic way to create a variable is to use `<cfset>` like so:

```
<cfset myVariable = "This is data being held by myVariable">
<cfoutput>
#myVariable#
</cfoutput>
```

Viewed within a browser this would become:

```
This is data being held by myVariable
```

The line "This is data being held by myVariable" is stored in a variable called `myVariable`.

*With some programming languages you will have to define what type the variable will be, whether it will it hold a number, a string or some other supported type. With CFML you don't have to worry about data types, and therefore CFML is known as a **typeless** language.*

Tags

Tags are the CFML that begins `<cf>` `<cfoutput>` and `<cfset>` which we've already used are ColdFusion tags. A list of the many tags can be found in the Studio help file, and it's definitely worth going through the list of tags and finding out for yourself just how much ColdFusion can do. Often people assume that ColdFusion can't carry out some action but chances are there is a tag or function (explained later) which can do what you require.

Tags can be broken up into categories as follows...

- ColdFusion Forms Tags
- Database Manipulation Tags
- Data Output Tags
- Exception Handling Tags
- Extensibility Tags
- File Management Tags
- Flow-Control Tags
- Internet Protocol Tags
- Java Servlet and Java Object Tags
- Variable Manipulation Tags
- Web Application Framework Tags

Let's work through some of the basic ColdFusion tags.

Flow control with tags

The tag `<cflocation>` allows a page to redirect to a different URL, which may be another ColdFusion template or web page.

1. Open a new page in the editor, File > New, and select the Default Template, and insert the text below between the `<body>` tags:

    This is a line of text from page1.cfm

2. Save it in your web root as `page1.cfm`.

3. Create another new page in the same manner and enter the following code:

```
<!DOCTYPE HTML PUBLIC "-//W3C//DTD HTML 4.0
Transitional//EN">

<html>
<head>
      <title>Untitled</title>
</head>

<body>

<cflocation url="page1.cfm">
This is a line of text from page2.cfm
</body>
</html>
```

4. Save this template as `page2.cfm`.

Now if you open `page2.cfm` in a browser you will then find the URL changing and `page1.cfm` displayed. This is because the `<cflocation url="page1.cfm">` has redirected the page from itself to `page1.cfm`. We don't get to see whatever was on our original page.

This can be useful, especially when used with an *IF...THEN...ELSE* decision, to send the user to different URLs depending upon some criteria. But page2.cfm is doing nothing of much use in our example, we'd be as well to simply view page1.cfm to start with.

We can get to see page2.cfm's contents as well, by including page1.cfm inside, <cfinclude> is the tag that allows you to include one web page with another.

5. Open up page2.cfm and delete the line:

    ```
    <cflocation url="page1.cfm">
    ```

6. And in its place type:

    ```
    <cfinclude template="page1.cfm">
    ```

7. If you now open page2.cfm in a browser you will see the text from page1.cfm, as well as the text from page2.cfm. Note that this time the URL has not changed.

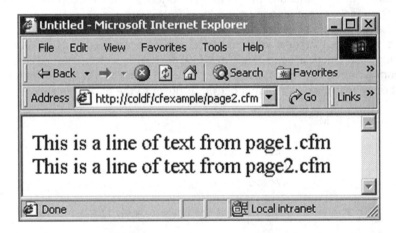

page2.cfm has included the content of page1.cfm and displayed it to screen.

As you can see tags allow for a great deal of functionality in a very small amount of code. Also you can see now how easy it is to both read and write CFML, which makes development of ColdFusion sites relatively easy task. This book contains an appendix with a brief description of many of the CFML tags you'll come across.

Functions

Functions allow you to alter, or manipulate data. At the start of this chapter we used a function to format the current time like so:

```
<cfset timeNow = #timeformat(now())#>
```

Here we used a function called timeformat. What timeformat does is allow you to take the current time and date and convert it into a more readable format. If we removed timeformat we would end up with the following.

```
The Time is {ts '2001-08-30 23:11:10'}
```

What timeformat did was it took the current date and time in its raw format and converted it into a friendlier format like so.

```
The Time is 11:11 PM
```

timeformat is just one of many functions, and we'll be using a fair chunk of them as we work through the book. For the rest, the ColdFusion documentation is comprehensive and the names of the functions themselves are often usefully descriptive of their purpose. When you feel up to it go and have a look.

Those functions that deal with numerical data are grouped by ColdFusion under the heading Mathematical Functions. They include the expected; sine, cosine, producing a random number, as well as some more unusual functionality. For example round is a function which rounds a real number up or down to the nearest integer.

The following CFML:

```
<cfoutput>
#round(2.7)#
</cfoutput>
```

Would yield 3 in our browser window, the nearest whole number being 3.

> In addition to built in functions there are another set of functions called User Defined Functions. These were introduced in Version 5 and allow you to create your own custom functions. This is beyond the scope of this chapter but is something to keep in mind for when you begin writing ColdFusion sites.

Operators

To do any serious programming you will have to come against operators. There are 4 types of operators in CFML:

- Arithmetic

- Boolean

- Decision

- String

Arithmetic operators

The simplest operators are those for doing your sums with. Here's a quick tabular summary:

Operator	Description
+ - * /	The basic arithmetic operators: addition, subtraction, multiplication, and division which are found in all languages.
+ -	Unary arithmetic operators for setting the sign of a number.
MOD	Returns the remainder (modulus) after a number is divided. For example, 11 MOD 4 is 3.
\	Divide an integer by another integer. For example, 9 \ 4 is 2
^	Returns the result of a number raised to a power (exponent). For example, 2 ^ 3 is 8.

To test this out you could try the following CFML:

```
<cfoutput>
<cfset number1 = 20>
<cfset number2 = 15>
<result = number1 + number1>
#result#
</cfoutput>
```

This would output 35 in the browser window.

Boolean and decision operators

These operators always return a Boolean value, that is TRUE or FALSE:

Operator	Description
NOT	Reverses the value of an argument. For example, NOT TRUE is FALSE and vice versa.
AND	Returns TRUE if both arguments are TRUE; returns FALSE otherwise. For example, TRUE AND TRUE is TRUE, but TRUE AND FALSE is FALSE.
OR	Returns TRUE if any of the arguments is TRUE; returns FALSE otherwise. For example, TRUE OR FALSE is TRUE, but FALSE OR FALSE is FALSE.
XOR	Exclusive or-either, or, but not both. Returns TRUE if the truth values of both arguments are different; returns FALSE otherwise. For example, TRUE XOR TRUE is FALSE, but TRUE XOR FALSE is TRUE.
EQV	Equivalence both true or both false. The EQV operator is the opposite of the XOR operator. For example, TRUE EQV TRUE is TRUE, but TRUE EQV FALSE is FALSE.
IMP	Implication. A IMP B is the truth value of the logical statement "If A Then B." A IMP B is FALSE only when A is TRUE and B is FALSE.

They are often used in combination with the decision operators, don't be afraid of the wealth of information here, the decision operators in particular read like English.

Operator	Description
IS	Performs a case-insensitive comparison of two values. Returns TRUE if the values are identical.
IS NOT	Performs a case-insensitive comparison of two values. Returns TRUE if the values are not identical.
CONTAINS	Determines whether the value on the left is contained in the value on the right. Returns TRUE if it is.
DOES NOT CONTAIN	Determines whether the value on the left is not contained in the value on the right. Returns TRUE if it is not contained.

GREATER THAN	Determines whether the value on the left is greater than the value on the right. Returns TRUE if it is.
LESS THAN	Determines whether the value on the left is less than the value on the right. Returns TRUE if it is.
GREATER THAN OR EQUAL TO	Determines whether the value on the left is greater than or equal to the value on the right. Returns TRUE if it is.
LESS THAN OR EQUAL TO	Determines whether the value on the left is less than or equal to the value on the right. Returns TRUE if it is.

This piece of CFML uses Boolean and decision operators

```
<cfset number1 = 1>
<cfif NOT number1 IS 1>
        FALSE
<cfelse>
        TRUE
</cfif>
```

<cfif> (more of which later) is used with <cfelse> and </cfif> here to form a basic *IF... THEN... ELSE* structure. This would return TRUE because number1 is 1 and the first condition is saying "If number1 is not equal to 1 then display FALSE else display TRUE". Since number1 is 1 then condition would return TRUE.

There are alternative ways of using decision operators, like aliases. They are...

- IS can be EQUAL or EQ

- IS NOT can be NOT EQUAL or NEQ

- GREATER THAN can be GT

- LESS THAN is also known as LT

- GREATER THAN OR EQUAL TO can be GTE or just GE

- LESS THAN OR EQUAL TO can be LTE or LE

So,

```
<cfif 10 GREATER THAN 9>
      TRUE
<cfelse>
      FALSE
</cfif>
```

(Which would display TRUE because "10 is greater than 9".) Could also be written as:

```
<cfif 10 GT 9>
      TRUE
<cfelse>
      FALSE
</cfif>
```

At this point we should mention just how important it is to get your order of operators correct. If they're not, the result returned could be different to what you expect it to be. For example you may expect:

```
100 - 50 * 2 / 10
```

to calculate the answer 10, but in fact it actually returns 90.

> This is due to something called **Operator Precedence**. When mathematical operations are carried out mathmatical operators have an order of precedence which means that some operators take priority.

To return 10 as the result, the calculation must be formatted like so:

```
((100 - 50) * 2) / 10 = 10
```

Grouping together sections of the sum has given the expected order of action. "100 minus 50 then multiply by 2 then divide by 10"

The precedence of operators is as follows...

- Unary +, Unary -
- ^
- *, /
- \
- MOD
- +, -
- &
- EQ, NEQ, LT, LTE, GT, GTE, CONTAINS, DOES NOT CONTAIN
- NOT
- AND
- OR
- XOR
- EQV
- IMP

String Operator

There is only one string operator. This is "&" which simply concatenates strings.

```
<cfset firstname = "Fiaz ">
<cfset surname = "Khan">
<cfset fullname = firstname & surname>
<cfoutput>
#fullname#
</cfoutput>
```

would <output>

```
Fiaz Khan
```

What has happened here is that the operator has strung together firstname and surname to make fullname. Note that it doesn't automatically include a space, so if one is required it'll have to be added as well.

Conditions

Conditional statements control the flow of your code. They allow you to make decisions and send the code in different directions. The experienced ActionScripters amongst you may be very familiar with conditional statements, but let's look at how they look in CFML:

The most common form for a conditional statement is:

<cfif>...<cfelseif>...<cfelse>...</cfif> like so:

```
<cfif expression>
    ...
<cfelseif expression>
    ...
<cfelse>
    ...
</cfif>
```

And just to make sure we've got it, a very quick run-able example:

```
<cfset number = 1>
<cfif number is 1>
    The number is 1
<cfelse>
    The number is not 1
</cfif>
```

Here, the code is saying "if the number is 1' then display the number is 1' else display the number is not 1".

Loops

Again, this should not be a new programming concept for most of you, loops allow you to repeat an instruction over and over again until a condition is met.

<cfloop>, the CFML loop tag, is able to form 5 different types of loops. They are:

- Index Loops

- Conditional Loops

- Looping over a Query

- Looping over a List

- Looping over a COM Collection or Structure

An index loop starts from one number and repeats, iterating the index number in steps until a second value is reached. This index loop will print out a list of numbers 1 to 5:

```
<cfoutput>
<cfloop from=1 to=5 index="number">
#number#<br>
</cfloop>
</cfoutput>
```


 being a HTML tag for a carriage return.

Conditional loops continue until a specified criteria is met you may refer to this as a *repeat-until* loop. You can also loop through record sets returned from queries, or loop through comma-delimited lists.

Posting data using forms

There will be many situations where you will have a form which, when submitted, will send data to other ColdFusion templates to process. For example you may have a "Contact Us" form which, when filled, sends the details via e-mail to a company. To be able to send data from a form to another ColdFusion template is a simple task. There are two ways of creating forms, either the HTML <form> tag or the CFML <cfform> tag. The <cfform> tag offers a great deal more functionality, and impressive data validation but for this example the <form> tag is enough.

1. Create a new page from the Default template and enter the following code between the <body> tags:

    ```
    <form action="process.cfm" method="GET">
        Year (yyyy)<br>
        <input type="text" name="leapYear"><br>
        <input type="submit"><br>
    </form>
    ```

2. Save it within your server's web root as myform.cfm.

3. Open another new Default template and insert the following code, again within the `<body>` tags:

```
<cfoutput>
<cfif isLeapYear("#leapYear#")>
     #leapYear# is a leap year.
<cfelse>
     #leapYear# is not a leap year.
</cfif>
</cfoutput>
```

Save this one in the same directory as `process.cfm`.

4. If you enter a year and click submit you should get a message telling you whether it is a leap year or not.

So, how does it work?

If we take a look at the code of myform.cfm we can see that it is very similar to a HMTL form.

```
<form action="process.cfm" method="GET">
    Year (yyyy)<br>
    <input type="text" name="leapYear"><br>
    <input type="submit"><br>
</form>
```

There are two attributes required for the <form> tag, they are action and method.

- Action: The URL of the page you are submitting to.

- Method: A method of accessing the URL specified in Action.

The action is straightforward, it is process.cfm. The method can either be POST or GET and you can see the difference in the URL. If you submit the form you will see the leapyear parameter being passed over as part of the URL. This is achieved using the GET method. This is ok for some situations but not for all. For example if you had a login page and when users submitted the form the login and password would be available for all to see.

Now change myform.cfm to read as follows:

```
<form action="process.cfm" method="POST">
    Year (yyyy)<br>
    <input type="text" name="leapYear"><br>
    <input type="submit"><br>
</form>
```

If you try and submit you will find that the leapyear parameter is no longer being passed as a URL variable but as a FORM variable. This is more secure when passing sensitive data around, you would not want passwords displayed in the URL.

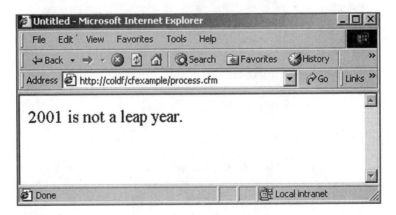

This is all well and good but try submitting with no year available or enter letters into the year text box. What happens is that ColdFusion Server throws an error. To remedy this we would have to validate form data (which will be explained later in the book).

Now that we have a basic understanding of some of the core CFML concepts we can now apply them to Flash and bring it all together.

ColdFusion and Flash: together at last

Flash and ColdFusion work together very well. But there are a two important issues when passing data between ColdFusion and Flash. The first main issue is white space.

When viewing ColdFusion templates in a browser the server tends to leave behind a lot of white space. Browsers can deal with this but Flash can't.

To get round this problem you will have to suppress all white space, you will have to use

```
<cfsetting enablecfoutputonly="YES">
```

at the very top of your template.

This tag stops the output of all text/HTML to screen thus, suppressing all white space.

*The other issue is data which is passed from a ColdFusion template to a Flash movie. Since this can take the form of almost any character we will have to **URLEncode** the data. This means converting all spaces and non-alphanumeric characters to there equivalent hexadecimal escape sequences.*

To do this you will use the function

```
#urlencodedformat(URL)#
```

this will turn, for example:

```
This is an example of a normal string with non-
alphanumeric characters!""££$$%%^^&&*!!!
```

into

```
This%20is%20an%20example%20of%20a%20normal%20string%20with%20non%2Dal
phanumeric%20characters%21%22%A3%A3%24%24%25%25%5E%5E%26%26%2A%21%21%
21
```

It is the second line that Flash can understand.

Leaping into Flash

In this example we will create a Flash form which will check to see if a year is a leap year, much like our last example. We'll rush through this a bit as you should be comfortable with the level of Flash we're going to use.

The Flash movie

1. Start a new movie in Flash, save it as `leapyear.fla` in your web root directory. Begin by adding two extra layers to the timeline. Name your three layers button, text and actions.

2. In the text layer, add two text fields. Using the Text Options panel, give the first text field the name `sendText` and set its type to be Input Text. Give the second text field the name `isleap` and set its type to be Dynamic Text.

3. In the button layer, create a button. You can either design your own, or else use one from a common library (use Window -> Common Libraries -> Buttons to open the button library). Right-click on the button and open its Actions window. Add the following ActionScript to the button:

   ```
   on (release) {
       loadVariables ("checkyear.cfm?year=" add
   ➥sendText, "");
   }
   ```

   This script will be called when the user has pressed (and released) the button. When this occurs, it uses the `loadVariables` action to pass the value of the `sendText` field to the ColdFusion template `checkyear.cfm` (which you will create next).

4. Finally, add the following action to the first frame in the actions layer:

   ```
   stop();
   ```

5.   Although not strictly necessary in this simple movie, a stop action will stop the movie at the first frame and prevent it from looping. In more complex movies a stop action is often used to wait for user input before continuing along the timeline.

Your movie should look something like the illustration below:

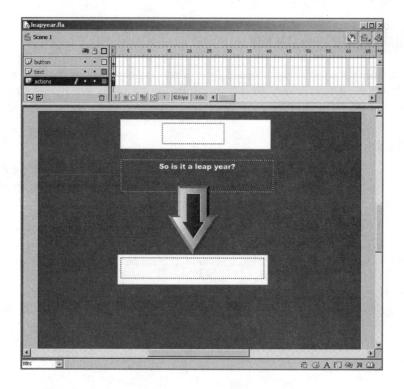

The ColdFusion template

Now we must build the ColdFusion template to process the year being sent from the movie and respond.

6.   Create a new page in Studio and delete all default HTML.

7. Insert the following code:

```
<cfsetting enablecfoutputonly="Yes">
<cfif isnumeric(year) and isleapYear(year)>
<cfset output = "&isleap=Yes&result=ok&">
<cfelse>
<cfset output = "&isleap=No&result=ok&">
</cfif>
<cfoutput>#output#</cfoutput>
```

8. Save the file as `checkyear.cfm`, in the same directory as your Flash FLA. Let's test our system.

9. Publish your Flash movie, along with its HTML page (by default SHIFT+F12).

10. Open the Flash movie page in a browser, `leapyear.html`.

You should get something like:

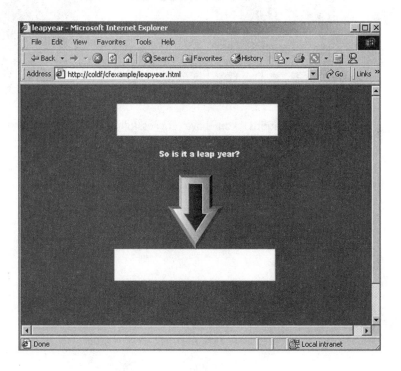

Enter a year into the top box then click on the arrow to see if the value entered is a leap year like so.

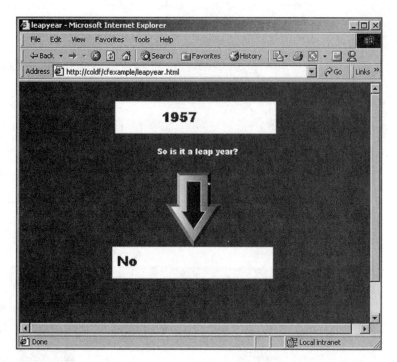

Congratulations, you have successfully created your first Flash and ColdFusion application!

Case study

In the last chapter's case study section we built a movie clip and buttons for our forum. In this chapter we're going to build the Flash basis within which our forum will live. Reopen your `forum.fla` and we'll get to work.

The frame

1. We'll start by changing one of the properties in the Movie Properties box. You might remember that when we created some of our buttons in the previous chapter I mentioned that they would be displayed on a black background in the final movie. Let's change the background to black now.

2. We're going to call the main scene in this movie forum, so using Modify>Scene change the name of the scene from Scene 1 to forum.

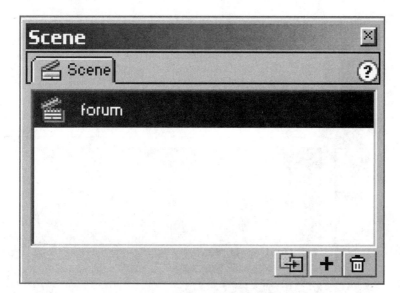

3. Name the default layer of the movie frame as that's exactly what we're going to put on this layer. Make a keyframe on frame 1 of the movie and select the Rectangle Tool. Now open up the Stroke panel and set the color to red and the stroke width to 2. We want our rectangle to act as the frame of our movie, so set the fill to none in the Fill panel. Before we draw the rectangle there's one final thing we need to do. We want our frame to have rounded corners and we achieve this by using the Round Rectangle Radius option. Set this radius to 10.

4. Now we've got our options for the rectangle completed, we can actually draw it on the stage! Draw a rectangle on the stage that is 495px by 355px. Once again we can use the Info panel to set the sizes precise. We'll then use the Align panel to center the frame on the stage.

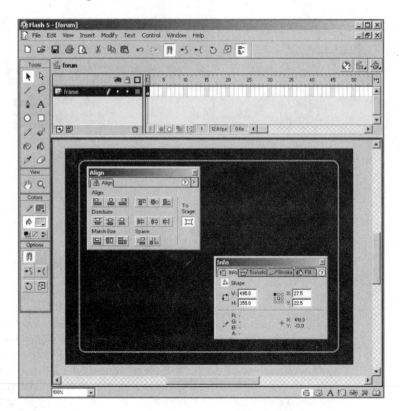

5. We're going to have a horizontal line running across our frame from one to the other. Make sure you have the Snap to Objects option selected and draw a line horizontally from the left side of the frame to the right. Set the y position of this line to 325 in the Info panel.

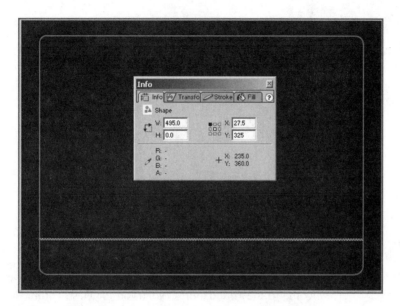

6. Insert a frame (Insert>Frame) at frame 50 of our frame layer, as this is how long we want the movie to be for the moment. We'll then add keyframes at frames 45 and 46. Select frame 45 and create a motion tween *on* this frame, and a second motion tween between frames 1 and 45.

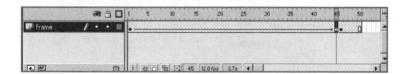

7. On frame 1 select the Effect panel and set Alpha to 0%. This will make our frame fade in from frame 1 to frame 45. On frame 46 we're going to use the Paint Bucket Tool to flood fill the segregated area at the bottom of our screen. We'll make this area white.

8. We're now going to add the text at the top of the screen for our forum's heading. In the Character panel set the font as Arial, the size as 17pt, the color as white and make sure that the bold option is selected. Using the Text Tool just under the top of our frame, type the heading of our forum: Welcome to the Foundation ColdFusion for Flash Forum. Align the text box to the center horizontally then you've finished typing the text. We're also going to place the first of our buttons on the stage now so drag the back button (bnback) from the library and place it at the left hand side of our white area.

9. We've now finished the frame layer and we're going to build a second layer to work with this layer. Insert a new layer above the frame layer and change it to a mask. We'll call this layer mask so we don't forget what's on it! Select the Rectangle Tool and change the corner radius back to 0. Draw a rectangle from the top left corner of the stage that stop just above the white area. The fill color doesn't matter as this is a mask and won't be seen (I've used blue anyway, with no stroke). I drew the rectangle with the movie on frame 46 as I could see the whole frame at this point (due to the alpha fading in), but make sure the rectangle covers the whole timeline.

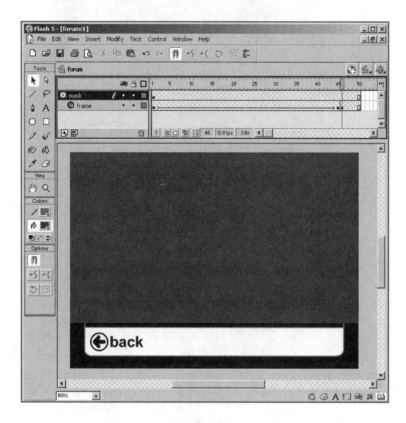

10. Insert a keyframe at frame 46 of the mask. Create a motion tween between frames 46 and 50, and then make frame 50 a keyframe to make the tween active. On frame 50 select the rectangle and choose Modify>Transform>Scale. (Make sure that you haven't gone into the tween edit mode.) Drag the bottom handle of the rectangle so that it's over the bottom of the frame. When the movie plays only the frame above the white area will be visible, until the motion tween when the rest will come into view. Once you've scaled the rectangle on frame 50 make this layer hidden so we can see the frame to help edit future layers.

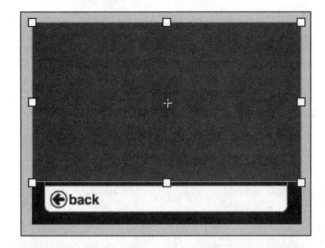

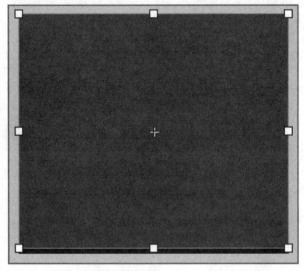

11. Create a new layer above the mask and call it actions. On this layer we'll have the actions and labels of the movie. Put a `stop` action on a keyframe at frame 50 of this layer. Preview the movie now and you'll see the effect that our mask achieves.

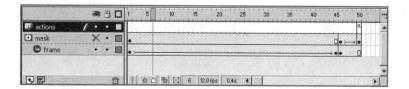

We've now finished the actual frame section of the case study and the next exercise will create a ball that follows around the outside of the frame.

The moving ball

1. Click on frame 45 of the frame layer on the timeline. The red outlined frame shape should be selected on the stage, copy this. Now make a new layer between mask and actions, and call this layer ball guide. Select a frame on this layer and paste the frame shape onto this layer using Edit>Paste in Place. This should span across the entire timeline on our new layer and be placed exactly over the original frame shape on the frame layer. Lock the frame layer so that we don't make alterations to this by accident, and delete the bottom two horizontal lines and bottom corner of the frame shape on the ball guide layer. Change this layer to a Guide layer. Finally, with the entire red guide line selected, break it apart (Modify>Break Apart). This is vital to the functioning of the line as a guide.

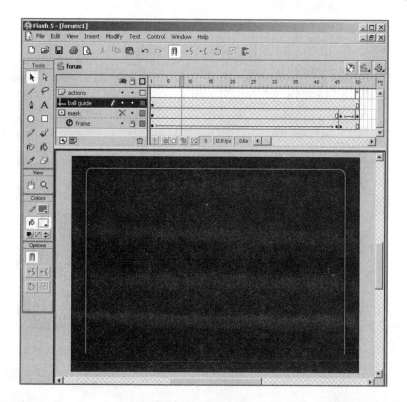

2. Create another new layer and drag this one under the ball guide layer. We'll call this layer ball, as this is where we're going to put the ball that is to be guided.

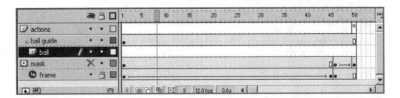

3. On the new ball layer choose the Oval Tool and draw a circle that is 15 pixels in diameter (red color, no stroke). Make sure that the ball is covering all 50 frames of the movie. On frame 1 drag the ball to the start of the red line on the left. Make sure that you have Snap to Objects selected so the ball sticks to the end of the line. Our next step is to create a motion tween between frames 1 and 50. This tween will appear incomplete as we haven't made the end keyframe yet. Make this keyframe at frame 49.

4. On frame 49, place the ball at the other end of the guide line (you might need to temporarily hide the frame layer to do this as the red frame has faded in by frame 49). As long as the ball has attached to the line properly we should see the ball move around the guide line when the movie is previewed. We want the ball to have disappeared by the end of the movie so delete the instance on frame 50. Preview the movie clip and watch the ball fly around the line, the frame fade in, and the mask side away to reveal the bottom white area. We've nearly finished!

5. Our last step of the case study for this chapter is to add the preloader movie clip. Add a new layer above the ball guide and name this layer loading movie clip. On this layer drop mcpreloader onto the stage so it fills all 50 frames. Finally, align this movie clip to the center of the stage.

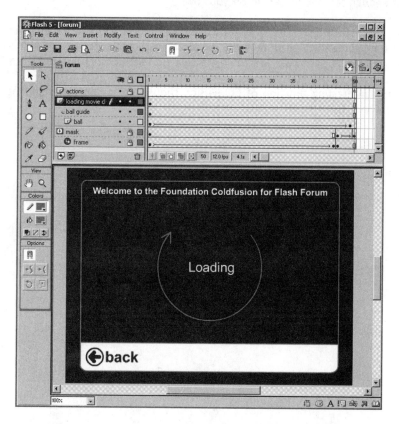

We're now at the end of the case study section for this chapter. Take a few moments to preview the movie and watch how the features we've been building fit together. In the next chapter's case study section we'll be building a database that will allow us to integrate this Flash interface with ColdFusion.

Summary

These are very simple examples but do show in a few lines of code what you can do. We have only scratched the surface with CFML, but we'll continue to delve and anyway, we've learnt enough for you to pursue on your own.

Again I can't stress any more, how good a source of information the help system is. Simply spend time going through all tags and functions to grasp the power of ColdFusion and the potential it has for allowing you to create very powerful ColdFusion powered Flash sites.

The most interesting function of ColdFusion though, is its database handling, and that's exactly where we're heading next!

4 Database Design

What We'll Cover in this Chapter

- *What **databases** are and how they are structured*

- *How to design and build a workable database*

- *Connecting databases as **data sources** to ColdFusion*

- *Accessing these data sources from CFML and Flash*

Now, we'll run over some basic database principles in the first part of this chapter – issues such as database types, good database design, data structures and the prime database vendors. I know we did a little of this in Chapter 1, so this is to firstly to remind you of that, and secondly to flesh out some of those concepts. There is an exercise at the end, in which we build a simple database.

In the second part of this chapter, we'll look at the database connections. This culminates in the creation of a potential connection to our practice database – although we will not actually connect it to a ColdFusion template until the third part of the chapter, where we look at the basic CF tags used to read data and how we use them in a template-driven web page. We'll also explore the fundamentals of SQL, the Structured Query Language. This part is quite exciting because, as part of our ongoing exercise, it culminates in the display of database information in Flash!

The fourth and last part begins with basic instruction on the use of forms in ColdFusion, and goes on to explain the principles of writing the form data into the database. We have a few simple stand-alone examples for you in there. Eventually this chapter ends with the final part of our exercise – a Flash interface that reads and writes data to and from a Database.

Database Essentials

The database world is, as we said already, full of acronyms. These could trip you up when reading something a little technical, so let's get rid of a few of them right away. Common as they are, it is surprisingly difficult sometimes to get an explanation. The number of IT workers I know who work with Win NT and don't know what the NT stands for! (New Technology). There are too many TLAs (three letter acronyms) and FLEAs (four letter extended acronyms) to worry anymore about their overuse for TWAIN (technology without an interesting name). So here is the Bluffer's Guide to DB TLAs (...hey, you're catching on...)

Any time the **DB** bit pops up, it's a database term. So just try to remember the other bits. **R** is relational, **A** is administrator, **MS** could be management system or Microsoft – if it is in front, it's usually Microsoft. Sometimes the **M** by itself can mean Microsoft too.

And so the following, while daunting at first, are actually quite easy:

- DBA – Database Administrator

- RDBMS – Relational Database Management System

- MSDB – Microsoft Database

- MDB – the usual Microsoft Database file acronym

- MSDBA – Microsoft Database Administrator.

File Structures

The database's file structure is like a grid. Rows extend across the database, punctuated vertically by columns. DBAs like to refer to their structures in particular ways, so we'll do the same and call the rows **records** and the columns **fields**.

The records are absolutely always horizontal! Each record contains information about one thing: if it's a person, then the information about name, card details, address etcetera extends along the record, existing in those fields. If you come across a page of information that's laid out vertically instead, or even in little neat blocks, warning bells should ring. It needs to be in neat long rows. These record and fields make up a **table** of information.

Not all the information in the database is in one table. A single database quite often will have three or four tables. It doesn't have to – your database could contain just one table, or it could contain dozens. This is where databases become **relational**, which we'll explain in a few paragraphs time.

Purpose and function

There must be a good reason for using a database. Reading and writing from them is time-consuming (in relative IT terms), so there has to be a rationale. With the prevalence of cookies – tiny text files that store information on the user's PC for a web site to pick up and use – and our ability to pass data from page to page with **GET**, **POST** and **Session** variables, we really need to use databases as efficiently as possible and attempt to complement what we already have.

Also bear in mind the various governments' rules of database use worldwide. A database that accumulates personal details can possibly compromise an individual's private life, and there are laws that encourage us to keep data updated and fresh.

Let's make a few assumptions now: we are a small business, and have a database of loyal customers. On there we have their names, addresses, purchasing preferences, and so on. On anther database we store our inventory. By comparing the number of customers and the products they like to purchase, looking at the purchase history for the same period last year and the year before, and looking at the current stock levels we can place an order with the manufacturer that ensures as little leftover on our shelves as possible. We can even tell if the manufacturer has stock themselves by perhaps pointing our browser to their Extranet (the art of their network they allow certain third-parties to access) and seeing their database via a web page.

What makes this all possible is the use of *databases*, *related* database *tables*, a method of actually *querying* the database, and the use of *dynamic web pages* to display the results of the database query.

Database vendors

Microsoft, who some think leads the pack in so many IT areas, is ranked third or fourth in the world of the database vendor. Way up there is Oracle and their Oracle 8i product – a powerful database for large companies with databases that measure in the hundreds or thousands of megabytes.

Sybase is another big vendor, supplying a similar market to Oracle, not to mention all the mainframe database vendors. Not relevant at all to us here and now, but it all goes to show that databases – and database web site integration – is big business indeed.

Moving down a notch to the SME (small to medium enterprise) market, we have Microsoft's SQL Server, the Unix/Linux product mySQL, and various other powerful databases with SQL often used in the name. We'll explain SQL properly in the third part of this chapter.

Moving down even further, into the realm of the common person and becoming totally relevant to us now, are the products like Microsoft Access, FileMaker Pro and dozens of other small, inexpensive database solutions.

But Microsoft Excel is not in our list – note that an application like Excel is a spreadsheet and therefore does write tables, but this doesn't comprise a database proper. You'll see in the very next part that this doesn't prevent us from accessing an Excel file, or even a `.txt` file, for use in our ColdFusion template.

Let's now summarize and also establish a working platform for the examples used in this book: we assume that the majority of developers are testing on Windows 95/98/NT/20000000, and that Microsoft Access is the database most likely to be present on that platform. Examples and screenshots in this chapter will be from Access 2000, but the rules for Access 97 are virtually identical. Other databases will follow extremely similar rules too.

The most important thing to understand from the vendors is their database's level of compatibility. Does it conform to some agreed standard, like being able to work with OLEB and ODBC? We'll talk about these in the second part of this chapter. There are methods to make almost any database work under almost any circumstances, but the road can be long and rocky. We choose our database and database vendor with care very early on in the development process!

Macintosh users

You're probably aware already that ColdFusion Server 5 doesn't run on the Mac. This doesn't mean that a Mac *database* can't be used. A table of data is a table of data is a table of data – it's the *connection* to that database that is a challenge. Later we'll talk about the most common connection types. I'm afraid though that there may be no easy answer for the Macintosh database.

Types of database

Now that the vendor issue is a little clearer, let's take a closer look at the types of database and what it is that makes them so different. We'll look at comma-separated files, flat-file databases, relational models and the advantages of full-blown database servers in the points to follow.

CSV comma-separated values

Comma-separated value files are the cornerstones of digital spreadsheets. All it means is that the data in a row is separated by commas. The rows are separated by one another with carriage returns. So this file...

Name, Age, School (RETURN)
Bob, 17, Windsor High (RETURN)
Jane, 17, St Mary Convent

...is a spreadsheet with three columns (fields) and two rows (records). The first row holds the field labels, in this case. If this file were typed up in MS Word and saved as a text file, it could then be opened in Excel and would appear as a spreadsheet.

It may not then surprise you to know that, given a suitable set up connection (which we'll discuss in detail soon), ColdFusion could access a `.csv` easily.

Flat-file

Flat-files are basic spreadsheets. In other words, they are the opposite of relational databases – they have no tables-that-connect-across-to-tables. Information is presented in grid-like form, and is accessible to ColdFusion. But these types of databases aren't efficient, not even for our simple example later in this part of this chapter. Excel is a classic example of a flat-file data structure.

I'd like to share a tip with you, though. Often, when Access simply won't behave or when I can do a filter/search/other odd thing in Excel but not Access, I have performed my task on a subset of my data in Excel and then copy-pasted the result back into Access. Always useful to have Excel around, especially if you aren't planning on becoming an Access guru!

The relational database model

At last, we are where we want to be – the relational database is the starting point really for any data-driven web project. We have touched on the concept of *relational* so many times so far, let's bring it all together in a summary.

A database that uses more than one table to store pieces of data that otherwise would be duplicated in some records, and yet retains all the links from the related record to that data, is considered relational.

A classic example: a builder has a hardware inventory. In that inventory are the descriptions for the products.

Partname,	Quantity	Description	Cost
Red Spade	1	Digging-stick	1.99
Blue Spade	3	Digging-stick	1.99
Bob's Hardhat	1	Bonedome	2.99
Wendy's Hardhat	1	Bonedome	2.99

Now, this is the problem: This database contains some information more than once. What's required is another table, turning this into one database with two tables. One would be titled stocklevel and the other stockdescription. Stocklevel would contain 4 records of two fields each, stockdescription would contain just two records of two fields each: Total 12 pieces of data, as opposed to 16.

Now, that's not quite true yet. These records don't now understand their relationship. To establish this, we'd have to have a lookup field in one table and some kind of field to actually look up in the other. This would make the database structure even bigger, and destroy the point we are trying to make.

But imagine if this current flat-file data structure had ten thousand records with ten fields in each, and every other field had the some piece of information that was repeated at least in every few records. We'd certainly save space, and search-time, with a relational database.

For the exercise at the end of this part of this chapter, we'll guide you through the steps to make a sample database in Microsoft Access 2000. If you have Access 97, that will do also. Access is what is known as a file-based system – that means that data is stored in a filing system, just like the folder structures we are used to in Windows or Mac.

True database servers

That file-based system of Access is certainly easy to follow and set up – we need hardly think about it after a few goes – but it's not efficient when it comes to dishing out the goods to every visitor on your site. Access is not geared to lots of *concurrent* connections – lots of requests for service at the same time. After a small handful (and this can't be quantified here – it's dependant on the efficiency of the connection, the size of the database, the number of fields, the types of query...) of users, things slow down.

Enter a fully-fledged database server, like SQL Server. Outwardly, the data structures appear very similar to Access's. But it's rigged differently inside, able to hold masses of data and handle dozens if not hundreds of concurrent requests.

SQL Server, (pronounced sequel) is at version 2000. We won't delve into anything like this level of database server here, but remain assured that the terms we will use are just as useful when playing with the big toys. These types of database start at many hundreds of dollars, and go right up in price!

Good database design

It's important to plan ahead with databases. You'll know how important planning is in your Flash work. So too in database design. If you don't plan properly, some parts may be hugely successful but others will fail, and the database may come crashing down under your inconsistencies. Plan now!, and plan to upgrade too. Try to build a solution, not a future problem. Talk to DBAs for tips and wrinkles, you know the slang now, so practice and learn.

Establish a naming convention

Decide early on about your naming system – do it on paper before going to screen even. As the field names materialise and the tables prove their existence and the database earns a name...bam! Something goes wrong...the same word is used twice for a field and a table, perhaps. This type of thing can really confuse later on, so work it out on paper first. Call things logical names, avoid words that look the same, keep words short (less chance of typos later). Here's a proposed list – note that these are not rules, simply guidelines:

- Lower case only, even for first letter

- Short names

- No spaces – use underscores instead. This *is* a rule!

- No ambiguity (**login** in one place, **username** in another...)

Here's part of mine, for what it's worth:

- Lower case only for field names

- Short words always

- For tables; the word `table` tagged to the end of the name (because I can use a Search feature in my text editor to find references to a table later, even if I forget what I called it).

Normalizing the database

Normalizing a database is really what was illustrated with our builder example we just saw. Normalizing means that the database is analysed for repeated elements, and is spread out into smaller related tables. Access actually has a wizard that does this automatically, as we'll see.

A database that is normalised is, as we have seen, a relational database. The relationships between the tables are paramount, and are achieved with an extra field in each table. These fields are known as the:

- **Primary Key**

- **Foreign Key**

By linking records to each other via their primary and/or foreign keys, we create relationships. These relationships could link one record to many records, or vice versa. The types of relationships are:

- One to Many

- Many to One

- Many to Many

- One to One

The two records in our builders stockdescription table would have enjoyed many to one relationships with the four records in the stocklevels table.

De-normalization

The term de-normalization may come up too in a casual dialog with your DBA. It can be that some databases become more unwieldy, or just plain slower, when they are supposedly ultra-efficiently normalized. Sometimes it is worth having the data repeated a few times, if it means that the data server software does not have to go off and open another table just to pick up an employee's payroll number (for example).

Keep it simple

In database design a good rule is to keep things as simple as possible, here are a few common-sense pointers for you to build on:

Don't plan to store data that is not necessarily required – in the databases of the world, an alarming percentage of data is not required and is becoming outdated. If the person's middle name or middle initial is unimportant, don't make a field for it and don't ask for it in the web form.

Don't store data that could be calculated - such as a person's age as well as their age. The second can be calculated from the first. This goes for addresses as well, provided you have access to the software that knows an address from just a postcode reference: it may be that all that is required is the zip code and house number in a database, which can then perform a lookup to a third party's country-wide zip code/address database.

If a piece of data is not really an issue, don't ask for it and don't store it – having too much data can really be a headache sometimes.

Now it's time to get a bit of hands-on practice and to practice what we preach.

We're about to build a very simple, small database with two small tables. It will be easy to stay within the guidelines above at *this* stage! To keep it lighthearted, what say we build on the builder example? This data will eventually be read from Access into Flash via ColdFusion, and then added to via a Flash interface and a ColdFusion insert template. So let's begin by creating the database: fire up Access on any Windows workstation and follow the steps below:

A place for everything, everything in its place

Back in Chapter 3 we covered the basic server setup – the directories, URL-mapping and so forth – that allowed your local machine to simulate a web server environment and access pages with the HTTP protocol. If all went well, then you now have a folder called `cf3` in the web root directory `c:\inetpub\wwwroot\cf3` on the web server. This folder should be set up in PWS (Personal Web Server) or IIS, and have an alias (a web name).I will assume that your web alias is also `cf3`, as is mine to make it easy to remember.

As an example if your server was called `coldf` your web alias would be `//coldf/cf3`

If this is not how your set up is now, backtrack and make it so. If there is already a lot of clutter in that folder, a good tip is to create a subfolder called disabled and sling all the junk in there temporarily. Those pages will stop working, but you can always put them back in the parent folder later and make everything tick as normal. We're just clearing some space for our little one-off exercise.

This is important now because we must save our database somewhere in just a few minutes, and c:\inetpub\wwwroot\cf3 is as good a place as any. In real life though, never save the database in an obvious place like the root folder. To a cracker (a malicious hacker) this would be the digital equivalent of leaving your briefcase on the car seat!

Another little tip: make a shortcut to the c:\inetpub\wwwroot\cf3 folder on the web server, and put it on the desktop. Open the folder and then minimize it, so it appears in the taskbar. Saves a lot of mouse mileage later.

Building a database

1. Launch Access and choose the radio button new database at the prompt. It already wants to know what to call the database – this is where, in a hurry, you might accidentally use the name you actually meant to use for the table, etc. We've planned this one, and a good name to use might be bobstock. Save it into that c:\inetpub\wwwroot\cf3 directory on the web server.

   In the window that appears, you have a couple of ways to go. Because other chapters will show you the use of the create table in design view option, we are going to use the other create table by entering data option. Just for a change of scenery, you understand, and because we do not have to worry too much about data types for this example. (Sometimes the fact that data is a number or a word, empty or filled, etc, is a concern. This is where data types have to be configured)

2. Choose the create table by entering data option now, and a table will appear:

3. Lets call the first two fields partname and quantity. Double-click on field one to rename it partname, then do

the same for field two – quantity. Enter the same information that we used earlier. This time we are going to spread our data out over two tables, so we just want the first two fields:

Red Spade	1	Digging-stick	1.99
Blue Spade	3	Digging-stick	1.99
Bob Hardhat	1	Bonedome	2.99
Wendy Hardhat	1	Bonedome	2.99

4. Now simply save and close the table. Name the table stocklevel when you close it. Right on cue, up comes a window that says words to the effect that without a primary key, this will never be part of the world of relational databases.

5. Allow Access to now automatically create a primary key for you, and you are done.

stocklevel : Table

ID	partname	quantity
1	red spade	1
2	blue spade	3
3	Bob hardhat	1
4	Wendy hardhat	1
(AutoNumber)		

So far this is a quick and easy way to get a table going!

6. Close the table, and do exactly the same for our second table. Here is the information you need for that second table:

stockdescription : Table

ID	partname	description	cost	sell
1	spade	digging-stick	1.99	2.99
2	hardhat	bonedome	2.99	4.99
(AutoNumber)				

7. Save and close the table, allowing Access to create the extra primary key field.

> *In Access a created primary key is an* autonumber *field that increments as records are added.*

In truth, we're not concerned with the relationships overmuch. I always allow a table to give itself a primary key, because I can always remove it later when the database goes live. The field is automatically called ID and can be useful when running a quick test on the table, testing a search function (for example) without being able to remember what data was actually in the table to be searched. I know that every table in every database in current development on my desk has an ID field, and it increments up sequentially and numerically.

Let's look at the relationships anyway. We are not going to tell Access about any relationship at this point. Instead, we can run a **query** across the second database and pull out, for example, all goods that made a profit of $1. Then, armed with that information (in this case, spade), we can run a query across the first database for all records with the word spade somewhere in the partname field. This would bring up two records, and we'd then know that we have two spades with a potential $1 profit each. By my math that makes up a potential $2 worth of profit lying around.

So there's our informal one-to-many relationship, without our needing to set it up in Access properly with a proper foreign key. All we need do is learn to write a query that does all the little queries in one, and then run it from the ColdFusion or Flash page. It's outside the scope of this book to instruct on the finer points of Access, so we'll leave it all there for now.

The database exists, it has a filename and it has two tables full of data that ColdFusion (and therefore Flash) can access. So now we need to make the connection to the database.

Connecting to the database

The next bit is very much Windows-centric. We're going to use the tools in Windows to create our connection to our sample database eventually. But first, some background on what we are about to do and the alternatives available to those whose platforms do not support the more typical connection methods

Web applications and databases

What's the relevance of the connection, we must ask first. Why does a database need a connection, must it be real-time or just every other day, must it be on the same machine?

A connection is vital because of the way queries are thrown back and forth, and the fact that there are so many database standards out there. The connection is a system of drivers and rules and protocols that enable a standard connection to a database. We don't simply 'point' to the database the way we point a web-link to an image file or PDF document.

That said, once the hard work of setting up the connection is done, the rest is a breeze. It's a case of investing time now for a quick 'n' easy connection when one is needed.

The database connection is very much a real-time connection. *So* real-time, that we have to worry about two people accessing the same record at the same time and updating it differently (resulting in database chaos, and the reason for cursor locks and database locks).

Generic framework for a web application

Working now with a set of common assumptions, here follows a possible sequence of events in the life of a Microsoft-hosted ColdFusion site.

The visitor's web client (probably Internet Explorer or Netscape Navigator) is pointed to a URL and requests the page from the web server.

The web server software, in our case IIS (Internet Information Server) handles the request and maps the URL (web address) to the real page in the real folder on the hard disk.

If the page address contains the file extension .cfm, then ColdFusion Server is automatically brought into play by the system's registry. The page is now really referred to as a template in ColdFusion circles. The template subjects itself to the processes of the ColdFusion Server:

ColdFusion Server looks through the text file for any CFML tags. Those it finds it acts upon, carrying out the pre-defined instructions built into ColdFusion Server. All CFML in the template is executed and replaced with HTML - and JavaScript where relevant.

Where a CFML tag requests information from a database, ColdFusion Server looks up the location and connection method and then runs the query on behalf of the CFML template. The resulting data is then slotted into the regenerated page, along with the HTML. This is a clue as to why the pages are called templates: identical layouts can look very different with different data – one template can generate a great many variations in look, feel or content through an almost unlimited number of data combinations.

The visitor's web client is fed the finished page. The CFML is no longer in this fresh *copy* of the original template

SME web applications

In the small-to-medium enterprise, all of the above may take place on just one machine. The web server would be an application server (generating pages with dynamic content). It would also be the database server, receiving queries via connections within its own internal structures. And it might be the mail server too, running specialised mail server software such as Microsoft Mail, Exchange or Notes.

As you can probably guess, this can be a tremendous load for a server running a busy site. Part of the solution is to outsource your worries – have a third party rent you a part of a machine, a whole machine or simply a network connection to your machine (in their space). This leaves the SME free to pick the right bandwidth and tools for the right job, possibly spreading the load out across more than one machine.

Corporate-level web applications

This load-balancing is a solution in-house, too. The database server doesn't have to be on the same machine. In fact it makes good security sense for it not to be. Equally the mail server will have different loads and is an important part of your infrastructure, so might be safest on a separate machine.

For the large-scale web site, this is without question. Next time you search on www.google.com, have a look at the understated statistics in its main screen. "1, 320, 847,000 pages indexed. Your search took 0.14 of a second". How on earth do 1.3 billion web pages get searched in one-sixth of a second? Easy – racks and racks of very powerful Database Servers, working together to handle incoming work shared out by a highly structured Web Server system. The whole thing is a web application.

Outsourced data servers

For the developer, or even the small business person (salesperson, web designer or window cleaner), the notion of an own-hosted web site is probably a little impractical.

The best bet for a small development set-up, other than a non-connected testing workstation like the development PC that you will run these exercises on, is to get hosted with a commercial web host. Beware of the hidden costs, such as a domain name transfer cost, and note that your web host should offer some kind of database service if you are to run a web application. In the UK, 50MB of web space and an Access database connection can be had for around £25/month, if Windows is acceptable to you. In the US, this is far more competitive still.

Unless an absolute monster with tens of thousands of records and a dozen or more fields your database is unlikely to swell too much. Perhaps 1 to 5Mb. The upgrade from Access to SQL Server isn't as fraught with danger as some database upgrades, so be prepared to start small and size up when you need to.

Types of connections

Connection methods is where it can get a little hairy. Reading through the newsgroups, especially ASP and UltraDev forums, it's interesting to see how many hacked solutions are out there. We'll run though a few here. But from the outset let me put your mind to rest – we're going to focus later on the ODBC connection using a DSN. We'll explain those acronyms in a page or so, but for now we'll simply say that ColdFusion does an excellent job of making the connection process painless with ODBC and DSN. We have the ColdFusion Server Administrator and the RDS to thank (refer back to Chapter 1 for a refresher on this if you like).

For now, let's look at the options. We're not trying to be definitive here – entire books have tried and failed at that! Once some of the more familiar terms are expanded on a little, we'll pull it all together by actually making the connection to our sample database, bobstock.mdb

ADO and connection strings

A connection string is simply a pointer to some pre-defined object, enabling the web application to then use that connection to send and receive data. The object (an object being a lump of code that does a particular connection job or more clearly identifies a final element) could be the database itself.

It's nowhere near as simple as that, of course! Microsoft make it a little easier by giving us ADO – the ActiveX Data Object. This handles a lot of the connection-code for us, making some connections very easy indeed. In fact we'll use ADO without realizing it later.

OLE DB

OLE stands for **Object Linking** and **Embedding**. The DB of course stands for database. This is a Microsoft technology that once again depends on other pre-written pieces of code **objects** to make the connection process smoother. And again, you'll use OLE DB later on without really realizing it. This process of transparent technology layers happens a lot. Only when a thing is *not* there do we realize its (non) existence. Which makes MDAC quite important:

MDAC 2.x

MDAC stands for Microsoft Data Access Components. Currently at about version 2.7, it is recommended that you install at least version 2.5 on a Windows machine that you plan to use for database access via a web application.

MDAC is not one thing, it is a package that updates many transparent technology layers at once. Kind of like taking the car in and asking for a new service to be fitted – it is not a single thing that is fitted, but several smaller things.

ODBC

The Open Database Connectivity (ODBC) driver is where it starts to get a bit more visual. This driver, or actually this *set* of drivers, provides a well-supported, standardized method of accessing a database.

MDAC updates the list of ODBC drivers. Also, when installing a database-oriented piece of software, ODBC drivers are usually installed or updated.

Acronym alert, DSN: It stands for Data Source Name, and we'll use it later a lot to point to our database.

ODBC driver

The ODBC Driver provides a front end to the database – a doorway or communications panel for other bits of code. By standardizing the access to the database, the way is clear for different technologies to connect to different databases.

In some ways it's like a printer-driver for your printer. Without it, the PC would require some clever coding to get it to print to the printer. But with the driver – no worries! It's important to remember that the ODBC setting that we make is a driver setting and is not the database itself in any way.

ODBC and OLE DB

We pay a price for this ease-of-connection. In truth, it is OLE DB that is more at the core of the connection, and the ODBC driver simply gives us more of a handle on the process. It is possible, in fact, to connect without using ODBC. An example of an Access OLE DB connection might be:

```
Provider=Microsoft.Jet.OLEDB.4.0; Data
➥Source=c:\inetpub\wwwroot\bobstock.mdb
```

It points to the database, yes, but employs a number of built-in objects to aid it in the actual connection process. It doesn't simply trigger the database in the way we double-click a desktop icon. We're not going to use the ODBC-less OLE DB connection string method, as it is known, in our example today.

Data Source Names (DSNs)

Once a database has been created and the ODBC driver is ready to be configured to access the new database, there comes the issue of a name for this source of data. We don't wish to name the ODBC driver, as it isn't the database, so we name the configuration setting for the ODBC driver, and refer to this as the DSN.

This DSN becomes our pointing-stick for quite a lot of the time when we work with ColdFusion and databases, so choose a name with care and do so early on in the data design process. I usually also add `dsn` as a prefix to the DSN name and then capitalise the first letter of the rest of the name, to make it easily identifiable in the code. And it's a good idea to name the DSN after the database as a rule (if you have that luxury) as it makes it so much easier to remember in six months time! Thus a database called Members might have a DSN called dsnMembers

ODBC Text Driver

To point out the potential of the ODBC plus DSN partnership, note that it's quite possible to set up a connection to a text file. With only a small variation on the steps we are about to follow in the next exercise, it is possible to connect to a number of simple file formats – including .txt. and the `.csv` file format we mentioned earlier.

And now, time to set up an ODBC connection to our database and to give it a DSN

Just to confirm, we have a database file called `c:\inetpub\wwwroot\cf3\bobstock.mdb`. Great, let's begin.

We will set up the ODBC driver from the settings panel in Windows. Note that if you still have the Access file open, now would be a good time to close it. ODBC will simply report an error if a new connection is attempted on an open database.

Setting up a connection

1. If you are running Win95/98, call up the ODBC Data Sources 32 Bit application from inside the Start>Settings>Control Panel> folder.

2. On Win2000/NT, hunt inside the Start>Settings>Control Panel> Administrative Tools> and launch the Data Sources (ODBC) icon.

    The driver actually already exists, we simply have to configure a new instance of the right driver for the right database with the right permissions. Looking at the window, see that the System DSN tab is selected, not the User DSN tab. User DSN is only used for single connections, such as for a personal intranet site that you wish to control.

    Don't be concerned about much else. The list in the main part of the window has nothing to do with what we are about to do – those are DSN's which have *already* been set up.

3. Click Add

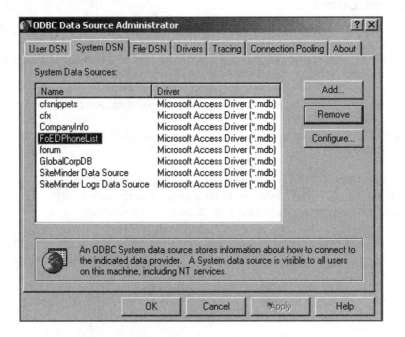

Source

This next window, titled Create a new Data Source, is likely to be quite busy with ODBC Drivers for ColdFusion labeled Merant. This will be good to see – it indicates that you have already installed ColdFusion Server – but for our example we are simply going to use the standard English Access driver (pictured as selected, below)

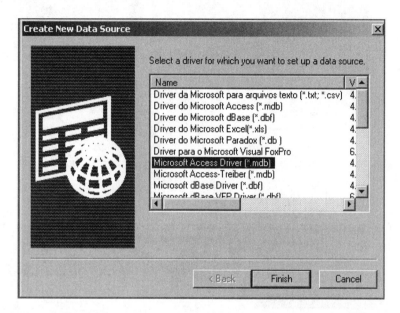

Remember what we said about linking to other types of files with the help of ODBC? This is probably the stage at which a different direction might be taken for a different database type, flat file or even plain text file.

4. Select the Microsoft Access Driver, and click Finish

    We are not yet finished, but certainly are on the home leg.

    This ODBC Microsoft Access Setup screen is where the database is *almost* selected, and the data source name filled in. Note that no description is actually required. We're going to click select in a few seconds, but for now look at those other options – create, repair and compact. These are little database utilities, coming in handy if you find yourself without a copy of Access and a database to fix or compact.

    Ignore Advanced and Options - these switch on things like password protection for the database. We'll leave ours open.

5. Type in the Data Source Name as dsnBobstock

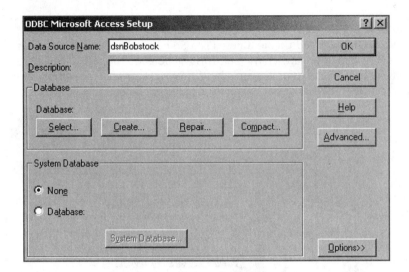

6. Click Select now.

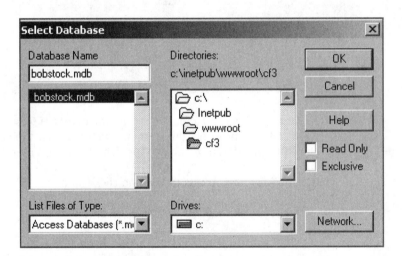

It is getting easier and easier now.

7. Select the database from the path c:\Inetpub\wwwroot\cf3, and click OK.

8. Simply click the OK buttons until all dialog boxes are gone.

9. Make sure the checkboxes read only and exclusive are unchecked – otherwise Flash and ColdFusion won't be allowed to write to the database!

Now begins a journey back in time. The screens you went through will all reappear. The database now has a driver configured, and the source of the data itself has a name – dsnBobstock. Congratulations, the connection is there and ready to use. Now for part three of our chapter, and some ColdFusion at long last!

ColdFusion Server Administrator

Well done, you have hopefully created a DSN. If you haven't, or if you wish to do it again, follow the instructions below to use the Administrator to avoid the long-winded processes of the Windows ODBC manager.

We went down that road for the journey, not the destination. It certainly is good to see the set-up of ODBC, database selection etc. from the Windows point of view, and I hope it has shed some light.

Now let's test it in the ColdFusion Administrator. You'll see that this one-stop window can be used to do everything that we did in the Windows ODBC Manager, and it is this Administrator that you'll probably want to use next time.

Adding the datasource to ColdFusion Sever

1. Open the Administrator now by right-clicking on the blue icon with a lightning bolt in the tray at the bottom of the screen.

    If ColdFusion Server 5 is installed on a different machine logon by typing \\servername\cfide\administrator into the address bar of your browser.

2. Choose ODBC Data Sources from the left-hand Navigation Panel.

3. Find our DSN dsnBobstock and click verify to check all is well.

    While you're here, notice that the add button launches a single screen into which the core pieces of information can be entered to set up a DSN. This is precisely why we have gone the long way round first – you may not ever use the Windows method again, and it is always useful to have done it once at least to appreciate the efficiency of ColdFusion.

Writing to ColdFusion and Flash from the database

This third section finally lets us get our teeth into a little CFML, and a bit of Flash ActionScript too!

We'll look initially at the tag that does most of the work for us, <cfquery> , then we'll discuss SQL, or Structured Query Language. A query language allows us to interrogate the database for the information we want.

Query basics

First off, we're going to write data simply to a ColdFusion template. That will be half the battle won. Core to the whole process is the tag called <cfquery>. Then we'll use <cfloop> to loop through our records with some control.

This tag runs the query on the database, using the setting we made last chapter. Inside the tag itself are the variables and their values

```
<cfquery name="bobsbits" datasource="dsnBobstock" dbtype="ODBC">
        SELECT partname FROM stocklevel
</cfquery>
```

The datasource is the name that we set up, in our case dsnBobstock. A *name* is also required for the query we are creating in the template, as well as the database type *dbtype* which is ODBC in our case

The tag is a tag-pair, in that it must be closed off with a matching tag.

In-between the opening and closing tags is the SQL. Now, we will look at SQL properly in the next exercise. For now, it will read very much like English, thank goodness. In our case we said that we want to *select* the partname field *from* the stocklevel table.

Exercise with <cfquery>

1.   Type the following using ColdFusion Studio, or another text editor

```
<html>
<head>
<title>
        Reading the Bobstock Database with ColdFusion
    </title>
  </head>
<body>
```

```
    <cfquery    name="bobsbits"    datasource="dsnBobstock"
dbtype="ODBC">
        SELECT partname FROM stocklevel
    </cfquery>
    <cfoutput query="bobsbits">
        #partname#
    </cfoutput>
  </body>
</html>
```

2. Save as `c:\inetpub\wwwroot\cf3\default.cfm`.

3. Run the file from your browser.

    Did that run okay? You should have seen the four partname records in the database appear in a line.

4. View the source code - `View` > `Source` menu in Internet Explorer or View>Page Source in Netscape Navigator

    You will see that there is no **CFML** in the final result.

Integrating repeating HTML elements

Well, you saw that ColdFusion needs no prompting to bang out the whole range of records for that field and that table. Point and shoot, and ColdFusion does the rest.

Later we'll use SQL to control that. For now, let's look at integrating a little HTML into the dynamic areas of the template.

The `<cfoutput>` tag basically looped around for every record it found in the range specified in the simple SQL query we wrote. We can use this feature to our great advantage – with no more ColdFusion scripting, we can change the heart of it to the following by adding just a few HTML elements such as line breaks and horizontal rules:

```
<cfquery name="bobsbits" datasource="dsnBobstock"
➥dbtype="ODBC">
    SELECT partname FROM stocklevel
</cfquery>
These are the parts:
<p>
<cfoutput query="bobsbits">
    #partname#
<hr>
</cfoutput>
```

Everything within the repeating <cfoutput> tags repeats as well, while the rest of the HTML behaves normally.

This is something you can really play with, before we move on to <cfloop> and then onto some SQL queries

<cfloop> with <cfquery>

In Chapter 2 you looked at the potential behind the <cfloop> tag. Good news folks – it works in just the same way with data too. In this example, <cfloop> has been used with <cfquery> to generate records and then number them.

This would be useful to display the number of records that have been found in a search, or some other logical data that works with the database but is not stored in the database

```
<html>
<head>
</head>
    <body>
        <cfquery name="loops" datasource="dsnBobstock"
➡dbtype="ODBC">
                SELECT * FROM stocklevel
        </cfquery>
                <cfset mycount=0>
        <cfloop query="loops">
                        <cfset mycount=mycount+1>
                <cfoutput>
                        Part no #mycount#:#partname#<br>
                </cfoutput>
        </cfloop>
    </body>
</html>
```

A smattering of SQL

Structured Query Language is a surprisingly straightforward query method that allows questions to the database to be written right there inside the template.

We're going to cover SQL more properly in Chapter 6. For now, here are some basic pointers so that we can get our data to display with some semblance of control.

Some SQL Conventions

Best practice for writing SQL is to keep the values in lowercase and the commands in uppercase. This separates clearly the core SQL itself from the other shrapnel, making it easier to read.

The values we mention would be the field and table names in our database. The commands are a set of SQL instructions which are run past the database to pick out a subset of data based on the database values we enter.

We created a database with two tables: stockdescription and stocklevel. Using the screenshots of those fields from earlier in the chapter, adapt the SQL to match some of the examples to follow. You'll also want to add some HTML formatting in some cases, because we're going to get all sixteen records up at some stage too.

Calling all fields and tables

- To call up all fields in a table, the asterisk (*) is used.

- To call up all tables, SELECT them and separate the names with commas.

- So, the SQL to call up all records in all fields in all tables is:

```
<cfquery name="loops" datasource="dsnBobstock' dbtype="ODBC">
        SELECT * FROM stocklevel, stockdescription
    </cfquery>
```

This puts all fields in all tables at the disposal of the template. Don't forget to actually call the fields up with the `<cfoutput>` tag and the usual `#fieldname#` delimiters. Otherwise you'll see nothing change!

This certainly works – but it also illustrates the need for a more careful approach to showing all data. What you will see if all records are displayed, is that fields with the same name in different tables display one after the other. Repeating fields cause other fields to repeat. Mayhem! Hmm... what we need is a method of selecting specific records...

Specifying More Query Parameters

We are not trying to be a definitive guide to SQL here, so will list just the most basic and useful commands for you, and experiment with them over the page with some examples.

SELECT	Get the fields listed
*	All fields
FROM	From the table/s listed
WHERE	The search clause...
LIKE	A logical operator
=	An absolute operator

Put it all together, and we have statements like:

```
SELECT dues, lastname FROM memberstable WHERE dues = 0
```

Which would call up the surnames for all the members in our table that are paid-up (thier dues being 0).

Later, in Chapter 6, we'll take a much closer look at SQL. We will use it to a small extent now so that we have some control over the display of records in our ColdFusion templates.

Querying our Database

It is most likely that you will first want to limit the records to one or a few very specific records – perhaps according to a search. We'll look at that first, using the WHERE command and various **operators**.

WHERE fieldname = value

Here is the WHERE command being used to equate directly to a value in the partname field: In this case the operator is the equals sign. Note the single-quotes used around the value being searched on – SQL can be pretty picky about that!

```
<html>
<head>
</head>
    <body>
        <cfquery name="mysearch" datasource="dsnBobstock"
                dbtype="ODBC">
            SELECT * FROM stockdescription
            WHERE partname='spade'
        </cfquery>
        <cfoutput query="mysearch">
            #partname#
        </cfoutput>
    </body>
</html>
```

Wildcards and logical operators

Here is the WHERE command again, this time being used to equate less directly to a value in the partname field in the *other* table: The operator is now a logical operator, LIKE. We have used it with some **wildcards** (and also %).

Logical operators are more English like, and a little bit fuzzy. We use them to compare records very basically sometimes, instead of perfectly or precisely.

This example pulls out all values in our stocklevel table that have any reference to spade in them

```
<html>
<head>
</head>
    <body>
        <cfquery      name="mysearch"      datasource="dsnBobstock"
➥dbtype="ODBC">
            SELECT * FROM stocklevel
            WHERE partname LIKE '%spade%'
        </cfquery>
        <cfoutput query="mysearch">
            #partname#
        </cfoutput>
    </body>
</html>
```

A Test-write to Flash from the Template

Before we plough in too deep, here's a little something to tinker with: This lovely and simple example will get a result in Flash with *very* little work. Once this is done, there will be something on the screen to demonstrate the principles with.

1. In a new text document, type the following and nothing else:

    ```
    <cfsetting enablecfoutputonly="yes">
    <cfset var1="Hello Luther">
    <cfset var2=var1>
    <cfoutput>
    &var2=#URLEncodedFormat(var2)#&
    </cfoutput>
    ```

2. Save the document as `flashdata.cfm` and pop it into the `c:\inetpub\wwwroot\cf3` directory, on the server.

    Now create a single-frame Flash movie. It doesn't matter what it looks like, but it must have a dynamic text box named `var2` somewhere on the stage, and a simple button.

3. Now add this ActionScript to the button:

    ```
    On(release){
    loadVariablesNum("flashdata.cfm", 0);
    }
    ```

4. Save the file as `c:\inetpub\wwwroot\cf3\fusiondata.fla`.

5. Publish an HTML file to view the Flash movie within (go to the File>Publish Settings, look at formats and make sure HTML is checked – click publish)

    Browse to the HTML file `fusiondata.html` and click the button in the Flash movie. `Hello Luther` should appear on the movie stage.

Troubleshooting

Both Flash and ColdFusion can be incredibly sensitive about the tiniest of things, so this short example was meant as a test drive more than anything else. If it didn't display the data as expected, check the following:

- In Flash, text in the text box is *not* set to white and the text field *is* called var2.

- The Flash movie, the Flash movie's HTML file and the ColdFusion template are all loose inside the c:\inetpub\wwwroot\cf3 folder on the server.

- The loadVariablesNum action in Flash points to the ColdFusion template.

- Browse directly to the ColdFusion template – if an error comes up, check the syntax and spelling methodically.

Flash is sensitive especially about the data that it reads into itself. Spaces can be a problem, although you'll notice we use them in our example and URL-encode the result for Flash. Flash prefers URL-encoded content.

Now we'll run a Flash movie and pick up a database value determined by the SQL statement we made earlier. We'll run though it all from the top, so follow us now:

Now we'll simply modify the ColdFusion template that read the value Hello Luther into the Flash movie.

Find that file – it was called flashdata.cfm and you used it in the last exercise. Open up the text file and change it to the following:

```
<cfsetting enablecfoutputonly="yes">
    <cfquery    name="flashquery"    datasource="dsnBobstock"
➥dbtype="ODBC">
        SELECT    partname    FROM    stockdescription    WHERE
➥partname='spade'
    </cfquery>
    <cfoutput query="flashquery">
        &var2=#partname#&
    </cfoutput>
```

The changes are very small. Essentially we have done two things:

- Modified the SQL in-between the <cfquery> tag to give us a specific record by using the mathematical = operator and comparing the field with the value spade.

- Removed the <cfset> tags, as the database is setting the values dynamically now. We have simply equated var2 with the SQL statement, and made the variable common to an empty variable in Flash.

Reading database records into Flash: conclusion

By now you're probably wondering what all the fuss is about. And perhaps you're wondering what the *potential* really is. After all, getting Flash to read a database is okay, but if it relies on tweaking a ColdFusion template every now and then, then what's the point?

We have yet to learn to write to the ColdFusion template – and therefore potentially to the database - from Flash. Once that is possible, Flash will be able to generate queries of its own and the ColdFusion will become properly transparent.

Writing to the database with ColdFusion and Flash

Well, this section is so much easier with so much ColdFusion and database terminology under our belts. And you've seen how straightforward it can be if we take the trouble to cross the t's and dot the i's – to make up for the sometimes particular natures of both Flash (reading URL-encoded text) and ColdFusion templates (a typo will result in a complete page failure)!

The main player now is the <cfinsert> tag. A potentially complex tag, by ColdFusion standards, this tag will be looked at in detail now. We'll use it to eventually push data into the database.

Finally, at the end of this chapter, we'll look at how the whole chapter can be brought together in a Flash Interface that drives variables in ColdFusion, automatically feeding database values back into Flash.

Syntax and Attributes

The syntax can be rather complex looking, but in fact is a simple series of name-value pairs. Those name-value pairs are the attributes, and there are some strict rules surrounding them. But in fact, there is an excellent indexed resource on the help section of ColdFusion Studio which lists all the attributes and the rules for the use of the <cfinsert> tag attributes.

Sample <cfinsert>

It really doesn't need be very complex anyway. This simple line will do it for us in these examples to come:

```
<cfinsert datasource="dsnBobstock" tablename="stocklevel"
➡dbtype="ODBC">
```

SQL insert

In fact there is another way of inserting data. Simply by using the <cfquery> tag and writing the right SQL command, we can insert data into our database. To illustrate, try the very next exercise: it is the same as what we did earlier in this chapter, in the section explaining about reading data into Flash/ColdFusio. Except that it now has an extra <cfquery> at the top with some SQL you may not have seen before

Data into the database with ColdFusion

We are going to focus on the <cfinsert> tag mostly here. But the following example gets a very quick result indeed, even though the method is not what we will use mostly. Have a go with it now and we'll come back to <cfinsert> when you're done.

Using <cfquery> with SQL

1.   Type the code below in a text editor and save it with the .cfm extension.

```
<cfquery name="insertquery" datasource="dsnBobstock"
➡dbtype="ODBC">
        INSERT INTO stocklevel
                        (partname,quantity)
                        values
                        ('skyhook', '2')
    </cfquery>
    <cfquery name="checkinsert" datasource="dsnBobstock"
➡dbtype="ODBC">
        SELECT partname, quantity FROM stocklevel
    </cfquery>
    <cfoutput query="checkinsert">
        #partname#:#quantity#
    </cfoutput>
```

Its function is simply to point to the database that we created, and insert a record into it. In fact, the record it inserts is hard-coded in (to save having to go through the process of building a form and form fields – too much for such a small example).

This exercise also reads back the updated fields, so you can see the result immediately. I recommend you run this a few times, but change the values in the text file each time. Later we'll do the same with <cfinsert>, but with a proper form.

Don't forget to add a sprinkling of <br>, <p> and perhaps some <hr> to smooth the data out Have fun.

That's it, nothing more to do but run it in a browser and see it write to your database.

Data into the database with Flash, *via* ColdFusion

Once again, we're streamlining it all down and showing just how little code is actually required once we get to this point. All the hard work of the past chapters has started to pay off.

What we'll do here is create a simple Flash form, and then use it to enter data into our database.

Setting up the Flash

1. Create a Flash movie, keep it to one frame and design it any way you like. But be sure to include:

- An input text box and call it partname

- An input text box and call it quantity

- A button with this ActionScript attatched to it:

    ```
    on(release)
    {
    loadVariablesNum('flashinsert.cfm", 0, "POST");
    }
    ```
    Save the Flash movie as
    c:\inetpub\wwwroot\cf3\flashinsert.fla on the server.

4. Publish your movie to create a flashinsert.html host page.

    Now close the Flash file and let's work on the ColdFusion template:

Setting up the ColdFusion Template

This one is even quicker.

1. Create a text file and give it two lines of information like so:

```
<cfparam name="partname" default="none">
<cfparam name="quantity" default="none">
```

2. Then add the last line, which contains the `<cfinsert>` command we saw earlier.

```
<cfinsert datasource="dsnBobstock" tablename="stocklevel"
➥formfields="partname, quantity" dbtype="ODBC">
```

The `<cfparam>` lines accept the values from the identically named Flash text fields, and pass them on. The `<cfinsert>` line actually tells the template where and how to send those values. Between the two of them, data is written to the database.

Don't forget the `formfields` parameter. This prevents errors by writing information to only the fields you specify. Otherwise Access may try to write non-existent data to a field it knows about (and you forgot about) and throw up an error!

That is it! It is very clean and neat, and it works.

After that it is a short step to again create a Flash page that picks up the new database variables, and in fact this could quite easily be the same movie that posts the variables in the first place. A total Flash front end...

A Flash front end

Let's now wrap this chapter up with a Flash movie that reads our database, displays the names and quantities of items in our builder's stock table, and then lets us add to that table via the same Flash front end.

First need a design:

The ColdFusion templates

The ColdFusion templates for this demo are really short and sweet. They are never seen, and are simply slaves to the Flash interface. There are two - one for pushing records into Flash, and one for inserting records into the database on Flash's behalf.

1. The first is called stockdata.cfm and is coded simply so:

```
<cfsetting enablecfoutputonly="yes">
  <cfquery    name="stockquery"    datasource="dsnBobstock"
  ➡dbtype="ODBC">
  SELECT    partname,quantity,    ID    FROM    stocklevel
  WHERE ÂID=#FORM.ID#
  </cfquery>
  <cfoutput query="stockquery">
        &partname=#partname#&quantity=#quantity#&
  </cfoutput>
```

Note that it is much the same as we have used previously, but also has the added ID field in the SQL query. This field is set to FORM.ID, which as you'll learn in later chapters, is our method of retrieving POST values from a form. In the case of the Flash movie, the values are in fact sent using a POST method, as we will explain at the end of this chapter.

The second template is called stockinsert.cfm, and its job is to receive POST values from the Flash movie, establish the database connections and setting, and insert the data into the database. Here is all the code for the template:

```
<cfinsert  datasource="dsnBobstock"  tablename="stocklevel"
➥formfields="partname, quantity" dbtype="ODBC">
```

It looks simple because we have already done all the work. The connection to the database is done, the fields are named correctly to match each other in the Flash movie and the <cfinsert> attributes contain the most vital information:

- Which table to use

- Which connection to use

- What fields to update

- What kind of database type to use

That's all! In fact, that is all the ColdFusion for this chapter. Now for a lot of ActionScript and design in Flash – much needed after so much code!

The Flash Layout

Now, the layout and design is open to your own interpretation. Use the movie name "stock" if you like, although the name is not really important. I suggest the following arrangement in the Flash movie

Here is what my layers and keyframes look like for this movie:

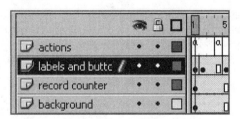

Frames 1, 2 and 5 are the keyframes on the graphical elementslayers.

1. On the *actions* layer, create **keyframes** at frames 1, 4 and 5.

    The two main **textfields** are *input* fields and live alongside the triangular buttons in the labels & buttons layer. They are labelled partname and quantity. They will display records *and* insert records. They are set up the same in every keyframe on that layer.

    In the record counter layer is a third textfield - this time dynamic - which displays the current ID number that we will later pass to the database to select a specific record.

2. Add two triangular buttons – one for forward, one for back. In frame 2 they both exist. In frame 5, only the forward button exists – where it becomes our insert record button.

3. **In frame 2** add a button to say "insert record" – this button belongs in keyframe 2, ready to be clicked while we scroll through our existing records.

4. Add the final button on frame 5 and label it back to browsing.

    That's all the graphics for now. Next - the actions in the frames!

5. In frame 1, a variable called ID is set to 1:

    ```
    ID=1
    ```

    This is going to be the variable that scrolls us through our records, and we want to start at the very beginning.

6. In frame 4 is an action that takes the movie back to frame 2 and plays

    ```
    gotoAndPlay(2)
    ```

    (we avoid frame 1 for a while as it will set ID to 0, and we might not want that all the time).

    That's all the frame actions. Next up are the button actions. Because this movie might well be played in a Flash 4 browser, I have kept the code to the Flash 4 style. If we went with Flash 5, however, we'd get rid of a lot of frames and frame actions and use movieClip events more.

You should have those triangular buttons in every keyframe on their layer. Totally ignore all the graphics and bits in frame 1 – they are there for show only.

7. Now add this code to the right-facing triangular button in frame 2

```
on (release) {
     ID = ID+1;
loadVariablesNum("stockdata.cfm",0,"POST");
}
```

8. Do the same for the left-facing button, except make the + into a –
Now look at the single triangular button in frame 5 and add this code to it:

```
on (release) {
     loadVariables ("flashinsert.cfm", "_root",
"POST");
}
```

Almost finished!

9. Now add the following code to the insert record button in frame 2:

```
on (release) {
partname="";
quantity=""
     gotoAndStop (5);
}
```

10. An lastly, add this code to the "back to browse" button in frame 5:

```
on (release) {
     gotoAndPlay (1);
}
```

Now let's look at the process, frame by frame: This is the best way to troubleshoot a Flash movie, by the way. Follow the code through and try to ask the same questions that Flash would ask as it moves forward. "Why must I stop here?", "How do I know the variable is re-set?" "What connects this variable to that object?" ... etc. etc.

Playback

The movie plays through frame 1, on to frame 4 and is returned to frame 2 again to loop over and over. As it passed through frame 1, a variable ID was set to 1. The dynamic textfield called ID picks up displays this at bottom-left.

Now the movie is looping through frames 2 to 4, and the triangular buttons are live. Clicking them will increment the variable ID, pass this value to the ColdFusion template stockdata.cfm and modify the SQL query in that template. The template will assign new values to the variables partname and quantity, and Flash will pick these changes up and display them in the .swf fields with the same names. But we are going to insert a record straight away, so let's click on insert new record...

Now the movie moves to frame 5 and stops. The textfields are empty because the action on insert new record set the fields to nothing (" "). We can type in a record....

...like so, and click on OK. An action on the triangular button calls up the ColdFusion template called stockinsert.cfm That template, as we saw earlier, uses a `<cfinsert>` tag with some specific settings to put these variables into the right tables via the right connection and into the right fields.

All done! Now browse your Flash movie and see the new entry, which shows that this record was inserted at ID 9 (Access does that automatically for you). Scroll back and forth to view other records.

This is a rough example. All the finishing touches are required, an `if..else` statement, in the ActionScript, to keep the ID from becoming a negative number and a warning when we are at the last record in the table. It is a platform on which to build and experiment. Enjoy!

Case study

As promised earlier, we're now going to generate the database to use in our forum. In our forum the database is as key a feature as the Flash and ColdFusion aspects. People will want to post messages and conduct interesting debates – no, honest, they will! All this information will have to reside somewhere, and that somewhere is in a database.

Database design can be a whole career in itself. Database methodologies are based upon they way that the data will be used. For our forum the main data viewed will be the list of posts, with each having any number of possible replies. Together the post and its replies make up a thread. This division between posts and replies lends itself to a database containing two tables that are linked together with a one to many relationship.

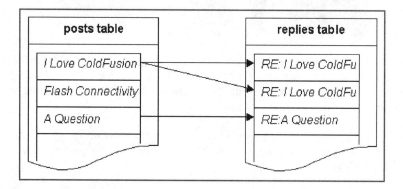

Right. On with the exercise.

Building the database

1. Open Access and create a new blank database. We'll save this as `message_data.mdb`, in a new folder called MessageBoardDB. The actual file name we use here holds no significance as ColdFusion will link to the database through an ODBC Data Source Name (DSN) that we're going to set up in ColdFusion Administrator. Make sure that your new folder is on the same machine as the server so that the data source can be linked correctly. Whilst the file name is not important, the names of the fields we'll create in the table certainly are as we'll be referring to them in both ColdFusion and Flash.

2. Create a new table using the Create table in Design view option.

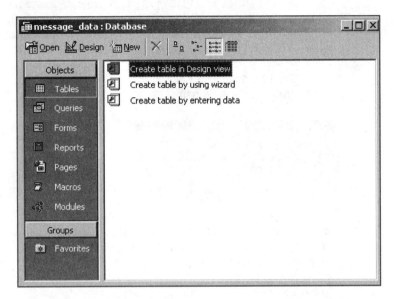

We'll now enter the field names and data types into this table. Make an entry for each of the following fields and the corresponding data type:

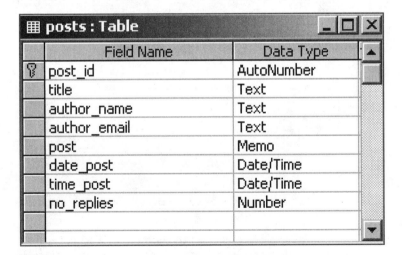

Each of these fields will contain data for each and every posting to our forum. Note that the first field, post_id, is generated automatically by the database. All the other fields will be input by code in our ColdFusion templates. If we now try to save the table, we'll be prompted for a table name. We'll call this table posts, for obvious reason. We'll then get a message asking whether we want to create a primary key. Click Yes here post_id will be made our default primary key, which is signified by a key symbol next to the field name.

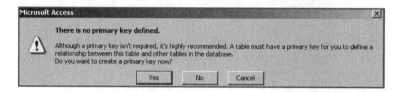

3.   On the copy of the database that I made I added descriptions to each field. (This file can be downloaded from the friends of ED web site.) This may seem a pointless thing to do for our simple database, but they're much like comments in code, when you come back later it's always best to have as much documentation as possible.

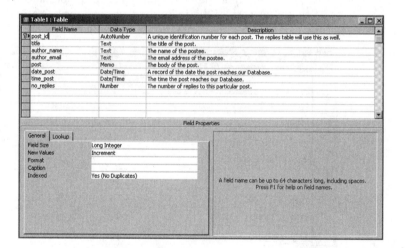

One thing to remember when choosing field names is that certain words are reserved and therefore can't be used. Most of these reserved words are used as SQL commands, *post* is one example of this. For a complete listing of these reserved words, Microsoft has a good knowledge base article that can be found at:

http://support.microsoft.com/support/kb/articles/Q286/3/35.ASP

With regard to naming conventions, I strongly suggest choosing one style and sticking with it. I tend to use underscores. Other common naming conventions include capitalizing the first letter, not using underscores and other combinations. For example, for the column name `author_email` many other developers would name this column `AuthorEmail` or `Authoremail`. Each one of these column names is valid. A constant style, whatever it is, can help eliminate errors and save you time as your applications become more complex.

4. We've now finished our post table, so close it and create another table within the same database. This table will be called replies. Follow the same process that we used to set up the posts table. This time the fields are slightly different:

Field Name	Data Type
reply_id	AutoNumber
post_id	Number
reply_title	Text
reply_name	Text
reply_email	Text
reply	Memo
date_reply	Date/Time
time_reply	Date/Time

This time it is `reply_id` that is automatically generated. You've probably noticed that `post_id` is on this table as well. This is our link between the two tables. Each reply will be to a specific post, and that post's ID number will be entered in the reply. Again, I've used the Description area to jot down notes on what each field is for.

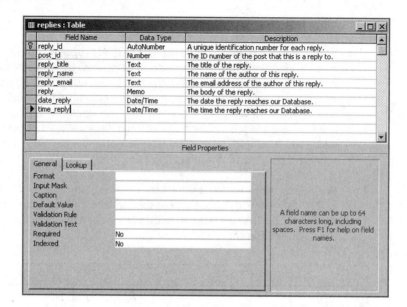

5. Once you've completed the information in the replies table and saved it we're almost done! I mentioned earlier that the file name wasn't important because ColdFusion references the database via an ODBC data source. Let's create that data source now. Open up the ColdFusion Administrator in your browser and log in.

6. Select ODBC Data Sources from the menu on the left. Next, click on Add, which will add an ODBC Data Source. Simple!

7. We now have to give the data source a name, or a DSN as it's commonly known as. We're going to call this board, and that is the name we use whenever we communicate with the database throughout the book. We need to also specify the route to our Access database file in the Database File field All there is to do now is click on Create.

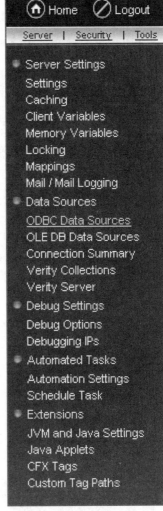

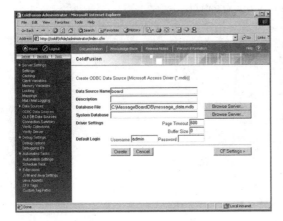

There, we've done it! Our database, even though it contains nothing, is all linked up and ready to go.

Remember to log out of ColdFusion Administrator as we've now finished the case study section for this chapter. In the next chapter we'll be creating the ColdFusion templates that will allow us, and the millions of people who want to talk on the forum, to fill it.

Summary

In this chapter we've covered the fundamentals of the way databases work, well at least as much as we need to know now! Also we've looked at how ColdFusion can look at the information in the database, and through CFML handle that data in a variety of ways. We've also talked about connecting the database to the outside world via ODBC and how data sources can be managed via the ColdFusion Server Administrator.

Most crucially we have seen how our data can be passed to and from a Flash movie. This means that however dull the data we can now the possibilities of presenting on the web in a form that is only limited by our creativity.

5 Forum Foundation

What We'll Cover in this Chapter

- *Building the basic templates for a message board application*

- *Inserting data to and requesting data from our data source*

- *Intergrating our Flash front-end with the CFML templates*

The ColdFusion templates

In order to build up our basic message board application we need to create six ColdFusion templates. Each one corresponds to a different state of the message board. Let's take a brief look at the templates before we build each one in turn.

1. **main.cfm** – the main template that will display all the titles of current posts, the author, date and time received, and the number of replies received for each post.

2. **new_post.cfm** – this template will contain a form that will allow visitors to the board to leave new posts.

3. **insert_post.cfm** – this template will process the `new_post.cfm` template by inserting the information into our database.

4. **new_reply.cfm** – this template will contain a form that will allow visitors to respond to any thread (or post) they select. The form will also be used to respond to replies that are part of the current thread.

5. **insert_reply.cfm** – like the `insert_post.cfm` template, this one will process the `new_reply.cfm` template by inserting the information passed in the form into our database.

6. **view_thread.cfm** – this template will allow us to view a particular thread and all of its replies.

Let's now build up each of these templates in turn.

main.cfm

We'll start by creating the central template of the forum. This acts as a home page for the message board with an index of the posts listed in a table. Our table will display five fields for each message as well as a link to view the post and any subsequent replies to it. The five fields we're going to display are:

- Number of replies

- Title

- Author (including their e-mail address as a link)

- Date of post

- Time of post

You'll notice that these headings correlate with the fields that we set up in the Chapter 4 case study database's posts table. We're going to pull the information from this database to display in the table.

Right, let's start building the template.

Building our main page

1. All of our templates are going to be built within ColdFusion Studio, so open this up now. Studio will open up with a new document (or **template** to use ColdFusion terminology) in the Edit window. By default this template will have the foundations of an HTML document, but we're going to build our template from scratch so delete this content to leave a blank window. We're now going to save this file as main.cfm. Create a new directory within the wwwroot directory of your web server (or a web directory if your not using the Windows IIS server), and call this directory forum. Save the file in this folder. By saving the file on the web server we can easily test our files – they have to be in the wwwroot directory or a subdirectory of this to function properly.

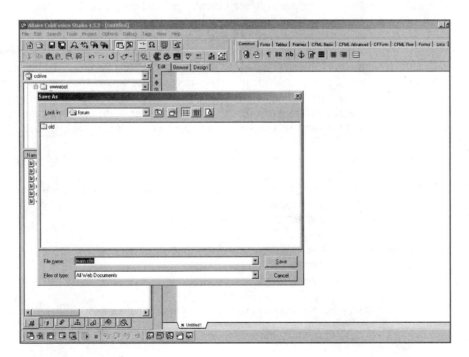

2. The first thing we're going to do is set up a query that will retrieve the data from our database so that we can display it in our table. We'll call this query current_posts. The query needs a name so that we easily reference the data when we want to output it into our table. In the Chapter 4 case study we gave our database a data source name (DSN) of board, so that's simply what we'll reference our data source as in this query. We set our database up as an ODBC data source in Administrator, hence this is our database type (dbtype).

```
<!-- query to get current posts for the forum -->

<cfquery name="current_posts" datasource="board"
➥dbtype="ODBC">
</cfquery>
```

Now seems the ideal opportunity to mention the comment tag in ColdFusion. Whilst similar in appearance to those in HTML, the ColdFusion Server strips ColdFusion comments out before rendering the template as an HTML document. What this means is that you never have to worry about anybody seeing your comments – so comment away! They certainly come in handy as your templates become more complex. They will help you figure out why you did what you did six months ago.

3. Now that we've got our basic query structure, the next step is to actually ask the database for the information we need to display. In order to do this we'll use some basic SQL commands. We'll be covering SQL in more detail in the next chapter, but as you'll see below the commands we're using here are self-explanatory. We want to *select* all the records *from* the posts table of our database, and *order* them in *descending* order so that the most recent posting is at the top. This is very easy to do:

```
<!-- query to get current posts for the forum -->

<cfquery name="current_posts" datasource="board"
➥dbtype="ODBC">
SELECT
*
FROM posts
ORDER BY post_id DESC
</cfquery>
```

(Note that the * symbol selects **all** as in many other programming languages.)

We've now got our data retrieved and waiting to be displayed, and the next step is to build the table where we'll display the data. If you're familiar with HTML you'll recognize the table tags that we use to build the table. Let's quickly look at a reminder of what each tag does before we get going.

<table>

The `<table>` tag defines the start of the table and as with all tags in a table has a closing tag (`</table>`). This tag take can take a number of attributes, and we'll be using `border`, `cellspacing` and `cellpadding`. The border of the table defines the thickness of the grid that divides up the table (a value of `0` would leave no border at all). The spacing value of a cell sets the space between each cell of the table, while the padding value sets the space between the content of a cell and its outside border. I find the easiest way of seeing exactly what effect each of these attributes has is to alter the values once I've completed the table and note the change in appearance.

<tr>

As with the database we created earlier, a table is divided up into horizontal rows. In our table we'll have a row at the top that defines column titles, and rows for each post record created in the database.

<td>

Each row in a table is divided up into individual cells, which are encased within `<td>` tags. Each cell of a table needs to be populated in order for its border to be displayed correctly. If the content of the cell should be empty we'll use an HTML space (` `).

Right, now we're refreshed on the construction of a table let's actually build it!

4. Let's set up a basic table with one row, containing our five column headings, after the `<cfquery>` statement that we've created. We'll also create one extra cell in this row, the reason for which you'll see when we come to the `<cfoutput>` statement.

```
<!-- the table -->

<table border="1" cellspacing="6"
➥cellpaddding="2">
    <tr>
            <td>Replies</td>
            <td>Title</td>
            <td>Author</td>
            <td>Date</td>
            <td>Time</td>
            <td> </td>
    </tr>
</table>
```

5. We now need to create a row for each record in our database, containing the data that corresponds to each heading in the top row. We'll use the `<cfoutput>` tag to dynamically generate each row. By putting the tags for a table row within the `<cfoutput>` tag we're instantly formatting each record we've collected from the database in the `<cfquery>`. In the opening `<cfoutput>` tag we state that we're outputting the data retrieved in our current_posts query.

```
<!-- the table -->

<table border="1" cellspacing="6"
➥cellpaddding="2">
    <tr>
            <td>Replies</td>
            <td>Title</td>
            <td>Author</td>
            <td>Date</td>
            <td>Time</td>
            <td> </td>
    </tr>

<!-- output all our data here -->

<cfoutput query="current_posts">

</cfoutput>
</table>
```

6. Right, it's time to add the table row formatting for each record and the code to produce the actual output. For each output we simply put the field name from the database that corresponds to the column title on our table.

```
<!-- the table -->

<table border="1" cellspacing="6"
➥cellpaddding="2">
    <tr>
            <td>Replies</td>
            <td>Title</td>
            <td>Author</td>
            <td>Date</td>
            <td>Time</td>
            <td> </td>
    </tr>

<!-- output all our data here -->

<cfoutput query="current_posts">
    <tr>
            <td>#no_replies#</td>
            <td>#title#</td>
            <td><a
href="mailto:#author_email#">#author_name#</td>
            <td>#DateFormat(date_post)#</td>
            <td>#TimeFormat(time_post)#</td>
            <td><a
➥href="view_thread.cfm?post_id=#post_id#">View
➥Thread!</a></td>
    </tr>
</cfoutput>
</table>
```

There are three things in this code that are worth mentioning. Firstly, we've combined the author's e-mail address with the author's name as a link. If the author's name is clicked on in the final table an e-mail message to that person will open up. The second thing to note is that we have special tags to output the date and time in the correct format. The third thing relates to the blank cell that we created with the headings. You'll see that we're using this column to provide a link to view the thread containing the posting and its replies. We'll be creating view_thread.cfm later in this chapter, but note that the relevant post_id for a post is appended to the address to make sure the right thread is called.

7. So, we've just got one more thing to add to complete main.cfm – a link to create a new post on the forum. This is simplicity in itself and links to the new_post.cfm template that we're about to create. Here's the full code listing for main.cfm:

```
<!-- code listing for main.cfm -->

<!-- query to get current posts for the forum -->

<cfquery name="current_posts" datasource="board"
➥dbtype="ODBC">
SELECT
*
FROM posts
ORDER BY post_id DESC
</cfquery>

<!-- the table -->

<table border="1" cellspacing="6"
➥cellpaddding="2">
    <tr>
        <td>Replies</td>
        <td>Title</td>
        <td>Author</td>
        <td>Date</td>
        <td>Time</td>
        <td> </td>
    </tr>

<!-- output all our data here -->

<cfoutput query="current_posts">
    <tr>
        <td>#no_replies#</td>
        <td>#title#</td>
        <td><a
➥href="mailto:#author_email#">#author_name#</td>
        <td>#DateFormat(date_post)#</td>
        <td>#TimeFormat(time_post)#</td>
        <td><a
➥href="view_thread.cfm?post_id=#post_id#">View
➥Thread!</a></td>
    </tr>
</cfoutput>
</table>
<p><a href="new_post.cfm">New post link</a></p>
```

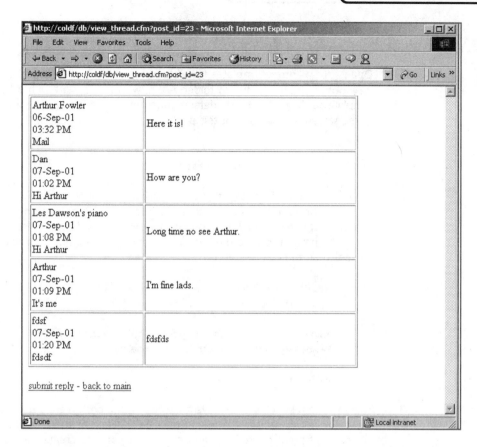

We've now completed the central template around which our forum will evolve. However, in order for the main page to display data from the database we first need to create some records in it. This is achieved by a combination of new_post.cfm and insert_post.cfm. The author of a post will enter the information into a form in new_post.cfm, which will then be passed onto insert_post.cfm, which will input the data into our database. Let's look at these two templates in turn.

new_post.cfm

This template will also contain a table for layout purposes, but the most important aspect is the form, which allows us to pass the data on to insert_post.cfm. With the exception of post_id, which is generated automatically, this template will define data for each field that we created in our database's posts table.

Creating the new post form

1. Open up a new template in ColdFusion Studio and save it as new_post.cfm in the forum folder. Again, we want to start with a blank template so delete the HTML default code. Let's put a few lines at the top of the screen to explain what this page is:

    ```
    <p><b>ColdFusion for Flash board</b></p>
    <p>Start a new thread here!</p>
    ```

2. Now we'll add the form tags that form the basis of this template. Any date we allow the user to submit within these tags can be passed on to our chosen destination, which in this case is insert_post.cfm. We're using the POST method to send the data as it allows a larger amount of data to be sent than the GET method.

    ```
    <p><b>ColdFusion for Flash board</b></p>
    <p>Start a new thread here!</p>

    <form action="insert_post.cfm" method="POST"
    ➥enctype="multipart/form-➥data">

    </form>
    ```

3. There will be four areas that we want the author of a post to enter data into: the name, e-mail address, title and post fields. Each of these inputs will live on a different row of the table that we're going to create. Let's start with the field where the author will input their name. You'll see widths specified in certain <td> tags, and these are the percentage of the table that a particular cell will take up. They're not really of a great importance but take note of their function. This row of the table consists of two cells: one consisting of text telling the author what should be entered, and the second an input box where they actually enter their name. Note that the input type is set as text, and the input name is set as author_name – the field name of the database where we want to insert the data.

```
<p><b>ColdFusion for Flash board</b></p>
<p>Start a new thread here!</p>

<form action="insert_post.cfm" method="POST"
➥enctype="multipart/form-data">

<table width="50%" border="1" cellspacing="2"
➥cellpadding="2">
      <tr>
              <td width="16%">Name:</td>
              <td width="84%"><input type="text"
➥name="author_name"></td>
      </tr>
</table>

</form>
```

4. The next row of the table takes exactly the same format. This time we substitute Name: with e-mail: and author_name with author_email.

```
<p><b>ColdFusion for Flash board</b></p>
<p>Start a new thread here!</p>

<form action="insert_post.cfm" method="POST"
➥enctype="multipart/form-data">

<table width="50%" border="1" cellspacing="2"
➥cellpadding="2">
      <tr>
              <td width="16%">Name:</td>
              <td width="84%"><input type="text"
➥name="author_name"></td>
      </tr>
      <tr>
              <td width="16%">e-mail:</td>
              <td width="84%"><input type="text"
➥name="author_email"></td>
      </tr>
</table>

</form>
```

5. You can no doubt guess what we're going to do for the title row! Yes, it's exactly the same format again with the relevant variables specified.

```
<table width="50%" border="1" cellspacing="2"
➡cellpadding="2">
    <tr>
            <td width="16%">Name:</td>
            <td width="84%"><input type="text"
➡name="author_name"></td>
    </tr>
    <tr>
            <td width="16%">e-mail:</td>
            <td width="84%"><input type="text"
➡name="author_email"></td>
    </tr>
    <tr>
            <td width="16%">Title:</td>
            <td width="84%"><input type="text"
➡name="title"></td>
    </tr>
</table>
```

6. The final piece of data that we want the user to enter is their actual post. This takes a slightly different format to the other three fields we've created. This is the data field that is likely to have the most content so we'll have this field spanning the whole of the table. We can do this by adding colspan="2" to the <td> tag. This means that this cell will span across both the cells that we've had in the preceding rows. I've also chosen to use the <div> tag to center this field – this is one way of doing this, you can use your preferred HTML method. Rather than using the <input> tag we're going to use <textarea> for this field. The name attribute of this tag has the same function as the <input> tag and we set this as post as this is the field name in the database. We set the size of the text box via the cols and rows attributes of the tag. So, let's add this code to the template:

```
<table width="50%" border="1" cellspacing="2"
➡cellpadding="2">
     <tr>
             <td width="16%">Name:</td>
             <td width="84%"><input type="text"
➡name="author_name"></td>
     </tr>
     <tr>
             <td width="16%">e-mail:</td>
             <td width="84%"><input type="text"
➡name="author_email"></td>
     </tr>
     <tr>
             <td width="16%">Title:</td>
             <td width="84%"><input type="text"
➡name="title"></td>
     </tr>
     <tr>
             <td colspan="2">
                     <div align="center">Post:<br>
                     <textarea name="post"
➡wrap="VIRTUAL" cols="70" rows="10"></textarea>
                     </div>
             </td>
     </tr>
</table>
```

7.   With any form we need to have some way of actually sending the data that the user enters. This is usually done through a Submit button, and that's exactly what we're going to do. We'll place it with its usual partner, the Reset button.

```
<table width="50%" border="1" cellspacing="2"
➡cellpadding="2">
     <tr>
             <td width="16%">Name:</td>
             <td width="84%"><input type="text"
➡name="author_name"></td>
     </tr>
     <tr>
             <td width="16%">e-mail:</td>
             <td width="84%"><input type="text"
➡name="author_email"></td>
     </tr>
     <tr>
             <td width="16%">Title:</td>
```

```
                              <td width="84%"><input type="text"
➥name="title"></td>
        </tr>
        <tr>
                <td colspan="2">
                        <div align="center">Post:<br>
                        <textarea name="post"
➥wrap="VIRTUAL" cols="70" rows="10"></textarea>
                        </div>
                </td>
        </tr>
        <tr>
                <td colspan="2">
                        <div align="center">
                        <input type="submit"
➥value="Submit">
                        <input type="reset"
➥value="Reset">
                        </div>
                </td>
        </tr>
</table>
```

8. We've finished the table, and nearly finished this template now. You may have noticed that there are actually seven fields in the database posts table that I said we needed to populate (remember that post_id is generated automatically), but we've only created inputs for four. That is because the other three pieces of data are sent as hidden data. The first one we're going to add is the number of replies (no_replies). As this is a new post the number of replies will initially be zero. So, we'll add the following line between the closing table and form tags. (Note that it has to be within the form tags in order for the data to be sent.)

    ```
    <input type="hidden" name="no_replies" value="0">
    ```

9. As we discovered when we create main.cfm, the value of the date and time is expressed differently to ensure a formatted appearance. We do this by using two in-built functions. For the correct time to be passed onto insert_post.cfm we use the following code:

    ```
    <input type="hidden" name="date_post"
    ➥value="#DateFormat(Now())#">
    <input type="hidden" name="time_post"
    ➥value="#CreateODBCTime(Now())#">
    ```

Notice that we've used CreateODBCTime to create the time rather than the TimeFormat we used earlier. This is because while TimeFormat can display the time correctly, it has problems actually setting the time correctly. One final thing to note is that we could put this code in <cfoutput> tags and it still wouldn't be displayed because of the hidden attribute. Here's the final code for this template:

```
<!-- new_post.cfm -->

<p><b>ColdFusion for Flash board</b></p>
<p>Start a new thread here!</p>

<form action="insert_post.cfm" method="POST"
➥enctype="multipart/form-data">
<table width="50%" border="1" cellspacing="2"
➥cellpadding="2">
     <tr>
             <td width="16%">Name:</td>
             <td width="84%"><input type="text"
➥name="author_name"></td>
     </tr>
     <tr>
             <td width="16%">e-mail:</td>
             <td width="84%"><input type="text"
➥name="author_email"></td>
     </tr>
     <tr>
             <td width="16%">Title:</td>
             <td width="84%"><input type="text"
➥name="title"></td>
     </tr>
     <tr>
             <td colspan="2">
                     <div align="center">Post:<br>
                     <textarea name="post"
➥wrap="VIRTUAL" cols="70" rows="10"></textarea>
                     </div>
             </td>
     </tr>
     <tr>
             <td colspan="2">
                     <div align="center">
                     <input type="submit"
➥value="Submit">
                     <input type="reset"
➥value="Reset">
                     </div>
```

```
              </td>
          </tr>
      </table>
      <cfoutput>
      <input type="hidden" name="no_replies" value="0">
      <input type="hidden" name="date_post"
      ➥value="#DateFormat(Now())#">
      <input type="hidden" name="time_post"
      ➥value="#CreateODBCTime(Now())#">
      </cfoutput>
      </form>
```

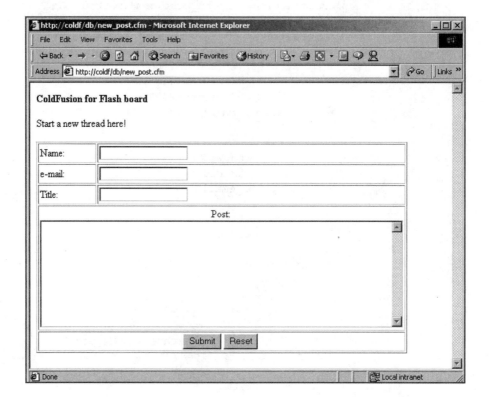

So, we've now finished our new_post.cfm template. Remember, this template passes the data on to insert_post.cfm, where the data is actually inserted into the database.

insert_post.cfm

This is the simplest of the templates and only has one meaningful line of code. When the Submit button is hit on the new post form, the data is sent to this template where it is passed on to the database by the following line of code:

```
<cfinsert datasource="board" tablename="posts"
➥dbtype="ODBC">
```

Very simple! There are actually two methods that can be used to add the data to our database. The alternate method to <cfinsert> is to a <cfquery> tag and the SQL INSERT INTO command. We saw this method in use in Chapter 4. The SQL option offers greater flexibility, but <cfinsert> is perfect for the application we're building here.

Let's take a look at three key attributes that the <cfinsert> command can take: datasource, tablename and formfields.

datasource

This is a required field and it's the name of the datasource that contains the table into which will we be inserting our data. In this case, the datasource is the database we linked to as board in the Chapter 4 case study.

tablename

This is also a required field and is the name of the table into which we'll insert our data within the database. For our message board this is the posts table. Note that when using <cfinsert> we're limited to inserting data into just one table per <cfinsert> statement. For instance, if our form was being used to insert data into the both the replies and the posts tables, we couldn't use <cfinsert>. This tag only let's us specify one table name.

formfields

This is an optional attribute. If we specify certain fields, only those will be inserted into the database. If we leave this blank, all form fields will be inserted into the database. For example, if we included the form fields author and post, the author's email, the post date, the post time and the number of replies would all be left out. If we left the attribute blank, they would all be included. By not including this statement in our tag we get the same effect as leaving the attribute value blank and all the fields are sent.

Sending the data to the database

1. Let's now build the template. Open a new template, delete the default content and save the file in the forum folder as `insert_post.cfm`. Let's add the `<cfinsert>` tag that we've just been examining. Note that we use the `dbtype` attribute again as we did earlier with a `<cfquery>` statement.

   ```
   <cfinsert datasource="board" tablename="posts"
   ➡dbtype="ODBC">
   ```

2. When this file is opened in a browser the user is confronted with a blank screen. Let's add some text telling the user what has happened:

   ```
   <cfinsert datasource="board" tablename="posts"
   ➡dbtype="ODBC">
   ```

   Thank you, your post has been inserted.

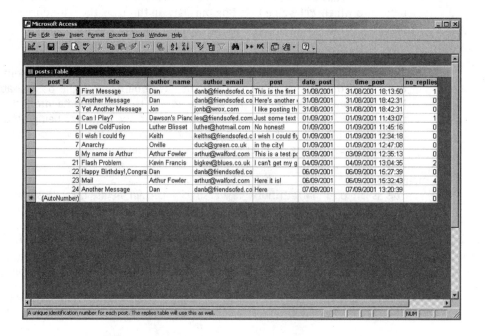

The final thing this page needs is a link back to the main board, otherwise the user will be stuck here with the only option being to use the browser's back button and refresh to see their post in the board.

```
<cfinsert datasource="board" tablename="posts"
➥dbtype="ODBC">

Thank you, your post has been inserted.

<cfoutput>
<p><a href="main.cfm">back to main</a></p>
</cfoutput>
```

4. Finally, for good practice we'll insert comments into the template so we can remember what's happening:

```
<!-- insert_post.cfm -->

<!-- insert the new post into the db -->

<cfinsert datasource="board" tablename="posts"
➥dbtype="ODBC">

<!-- tell the user that their post has been
➥accepted -->

Thank you, your post has been inserted.

<cfoutput>
<p><a href="main.cfm">back to main</a></p>
</cfoutput>
```

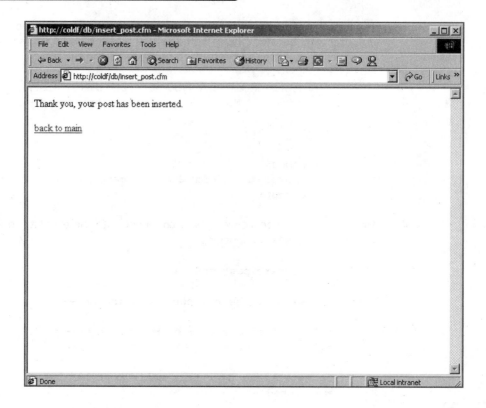

Let's check that the three templates we've made so far are working properly. Open up the main.cfm file in your web browser using the http://localhost or server path to the address. For example, if you're testing in the server machine the address will be something similar to:

http://localhost/forum/main.cfm

If you're using a remote server the address is via the server name:

http://*servername*/forum/main.cfm

Your database probably won't have any records in it at this point so you'll be greeted by an empty table. Click on the new post link and you'll see the form to add messages. Add some messages to the board and see them added to the main page.

new_reply.cfm

The new reply form is similar to the new post form, but does have some additions. This is due to the fact that while an original post is a standalone entity, a reply is implicitly linked to an original posting and any other replies to that posting. As a consequence we need to retrieve data about the original post and link our reply to that posting. As with `new_post.cfm` and `insert_post.cfm`, the new reply template works with `insert_reply.cfm` to input the information into the database.

The new reply template

1. Create a new ColdFusion template and this time save the file as `new_reply.cfm` (once again in the forum folder). You probably know what the next thing to do is – delete the default code. In the finished forum this template will be opened from the view thread page, and when the link is clicked the `post_id` of the original message is appended to the URL for use in the new reply template. We'll use this `post_id` in a `<cfquery>` to get information about the original posting:

   ```
   <!-- Run query to get info about the selected
   post -->

   <cfquery name="get_post" datasource="board"
   ➥dbtype="ODBC">
   SELECT
   post, no_replies, author_name
   FROM
   posts
   WHERE post_id = #post_id#
   </cfquery>
   ```

   As you can see, we're only interested in selected information about the original post. We need the author's name and their post so we have a reminder on screen of what we're replying to! The number of replies is needed as this value will be updated when the information is inserted into the database by `insert_reply.cfm`.

2. Once the above query has been used in a `<cfoutput>` statement the rest of this template is remarkably similar to the new post form we created earlier. Let's create our form and table, and add this output to the first row of the table. (Note that we called the query get_post this time.)

```
<!-- new_reply.cfm -->
<!-- Run query to get info about the selected
➥post -->

<cfquery name="get_post" datasource="board"
➥dbtype="ODBC">
SELECT
post, no_replies, author_name
FROM
posts
WHERE post_id = #post_id#
</cfquery>

<form action="insert_reply.cfm" method="POST"
➥enctype="multipart/form-➥data">
<table width="50%" border="1" cellspacing="2"
➥cellpadding="2">
    <tr>
    <cfoutput query="get_post">
        <td colspan="2">
        <b>Post: </b>#post#<br>
        <b>Author: </b>#author_name#
        </td>
    </cfoutput>
    </tr>
</table>
</form>
```

3. We now have the post and name of the original author at the top of the reply form, and we can get on with the sections of this table that actually deal with the reply. This code is almost identical to the table in the new posts form, except for the different field names that correspond to the replies table we created in the database.

```
<!-- new_reply.cfm -->

➡<!-- Run query to get info about the selected
post -->

<cfquery name="get_post" datasource="board"
➡dbtype="ODBC">
SELECT
post, no_replies, author_name
FROM
posts
WHERE post_id = #post_id#
</cfquery>

<form action="insert_reply.cfm" method="POST"
➡enctype="multipart/form-data">
<table width="50%" border="1" cellspacing="2"
➡cellpadding="2">
    <tr>
    <cfoutput query="get_post">
            <td colspan="2">
            <b>Post: </b>#post#<br>
            <b>Author: </b>#author_name#
            </td>
    </cfoutput>
    </tr>
    <tr>
            <td width="16%">Name:</td>
            <td width="84%"><input type="text"
➡name="reply_name"></td>
    </tr>
    <tr>
            <td width="16%">e-mail:</td>
            <td width="84%"><input type="text"
➡name="reply_email"></td>
    </tr>
    <tr>
            <td width="16%">Title:</td>
            <td width="84%"><input type="text"
➡name="reply_title"></td>
```

```
            </tr>
            <tr>
                 <td colspan="2">
                         <div align="center">Reply:<br>
                         <textarea name="reply"
➥wrap="VIRTUAL" cols="70" ➥rows="10"></textarea>
                         </div>
                 </td>
            </tr>
            <tr>
                 <td colspan="2">
                         <div align="center">
                         <input type="submit"
➥value="Submit">
                         <input type="reset"
➥value="Reset">
                         </div>
                 </td>
            </tr>
        </table>
        </form>
```

4. The last thing we need to do on this template is to insert the hidden
    inputs. In the new posts form we had a time, date and number of replies.
    This time we don't need to set a number of replies as this will be
    calculated in insert_reply.cfm. Instead we'll pass on the post_id as
    a hidden input. Where these lines of code are placed is not overly
    important as long as they're within the form tags and some output tags.
    This time we'll put it before the Submit button to prove this point. Here's
    the final code listing for this template:

```
<!-- new_reply.cfm -->

<!-- Run query to get info about the selected
➥post -->

<cfquery name="get_post" datasource="board"
➥dbtype="ODBC">
SELECT
post, no_replies, author_name
FROM
posts
WHERE post_id = #post_id#
</cfquery>
```

```
<form action="insert_reply.cfm" method="POST"
➥enctype="multipart/form-data">
<table width="50%" border="1" cellspacing="2"
➥cellpadding="2">
    <tr>
    <cfoutput query="get_post">
            <td colspan="2">
            <b>Post: </b>#post#<br>
            <b>Author: </b>#author_name#
            </td>
    </cfoutput>
    </tr>
    <tr>
            <td width="16%">Name:</td>
            <td width="84%"><input type="text"
➥name="reply_name"></td>
    </tr>
    <tr>
            <td width="16%">e-mail:</td>
            <td width="84%"><input type="text"
➥name="reply_email"></td>
    </tr>
    <tr>
            <td width="16%">Title:</td>
            <td width="84%"><input type="text"
➥name="reply_title"></td>
    </tr>
    <tr>
            <td colspan="2">
                    <div align="center">Reply:<br>
                    <textarea name="reply"
➥wrap="VIRTUAL" cols="70" rows="10"></textarea>
                    </div>
            </td>
    </tr>
    <tr>
            <td colspan="2">
                    <div align="center">
                    <cfoutput>
                    <input type="hidden"
➥name="post_id" value="#post_id#">
                    <input type="hidden"
➥name="date_reply" ➥value="#DateFormat(Now())#">
                    <input type="hidden"
➥name="time_reply"
➥value="#CreateODBCTime(Now())#">
```

```
                                          <input type="submit"
➥value="Submit">
                                          <input type="reset"
➥value="Reset">
                                          </cfoutput>
                                          </div>
                          </td>
                  </tr>
          </table>
          </form>
```

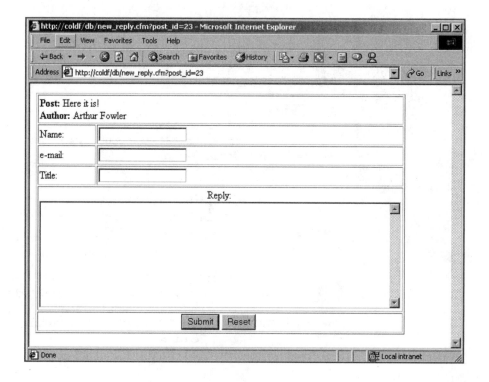

Now that we've created one half of the reply system let's move onto the template that inserts the data into the database.

insert_reply.cfm

This is our penultimate template and is the final piece we need too make sure all our data is posted into the database. This template is similar in nature to `insert_post.cfm` – well it would be as they do the same job, except for posting the data into the `replies` table rather than the `posts` table! However, this template does have additional code to update the number of replies (`no_replies`) in the `posts` table. Let's get on with it.

Inserting the reply data into the databases

1. Make a new ColdFusion template and save it as `insert_replies.cfm`. Let's put the insert command into the empty template. Remember, this time we're inserting the data into the `replies` table.

```
<cfinsert datasource="board" tablename="replies"
➥dbtype="ODBC">
```

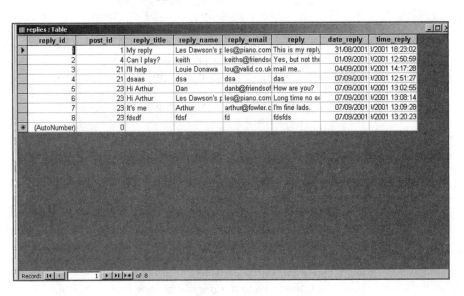

	reply_id	post_id	reply_title	reply_name	reply_email	reply	date_reply	time_reply
▶	1	1	My reply	Les Dawson's ¢	les@piano.com	This is my reply	31/08/2001	1/2001 18:23:02
	2	4	Can I play?	keith	keiths@friends₢	Yes, but not the	01/09/2001	1/2001 12:50:59
	3	21	I'll help	Louie Donawa	lou@valid.co.uk	mail me..	04/09/2001	1/2001 14:17:28
	4	21	dsaas	dsa	dsa	das	07/09/2001	1/2001 12:51:27
	5	23	Hi Arthur	Dan	danb@friendsof	How are you?	07/09/2001	1/2001 13:02:55
	6	23	Hi Arthur	Les Dawson's ¢	les@piano.com	Long time no se	07/09/2001	1/2001 13:08:14
	7	23	It's me	Arthur	arthur@fowler.c	I'm fine lads.	07/09/2001	1/2001 13:09:28
	8	23	fdsdf	fdsf	fd	fdsfds	07/09/2001	1/2001 13:20:23
*	(AutoNumber)	0						

Record: 1 ▶ ▶I ▶* of 8

2. We now need to add the code for updating the number of replies in the posts table. Remember that this figure is retrieved from the posts table to display in main.cfm. There are two sections to this code: a query statement, and an output statement containing a second query. Let's start by entering the first <cfquery>.

```
<cfquery name="get_replies" datasource="board"
➥dbtype="ODBC">
SELECT
COUNT(reply_id) AS no_replies
FROM
replies
WHERE post_id = #post_id#
</cfquery>
```

Before analyzing what the above code does, let's first think about what data can give us the number of replies to a message. The link between a post and its replies is that the post_id of the post is inserted into all replies to that message in the database. Therefore to count the number of replies we just need to count how many times the relevant post_id occurs in the replies table. The above SQL statement does this calculation. The new command to us in this query is the COUNT facility.

A COUNT command takes the following form:

COUNT (*Field Name*) AS *variable_name*

What this does is look for all instances of *Field Name* and sets the total number as the *variable_name*. (Note this looks for the number of instances of the *Field Name* and isn't actually concerned with the data in that field name.) In our example we're looking for the number of reply_id instances and we're going to set this as no_replies. If we left the code at this one line it would return the number of replies in the database, not for a single post. This is why we qualify the statement. We want to *count* the reply_id's *from* the replies table *where* the post_id is the same as our original posting (remember that the post_id was passed on to us by new_reply.cfm).

3. So, we now know how to get the number of replies to a post, but we still need to insert this number into the posts table so the figure is displayed correctly in main.cfm. This is where the <cfoutput> and second query comes in. Add the next block of code and we'll then look at what it does.

```
<cfoutput query="get_replies">
<cfquery datasource="board" dbtype="ODBC">
UPDATE posts
SET no_replies = '#no_replies#'
WHERE post_id = #post_id#
</cfquery>
</cfoutput>
```

As with all the SQL commands we've looked at so far this is pretty self-explanatory. Our get_replies query above calculated the number of replies to the post, so we start the output by collecting that data for use (query="get_replies"). We then use a query to actually insert the value into the posts table. We want to *update* the posts table by setting the number of replies (no_replies) to equal the figure we've just retrieved from the get_replies query. This figure only needs to be inserted for the actual posting that we're replying to, hence the need for the WHERE post_id = #post_id# statement. Once this code is processed the number of replies is updated with the correct value.

4. This template is nearly finished now. It serves its purpose in updating the database, but we need to add a link so that we're not stuck on this page. This time we'll send the user back to the thread they've just replied to. Note that we've used the <cflocation> tag this time as an alternative to an HTML link. Once we've added this code, and a few comments to remind us what we've done, we should have the following code in our completed template:

```
<!-- insert_reply.cfm -->

<!-- insert the new reply into the db -->

<cfinsert datasource="board" tablename="replies"
➥dbtype="ODBC">

<!-- update the number of replies in the posts
➥table -->

<cfquery name="get_replies" datasource="board"
➥dbtype="ODBC">
SELECT
COUNT(reply_id) AS no_replies
```

```
FROM
replies
WHERE post_id = #post_id#
</cfquery>
<cfoutput query="get_replies">
<cfquery datasource="board" dbtype="ODBC">
UPDATE posts
SET no_replies = '#no_replies#'
WHERE post_id = #post_id#
</cfquery>
</cfoutput>

<!-- send the user back to thread -->

<cfoutput>
<cflocation
➥url="view_thread.cfm?post_id=#post_id#"
➥addtken="No">
</cfoutput>
```

So, if the author of the reply clicks the link at the end of the insert_reply.cfm template they're taken to view_thread.cfm. Let's build this last template now.

view_thread.cfm

View thread is the last, but no means the least, of the templates that we need to build for our forum to fully function. On the forum's main page for each post we have a link to view the thread, and this is where that link will take us to. The view thread template needs to display all the relevant information for a post and its subsequent replies. Let's get on with building the last foundation of our forum.

Building the view thread template

1. As with all the other templates we want to start with a blank page. This time save it as view_thread.cfm. As the aim of this template is to display a post and its replies we'll start with two queries: one to retrieve the post data and one for the replies. We should be familiar with the format of these queries by now.

```
<cfquery name="get_post" datasource="board"
Âdbtype="OBDC">
SELECT
*
FROM
posts
WHERE
post_id = #post_id#
</cfquery>

<cfquery name="get_replies" datasource="board"
dbtype="OBDC">
SELECT
*
FROM
replies
WHERE
post_id = #post_id#
ORDER BY reply_id ASC
</cfquery>
```

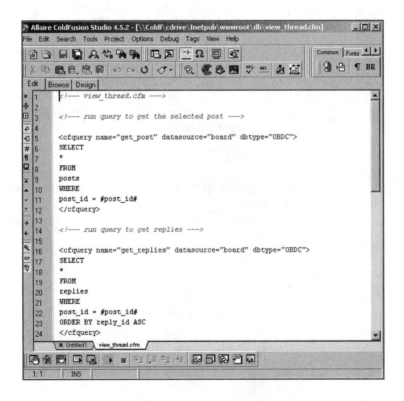

If we think back to the main.cfm template, we'll remember that the post_id was appended to the URL in the view thread link so that the right page was loaded. This also means that we have the post_id value to use in the above queries. The first query retrieves all the information (*) about the post by using the post_id. The second query uses the post_id in a similar fashion to what we did when we calculated the number of replies in insert_replies.cfm. All the relevant replies have the post_id as one of their variables so we can use this fact to pull the relevant data out of the replies table. This time we're ordering the replies in ascending order so they're displayed in the order they were made.

2. Now that we've retrieved the relevant data, our next job is to make the table to display it all. We divide this into two output queries: one for the post and one for the replies. Let's start with the basic table design and the post's output.

```
<table width="80%" border="1" cellspacing="2"
➡cellpadding="2">
    <tr>
    <!--- insert the post info --->
    <cfoutput query="get_post">
        <td width="19%" valign="top">
                #author_name#<br>
                #DateFormat(date_post)#<br>
                #TimeFormat(time_post)#<br>
                #title#
        </td>
        <td width="36%">#post#</td>
    </cfoutput>
    </tr>
</table>
```

Simple enough isn't it? We're just reusing code and techniques that we've used previously.

3. For adding the replies we use an almost identical structure. The major difference is that we insert the `<tr>` tags inside the `<cfoutput>` tags this time. While there is only one post, there are potentially many replies, so we need to ensure that a new row is created for each reply, hence we put the row tag inside the output tag.

```
<table width="80%" border="1" cellspacing="2"
➡cellpadding="2">
    <tr>
    <!-- insert the post info -->
    <cfoutput query="get_post">
        <td width="19%" valign="top">
            #author_name#<br>
            #DateFormat(date_post)#<br>
            #TimeFormat(time_post)#<br>
            #title#
        </td>
        <td width="36%">#post#</td>
    </cfoutput>
    </tr>
    <!-- insert the replies info -->
    <tr>
    <cfoutput query="get_replies">
        <td width="19%" valign="top">
            #reply_name#<br>
            #DateFormat(date_reply)#<br>
            #TimeFormat(time_reply)#<br>
            #reply_title#
        </td>
        <td width="36%">#reply#</td>
    </tr>
    </cfoutput>
</table>
```

4. Our last task is to add the links to this page. We need one link to take the user back to the main page, and one for the user to add a reply to the thread. Once these are added we can see our final code list for this template.

```
<!-- view_thread.cfm -->

<!-- run query to get the selected post -->

<cfquery name"get_post" datasource="board"
➥dbtype="OBDC">
SELECT
*
FROM
posts
WHERE
post_id = #post_id#
</cfquery>

<!-- run query to get replies -->

<cfquery name="get_replies" datasource="board"
➥dbtype="OBDC">
SELECT
*
FROM
replies
WHERE
post_id = #post_id#
ORDER BY reply_id ASC
</cfquery>

<table width="80%" border="1" cellspacing="2"
➥cellpadding="2">
    <tr>
    <!-- insert the post info -->
    <cfoutput query="get_post">
        <td width="19%" valign="top">
            #author_name#<br>
            #DateFormat(date_post)#<br>
            #TimeFormat(time_post)#<br>
            #title#
        </td>
        <td width="36%">#post#</td>
    </cfoutput>
    </tr>
    <!-- insert the replies info -->
```

```
        <tr>
        <cfoutput query="get_replies">
            <td width="19%" valign="top">
                #reply_name#<br>
                #DateFormat(date_reply)#<br>
                #TimeFormat(time_reply)#<br>
                #reply_title#
            </td>
            <td width="36%">#reply#</td>
        </tr>
        </cfoutput>
</table>

<!-- insert links -->
<cfoutput>
<p>
<a href="new_reply.cfm?post_id=#post_id#">submit
➥reply</a> -
<a href="main.cfm">back to main</a>
</p>
</cfoutput>
```

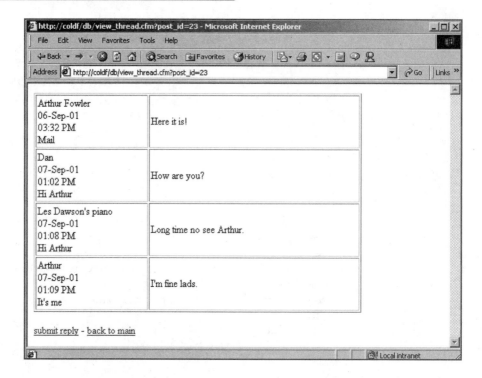

Test the forum now in your browser and it should be fully functioning. We've created a working message board out of ColdFusion. Well done!

In the case study section of this chapter we're going to integrate these templates with a Flash interface.

Case study

So far in the case study we've built up a Flash interface to house our forum and the database that will feed us with and eat our data. We're now going to prime two of the templates we've made in this chapter so that they can pass Flash the data variables. We'll then start the process of integrating these ColdFusion templates with our Flash interface. By the end of this chapter's case study section we'll have a Flash forum that can display our posts and their replies. But first let's get those templates ready.

Priming the Coldfusion templates

1. We'll be using the Chapter 5 templates again in Chapter 6, so we'll make duplicates of the relevant templates for use in the case study. Create a new folder within the forum folder that currently houses our templates. Name this new folder casestudy and make copies of main.cfm and view_thread.cfm in this folder. We'll deal with main.cfm first, so open up the newly duplicated copy of this file in ColdFusion Studio. The process of preparing this document for Flash is remarkably simple. When we built this template earlier in the chapter the main purpose of this template was to display a table of data. For our case study the only purpose is to allow for that data to be collected for display in Flash – we no longer need the table. The first thing we're going to do is remove all the table tags from our template. That is the <table>, <tr> and <td> tags, and their associated closing tags. We also remove all indentation at this point. The document we're left with should hold the following code:

```
<!-- code listing for main.cfm -->

<!-- query to get current posts for the forum -->

<cfquery name="current_posts" datasource="board"
dbtype="ODBC">
SELECT
*
FROM posts
ORDER BY post_id DESC
</cfquery>

<!-- the table -->

Replies
Title
Author
Date
Time
```

```
 

<!-- output all our data here -->

<cfoutput query="current_posts">

#no_replies#
#title#
<a href="mailto:#author_email#">#author_name#</a>
#DateFormat(date_post)#
#TimeFormat(time_post)#
<a href="view_thread.cfm?post_id=#post_id#">View
Thread!</a>

</cfoutput>

<p><a href="new_post.cfm">New post link</a></p>
```

2. Feel ruthless cutting all this code out? I hope not as we've only just begun! The only code that we'll pass to Flash will come from the <cfoutput> command. Any code that doesn't form part of this tag, or it related query, will be redundant as a consequence. We'll get rid of this code now. Once you've wielded your ax and slain this code we'll be left with the following:

```
<cfquery name="current_posts" datasource="board"
dbtype="ODBC">
SELECT
*
FROM posts
ORDER BY post_id DESC
</cfquery>

<cfoutput query="current_posts">
#no_replies#
#title#
<a href="mailto:#author_email#">#author_name#</a>
#DateFormat(date_post)#
#TimeFormat(time_post)#
<a href="view_thread.cfm?post_id=#post_id#">View
Thread!</a>
</cfoutput>
```

You can guess the power of Flash in displaying our data when it can reduce a once mighty forum to mere leftovers. Well, that's not quite the case as what we're left with is the most powerful part of the template. In a few more moves our streamline template will be the perfect partner for our Flash interface. But first there are two further pieces of code to remove before our main.cfm hits its perfect fighting weight. In the pure ColdFusion forum we had the author's name as a link to their e-mail address, but Flash can't interpret the data in that fashion so we'll strip away the e-mail link. The second thing we want to remove is the entire view thread link. In Flash we'll have an alternative way of showing the thread, so we won't pass this across. We'll also add a few comments to the template at this point so we can keep track of what the code is doing.

```
<!—- main.cfm —->

<!— query to get posts from the database —->

<cfquery name="current_posts" datasource="board"
➥dbtype="ODBC">
SELECT
*
FROM posts
ORDER BY post_id DESC
</cfquery>

<!—- prime the data to be collected by Flash —->

<cfoutput query="current_posts">
#no_replies#
#title#
#author_name#
#DateFormat(date_post)#
#TimeFormat(time_post)#
</cfoutput>
```

3.   Flash has a dislike of white space when liasing with a ColdFusion template. To get past this issue we can use the following line of code:

```
<cfsetting enablecfoutputonly="Yes">
```

As you might guess, this line means that only the output tag is enabled and serves to strip out the white space in the rest of the template. We'll have this as one continuous string in the output tag by the time Flash gets anywhere near it.

The data within the output tag is going to be expressed in the following format:

```
&variablename_#CurrentRow#=#variablename#&
```

Each variable string is attached to the next by an ampersand symbol, and this symbol also links the variables with the <cfoutput> tags. With any variables that are likely to contain strings of text we're going to send them within an URLEncodedFormat() command. This ensures that the text displays correctly in the Flash movie. The CurrentRow attribute ensures that a new record is printed for each row in the Flash movie. We'll now add the <cfsetting> tag that we looked at above and start to move the variables into the correct format.

```
<!-- main.cfm -->

<cfsetting enablecfoutputonly="Yes">

<!-- query to get posts from the database -->

<cfquery name="current_posts" datasource="board"
dbtype="ODBC">
SELECT
*
FROM posts
ORDER BY post_id DESC
</cfquery>

<!-- prime the data to be collected by Flash -->

<cfoutput query="current_posts">
&no_replies_#CurrentRow#=#no_replies#
&title_#CurrentRow#=#URLEncodedFormat(title)#
&author_name_#CurrentRow#=#URLEncodedFormat(author
➥ _name)#
&date_post_#CurrentRow#=#DateFormat(date_post)#
&time_post_#CurrentRow#=#TimeFormat(time_post)#
&</cfoutput>
```

4. We're going to add two more variable to the list. Firstly, we want to send the post_id. This was previously contained in the view thread link that we've removed. The second variable we want to add is thread_count. Our Flash movie will display 10 records on the screen at a time and will have a scroll button to view the rest. The thread count will tell Flash how many records there are so it can decide whether the scroll button should be active or not. Notice that this variable takes a slightly different format as we only require a single output from it, which is calculated with the help of an inbuilt counting function. We're also going to pass one final variable in a separate output tag. This variable is done=yes and will tell Flash that all the records are loaded. These tags should be added in the following format:

```
<!-- prime the data to be collected by Flash -->
```

...accepted by Flash, and also adding a <cfheader> tag at the top of the page that will allow the forum to be updated.

```
<cfheader name="Expires" value="#Now()#">
```

This template is now ready and waiting to be tackled by Flash.

```
<cfoutput query="current_posts">
&no_replies_#CurrentRow#=#no_replies#
&title_#CurrentRow#=#URLEncodedFormat(title)#
&author_name_#CurrentRow#=#URLEncodedFormat(author
_name)#
&date_post_#CurrentRow#=#DateFormat(date_post)#
&time_post_#CurrentRow#=#TimeFormat(time_post)#
&post_id_#CurrentRow#=#post_id#
&thread_count=#current_posts.RecordCount#
&</cfoutput>

<cfoutput>&done=yes&</cfoutput>
```

5. We finish this template by putting the first <cfquery> on one single line so that it is accepted by Flash. This template is now ready and waiting to be tackled by Flash.

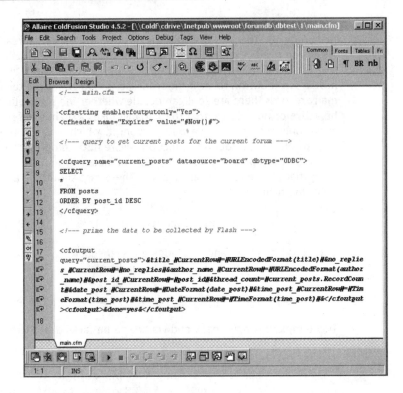

6. Now onto the second template, `view_thread.cfm`. This template is in a similar position to `main.cfm` in that it now has a redundant table. Apart from adding the `<cfsetting enablecfoutputonly="Yes">` line below the opening comment again, this template will remain unaltered until the opening table tag.

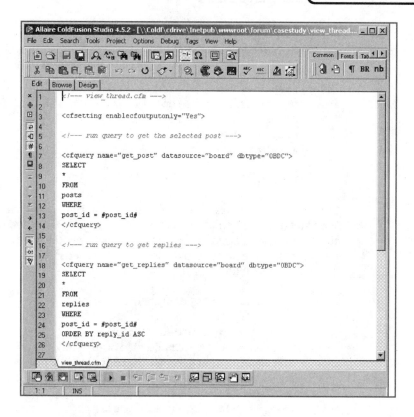

We still want to run the same queries to get the post and reply data. Our next step is to once again strip the table related tags from the template. This should leave us with three remaining `<cfoutput>` commands: one for the posts, one for the replies, and one containing links. We don't want the links output so delete this and any other remaining `<br>` tags. We should be now left with the two output tags that we're going to pass to Flash.

```
<!-- insert the post info -->

<cfoutput query="get_post">

#author_name#
#DateFormat(date_post)#
#TimeFormat(time_post)#
#title#
#post#

</cfoutput>
```

```
<!-- insert the replies info -->

<cfoutput query="get_replies">

#reply_name#
#DateFormat(date_reply)#
#TimeFormat(time_reply)#
#reply_title#
#reply#

</cfoutput>
```

7.   Our next task is to again prepare the variables into a format Flash can understand. We saw what the technique was in main.cfm and we'll carry out this technique again on the replies output now. For the posts output we will only be collecting one post so we don't need to include the CurrentRow attribute.

```
<!-- insert the post info -->

<cfoutput query="get_post">
&author_name=#URLEncodedFormat(author_name)#
&date_post=#DateFormat(date_post)#
&time_post=#TimeFormat(time_post)#
&title=#URLEncodedFormat(title)#
&post=#URLEncodedFormat(post)#
&</cfoutput>

<!-- insert the replies info -->

<cfoutput query="get_replies">
&reply_name_#CurrentRow#=#URLEncodedFormat(reply_n
➥ame)#
&date_reply_#CurrentRow#=#DateFormat(date_reply)#
&time_reply_#CurrentRow#=#TimeFormat(time_reply)#
&reply_title_#CurrentRow#=#URLEncodedFormat(reply_
➥title)#
&reply_#CurrentRow#=#URLEncodedFormat(reply)#
&</cfoutput>
```

8. There is one extra variable to add to each output this time. In the post output we want the pass the `post_id` on again, and in the replies output we want to add a variable that is similar to the `thread_count` we saw earlier. This time it's `reply_count` and it does the same job as `thread_count` but for the replies. Insert the following two lines into the relevant outputs:

```
&post_id=#post_id#
&reply_count=#get_replies.RecordCount#
```

9. Our last jobs is to do are put the output queries on a single line and add and output that signifies that the post and all its replies have loaded. Here i that line (it fulfils a similar function to the output at the end of `main.cfm`).

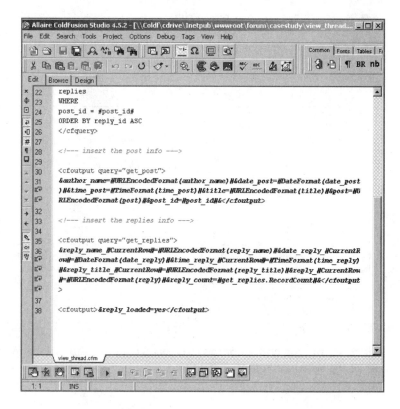

```
<cfoutput>&reply_loaded=yes</cfoutput>
```

We've now adjust the templates that are required for the case study in this chapter and can now move on to integrating them with Flash.

Integrating ColdFusion and Flash

We're now moving into the exciting part of the case study: the integration of ColdFusion and Flash to make a dynamic forum. The rest of our work in this chapter revolves around the `forum.fla` movie that we have been building up throughout the case study.

We can break the movie up into five sections that we are going to build in this chapter:

- The main timeline

- The forum movie clip

- The thread movie clip

- The duplicate posts movie clip

- The post movie clip

The clips all sit nicely together in a hierarchical structure that can be seen diagrammatically below.

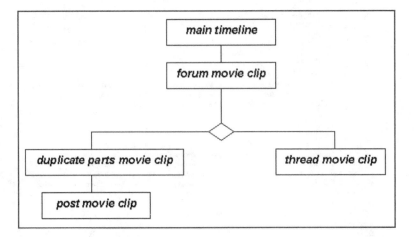

We're going to start at the bottom of this structure, as we need to include the clips form the bottom of the structure in those higher up.

Building the post movie clip

The post movie clip can defined as the equivalent of one record from our old `main.cfm` table. Open up the `forum.fla` file that we've been building up in previous chapters. Select Insert>New Symbol and we'll name the movie clip mcpost.

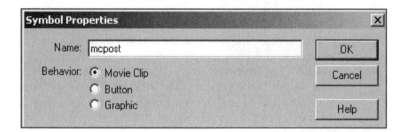

2. On this movie clip we're going to need five textboxes, that's one for each piece of information we're going to display in this movie clip. We'll now open up the Character panel and set the font style that we'll use for all the textboxes on this movie clip, namely: Arial, 12pt, bold, and white.

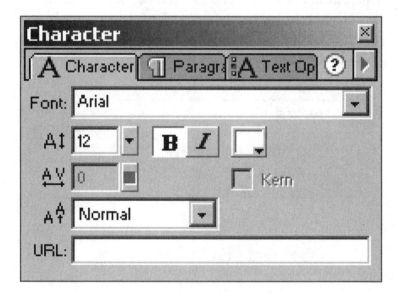

3. We'll now create the first, and smallest, textbox on the stage. This textbox will dynamically generate the number of replies to the post when displayed in the final forum. With the Text Tool now selected, click on the stage. Our textbox should be waiting for us to enter the text into it, but we're not going to! The content for this box, and all the others in this clip, will be dynamically generated. To achieve this we need to go back to the Character panel and time choose the Text Options tab. You'll be greeted with a fairly empty panel with Static Text selected from a drop-down menu. From this menu select Dynamic Text and you'll see a number of options appear. We want this box to only run over one line, so we need to keep Single Line selected in the next drop-down menu. I've made the Selectable checkbox should be unchecked so that the text is not selectable, but this is up to you. The most important aspect of this box is what we put in the Variable box. We want this box to display the number of replies, and throughout our ColdFusion templates and database we've referred to this as no_replies, so that is the variable name we need to enter here.

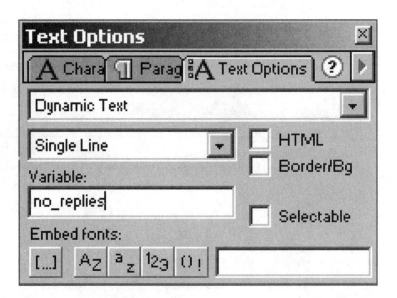

4. Once we've set the options for the textbox we want to resize it. Select the Arrow Tool and make sure the textbox we've just made is selected. Now open the Info panel and insert the width as 25 pixels and the height as 19.7. The height of our textboxes will remain constant throughout this movie clip – it is only the width that will vary in relation to the conentt we want each box to display. You may think that 19.7 is a strange value to choose, but my reasoning is simple: it's the default height that my Text Tool made when I first clicked on the stage. (It is possible that your default will be set at a slightly different value, but as long as we use that height constantly throughout the clip we wont have a problem.)

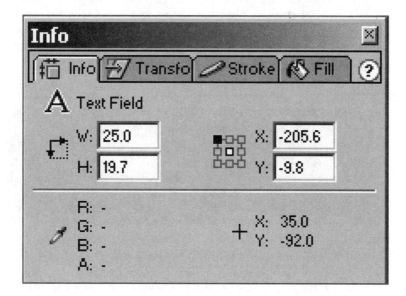

5. We'll now create the other four textboxes for this movie clip in the same way. The only things that we need to vary are the width of the textbox and the variable name. Let's now list these variable factors rather than going through each in turn and repeating information.

- title (width = 175)

- author_name (width = 80)

- date_post (width=65.7)

- time_post (width=55.9)

It is vital that we use the same variable names that we used in the main.cfm template for this to work. You may thing that some of these sizes are a bit strange using decimal values, I got them by typing out an example in the box an seeing what the width was.

6. So, we've now created our five textboxes and all we need to do now is arrange them on the stage. We'll arrange them left to right in the following order: no_replies, title, author_name, date_post and finally time_post. Put a slight gap between each textbox and then select all the textboxes on the stage. Next, open up the Align panel. Firstly, use the Space even horizontally button to make the gap between each of our textboxes even, and then Align vertical center to place the buttons in a row. Group the selection together now as we've go them positioned now we want them. Our final job for this layer is to center the group to the stage (Simply done in the Align panel again by now checking the To Stage button and using the Align vertical center and Align horizontal center buttons).

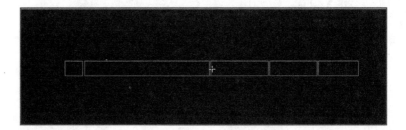

7. Rename Layer 1 as text fields and create a second layer above this called button. On this new layer draw a rectangle with no stroke over the two left hand textboxes on the text fields layer. The color of the rectangle is unimportant because where turning it into a button. Reselect the rectangle and convert it into a symbol (Insert>Convert to Symbol). We'll call this symbol bninvisible, because it's going to be an invisible button! In the new button's edit mode we'll see that the rectangle is on the Up state. On the timeline drag the con1ent so that it only lives on the Hit state and is therefore invisible.

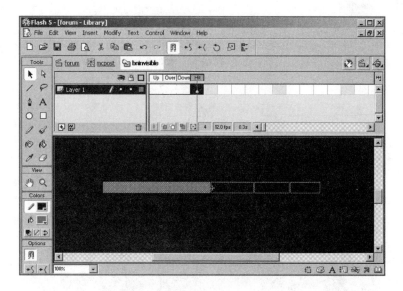

8. Our final act for mcpost is to add some actions to the button. Back in the edit mode for mcpost select the button on the stage and open the Actions panel (which should open in Object Actions rather than Frame Actions). Our button is going to be a link that allows the user to view the entire thread of the selected post. Our actions need to load the variables that we told view_thread.cfm to pass to Flash, and then go to the point in our movie that will display them.

    As the actions are on the button we need to add an on action first. In this case the event will be on(release). The next line of code will load our variables, and we need to include three variables with this code. Firstly the location of the variables (view_thread.cfm), secondly the movie level that we load the data into (Level 0), and finally the method used (POST). Our final line of code will tell the movie where to go next. For every clip in our movie we'll give it an instance name. This will allow us to refer to the route to that clip in a dot syntax form. The route for the movie to view the thread will be to go to the movie clip with the instance name forum and then to the frame labeled view_thread. We haven't create this movie clip yet as it's higher up our structure, but I'm sure you'll recognize the instance name and frame name when we get there, and know why they have to be named. The final code for our button should look like this:

```
on (release) {
    loadVariablesNum ("view_thread.cfm", 0,
➡"POST");
    _level0.forum.gotoAndPlay("view_thread");
}
```

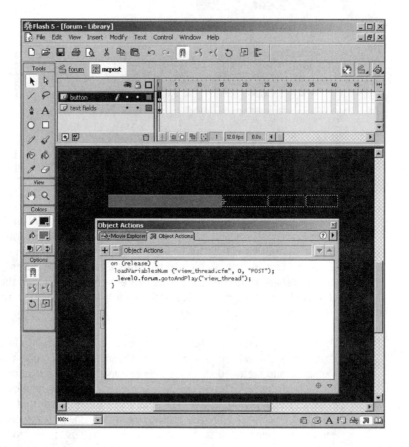

We've now finished the movie clip at the bottom of our structure and the next step up is to build the movie clip that duplicates mcpost and makes a copy for each record in our database. Remember that our Flash movie has no direct contact with the database, and all communication is done through our ColdFusion templates.

The duplicating movie clip

1. Make a new symbol and call it mcduplicate, giving at a Movie Clip state. On the default layer we're doing to place our mcpost movie clip that we're going to duplicate (you can see why we made it first now). Align this to the center of our stage and also name the layer mcpost as that is the only thing it contains. I mentioned that we're giving every movie clip and instance name, so call this instance post.

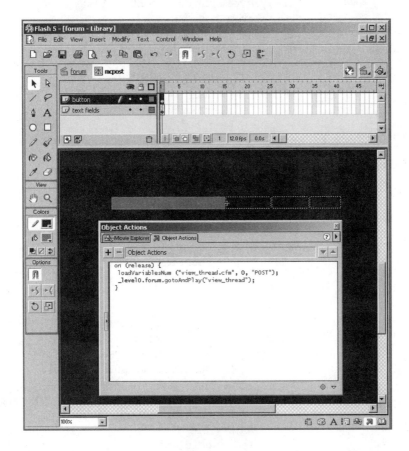

2. Make a second layer, onto which we're going to put the actions that will duplicate the post movie clip. Rename this layer as actions. Here's a full listing of the code that we'll enter into frame one. Take a look through this now, but wait until we know what it all does before typing it in.

```
stop ();
// set a value for x to use with our loop
x = 1;
position = 0;
setProperty ("post", _visible, false);
// while the number of headers is less than x -
➥run the loop to duplicate clips
// if there is more than 10 posts - only
➥duplicate 10 times
if (_level0.thread_count > 10) {
    while (x<=10) {
            duplicateMovieClip ("post", "post"+x,
➥x);
            setProperty ("post"+x, _y, position);
            this["post"+x].title =
➥_level0["title_"+x];
            this["post"+x].no_replies =
➥_level0["no_replies_"+x];
            this["post"+x].author_name =
➥_level0["author_name_"+x];
            this["post"+x].date_post =
➥_level0["date_post_"+x];
            this["post"+x].time_post =
➥_level0["time_post_"+x];
            this["post"+x].post_id =
➥_level0["post_id_"+x];
            position = position+15;
            x = x+1;
    }
} else {
    // otherwise, if there up to 10 posts -
➥duplicate for all of them
    while (x<=_level0.thread_count) {
            duplicateMovieClip ("post", "post"+x,
x);
            setProperty ("post"+x, _y, position);
            this["post"+x].title =
➥_level0["title_"+x];
            this["post"+x].no_replies =
➥_level0["no_replies_"+x];
            this["post"+x].author_name =
➥_level0["author_name_"+x];
            this["post"+x].date_post =
➥_level0["date_post_"+x];
            this["post"+x].time_post =
➥_level0["time_post_"+x];
```

```
                  this["post"+x].post_id =
➡ _level0["post_id_"+x];
                  position = position+15;
                  x = x+1;
          }
      }
```

There's a lot of it isn't there! But don't worry, it isn't as hard as it looks to understand. The first line of this code is a simple stop action. We've all probably seen these many times before and its only purpose here is to stop the movie looping over and over. We want to duplicate the post movie clip (remember that's the instance of mcpost on the stage) so that it makes an instance for each post we're going to retrieve. We're only going to display 10 records on the main page at a time (we use the scroll bar to view the rest), so we only want only to duplicate a maximum of 10 times.

As with any duplication in ActionScript we use an if loop to produce the required number of replicas. Before we start this loop there are a couple variables we need to set:

```
x = 1
position = 0
```

The first of these variables, x, will give an identifier to each replicated clip. We set this to 1 for the first replica. The position variable sets where the clip goes on the stage. If we didn't have this variable all the replicas would end up on top of each other. The variable before the loop deals with our original instance on the stage, post. Our first replica will sit on top of the original instance so we need to set the original instance's visibility to false:

```
setProperty ("post", _visible, false)
```

Now we can move onto the loop. There are two scenarios in our forum. The first one is that there are more than 10 posts, in which case we need to duplicate the movie clip the maximum 10 times. The second scenario is that there are 10 or less posts, in which case we only want to duplicate the movie clip for the number of posts that there are. We'll deal with the first scenario in the if statement and the second scenario in the else statement. The conent of the if and else statements is exactly the same after the while statement, so we'll only explain this once.

Let's now go through the if statement. We start by saying that this statement should only run if the thread_count variable that our ColdFusion templates pass to us is greater than 10. In plain English this statement will run if there are more than 10 records in our database. We'll later tell our Flash movie to load the data from ColdFusion into Level 0, so we need to tell Flash that this is where the thread_count data is stored.

```
if (_level0.thread_count > 10)
```

Our next job is to tell this statement to run only while our x value is less than our equal to 10. This way we create 10 replicas, as we've set x to start as 1.

```
while (x <= 10)
```

The rest of the code in the if statement will be run through for each of the 10 replicas that we make. This block of code starts with the code that actually duplicates our movie clip.

```
duplicateMovieClip ("post", "post"+x, x)
```

You'll see that there are three parameters set here. The first is the name of the clip we're going to duplicate (post), the second is the name we'll give to our replicated instance (we'll end up with post1, post2, post3, and so on), and the third parameter sets the depth of the clip in the movie. This third parameter only serves to load each clip at a different depth and is not of a great importance to us (whether it is x, $x+1$, or $x+2$ has no bearing on our final movie, as long as each clip ends up at a different depth).

The next line relates to our setProperty variable. As with when we made the original instance invisible earlier, this variable has the instance name, followed by what we're going to set. In this case we're setting the **y** value of the clip on the stage to the position variable. When we alter the value of the position shortly we'll make sure that each clip has a different y position and this will ensure that the clips appear in a list and not on top of each other.

```
setProperty ("post"+x, _y, position)
```

The next six lines of code serve to connect the textboxes of each clip with the actual conent that they will contain. Let's take a look at the first of these lines and see how it works:

```
this["post"+x].title = _level0["title_"+x];
```

The left hand side shows the easiest way of referring to the textbox with the variable `title`. Note how the instance name is again being used as part of a dot syntax statement. Let's consider the first duplicate movie clip as an example. The `duplicateMovieClip` command will give us an instance name of post1 and the title field of this post would be referenced to as post1.title using dot syntax, which is what the left hand side of our statement produces. So, the left hand side of the statement references the textbox where we want the data to be displayed, while the right hand side link this to the actual data. All our data is being loaded into level 0 of the movie so this is where the relevant information will be waiting to be retrieved. In our example we've used the value $x=1$ so the right side of the statement will retrieve `title_1`. If you remember back to `main.cfm`, you'll recall that we sent our data for the title as `title_#CurrentRow#`, and `#CurrentRow#` will produce exactly the same value as x here. All links in nicely doesn't it!

After we've written a similar statement for each of the textboxes in our movie clip, and added one for the `post_id` as well (which is needed for linking each post to its replies) we only have two lines left to look at in the `if` statement. These two lines update our variables for the next time the loop is run. The first one updates the `position` variable that we use to space out our clips. `position = position+15` will move each duplicated clip 15 pixels further down the movie making them appear in rows. If you want to space your clips out by a greater margin, this is the figure you'll need to change. The `x` variable is simply increased by 1, enabling us to create post1, post2, and so on.

The only piece of code we've yet to look at is the `while` statement within `else` statement. The `else` statement will only run when the condition of the `if` statement is not met, which is when there are 10 or less posts. In this loop we only want to duplicate the clip for the number of posts that there are, so this clip runs while the value of x is under and equal to the number of posts (`thread_count`).

```
while (x<=_level0.thread_count)
```

As the actual material of the `else` statement is the same as the `if` statement, we've now covered what all the code in this script does, and we can now enter the code into frame 1. As the content of two `while` statements is the same, you might want to copy and paste it to save time and typing energy.

```
Frame Actions
Movie Explorer  Frame Actions                                              ?
+  -  Frame Actions                                                      ▼ ▲
stop ();
// set a value for x to use with our loop
x = 1;
position = 0;
setProperty ("post", _visible, false);
// while the number of headers is less than x - run the loop to duplicate clips
// if there is more than 10 posts - only duplicate ten times
if (_level0.thread_count>10) {
 while (x<=10) {
  duplicateMovieClip ("post", "post"+x, x);
  setProperty ("post"+x, _y, position);
  this["post"+x].title = _level0["title_"+x];
  this["post"+x].no_replies = _level0["no_replies_"+x];
  this["post"+x].author_name = _level0["author_name_"+x];
  this["post"+x].date_post = _level0["date_post_"+x];
  this["post"+x].time_post = _level0["time_post_"+x];
  this["post"+x].post_id = _level0["post_id_"+x];
  position = position+15;
  x = x+1;
  }
} else {
 // otherwise, if there are up to 10 posts - duplicte for all of them
 while (x<=_level0.thread_count) {
  duplicateMovieClip ("post", "post"+x, x);
  setProperty ("post"+x, _y, position);
  this["post"+x].title = _level0["title_"+x];
  this["post"+x].no_replies = _level0["no_replies_"+x];
  this["post"+x].author_name = _level0["author_name_"+x];
  this["post"+x].date_post = _level0["date_post_"+x];
  this["post"+x].time_post = _level0["time_post_"+x];
  this["post"+x].post_id = _level0["post_id_"+x];
  position = position+15;
  x = x+1;
  }
}
```

We've now finished the duplicating movie clip! Before we go a stage higher in our structure we're going to build the thread movie clip that also feeds into the forum movie clip. This is the clip that will display the entire thread when the user clicks on the button we made in mcpost. It's that button which actually programmed to load the information from view_thread.cfm.

Constructing the thread movie clip

1. Create a new movie clip, naming it mcthread. This is the clip that will display the information from view_thread.cfm. We'll name the default layer movie clips and make this 25 frames long by inserting a frame at frame 25 (F5 on a PC). Drop mcpreloader onto frame one of this layer and center it on the stage. Now insert a blank keyframe at frame 15. Our loading movie clip will play while the user waits for the relevant thread to load.

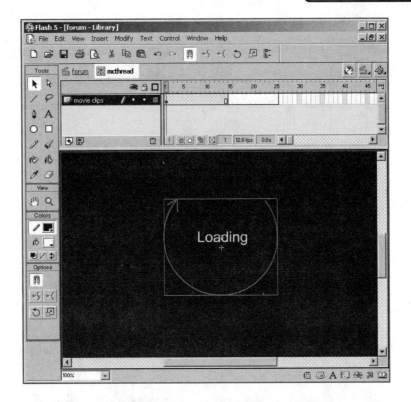

2. Create a second layer in this movie and name this text fields. This is where the actual dynamic text box that shows the post and its replies will be housed. Our loading movie clip is showing while the data is actually loaded so this textbox wants to appear at frame 15 when the loading clip stops. Make a keyframe at frame 15 of the text fields layer. In the Character panel set the font to Arial, the size to 18 and the color to white. With the Text Tool draw a textbox on the stage, and then open the Text Options panel where we'll make is a dynamic textfield. This time we'll make it Multiline and have the Word wrap on, as I'm sure that a whole thread will extend more than one line on most occasions. We'll call this variable body. We now want to resize the textbox and position it on the stage. Open the info panel and change the size to 350px by 200px, and the coordinates on the stage to x=-150.1 and y=-122.

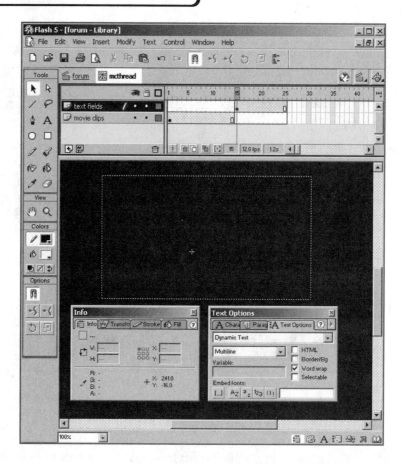

3. There's one more layer we need to create in this movie clip – the actions layer. On frame 1 of this new layer add a simple play action, and label the frame as retry.

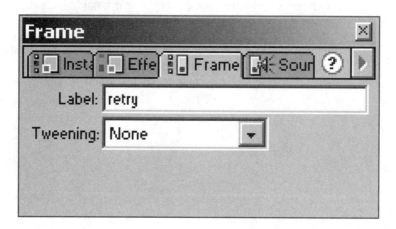

4. The next step is to add a keyframe 5. We'll label this frame as check and ad the following code:

```
if (_level0.reply_loaded == "yes") {
     gotoAndStop ("create_thread");
} else {
     gotoAndPlay ("retry");
}
```

When we modified the view_thread.cfm template, we added a new variable at the end: reply_loaded=yes. This variable was the last thing that this template passes to Flash, so if it's present we know that all the data has loaded into Flash, and if it isn't the data is still loading so we need to try again. So, the gotoAndStop action runs if all the data is loaded and sends us to the frame create_thread, which is what we'll label frame 15 shortly. (It's frame 15 that our textbox appears in.) It's the else statement that runs if the data is not loaded and sends us back to the frame labeled retry where we have our play() action.

5. Make a keyframe at frame 15 and label this create_thread. As we've already discovered, this frame is where all the data will be displayed in the textbox, so we need to write to code that formats the information on this frame of the actions layer. As we did earlier, we'll look at code first, examine it, and then type it. Here it is:

```
stop ();
body = "";
title = _level0.title;
author_name = _level0.author_name;
date_post = _level0.date_post;
time_post = _level0.time_post;
post = _level0.post;
post_id = _level0.post_id;
x = 1;
body = "Title: "+title+"\n"+" original post by
➥"+author_name+" on "+date_post+" at
➥"+time_post+"\n"+"\n"+post+"\n"+"_____
➥                      "+"\n"+"\n";
while (x<=_level0.reply_count) {
     body = body+"Title:
```

```
"+_level0["reply_title_"+x]+"\n"+" reply by
➥"+_level0["reply_name_"+x]+" on
"+level0["date_reply_"+x]+" at
➥"+_level0["time_reply_"+x]+"\n"+"\n"+_level0["re
ply_"+x]+"\n"+"_____
➥_____"+"\n"+"\n";
    x = x+1;
}
_level0.count = 0;
```

We start this code with a stop action to make sure the movie stop here. We don't want our thread displaying briefly and then disappearing as the movie loops. The second line of code introduces our body variable (the variable name we gave to the textbox).

Our next step is to define the variables that we'll be using in the post section of the textbox. As we're viewing a thread there will only be one relevant post, unlike replies where there could be many. All the information about our post has been loaded into level 0 and we therefore just need to link our variables to the data that is there:

```
title = _level0.title;
author_name = _level0.author_name;
date_post = _level0.date_post;
time_post = _level0.time_post;
post = _level0.post;
post_id = _level0.post_id;
```

Once again we include the post_id here as it is the link between a post and its replies, so is useful data to have. We're also going to set the x variable again here, this time for replicating replies rather than posts.

Our next step is to set the body variable to display our post and its details. The format that this takes it that any text we want displayed is contained within "" marks, and any variable just uses its variable name. There should be no spaces in the code, so we use a + symbol to join everything together. We'll use the underscore character (_) to make a line dividing the post any replies. To make a new line in the text we simply use \n.

```
body = "Title: "+title+"\n"+" original post by
➥"+author_name+" on "+date_post+" at
➥"+time_post+"\n"+"\n"+post+"\n"+"_____
➥_____"+"\n"+"\n";
```

So, at this point the textbox will display the post and its details, but we also want to include the replies and we don't know how many there are going to be. As with most things in ActionScript, when you're not sure you lose a loop to find out. We use a `while` statement here. We've been sent the number of replies as the `reply_count` variable (much like `thread_count` for the number of posts), so we'll use this figure in the loop. Our loop will run while the value of `x` (which we defined as 1 to start with) is less than or equal to the number of replies. In other words, it will run until every reply has been added.

$$while \ (x<=\_level0.reply\_count)$$

The content of the loop takes much the same format as the `body` command for displaying the post. The first difference is that any reply will be needed to be added to the original `body` (which just contained the post), so we create a new value for `body` using a `body=body+reply` format. By the time the loop gets to this point again if there's more than one reply, the first reply will have been added to `body` so won't need stating again. The second difference is the way our variables are called. For replies we use the following format:

$$\_level0["variablename\_"+x]$$

Once again this links the #CurrentRow# variable that we're passed with the value of `x`. For example, the variables of the first reply in a thread will be passed by ColdFusion with the following format `variablename_1`. This links nicely with our loop, which for the first reply will have `_level0[variablename_1]`. Once again the variable will all be found on level 0 so we call the variable from there. The value of `x` is increased by one at the end of the loop so it will then go and retrieve the next reply, or stop if there are no more. By the time our loop has stopped running we'll have all the replies and the post retrieved and formatted.

The code finished by setting `_level0.count` to 0. This value will be used by the scroll buttons that we'll add to the forum movie clip shortly. Now that we've examined the code and know what it does well type it onto the frame 15 actions frame. Now we've added all the code and labels to this layer we've completed this movie clip.

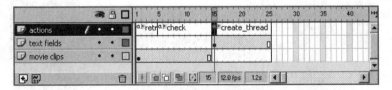

We can now take one step further up our movie clip structure to the forum movie clip where the different aspects of our forum come together.

The forum movie clip

1. Let's get on with our final movie clip. Create a new movie clip and name it mcforum. We'll start with the actions first this time, so name the default layer to actions. This movie clip is going to be 30 frames long, so enter a frame at that point. On frame 1, label the frame as forum_main and enter the following code:

```
stop ();
_level0.reply_loaded = "no";
```

The stop() action is self-explanatory, and the second line set the reply_loaded variable to no. The reason for this is that if we've looked at one thread reply_loaded will be set to yes. If we want to look at a further thread it will still be set to yes before the reply has been loaded. So, we need to reset this value for the thread to be viewed at the correct time.

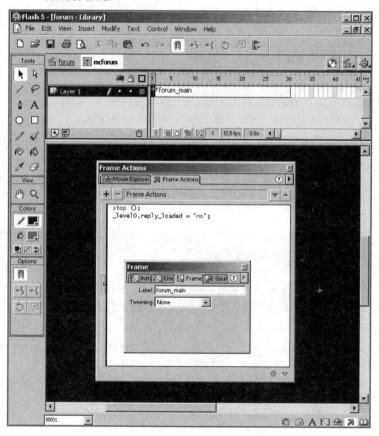

2. The only other action on this layer is a `stop()` action on a keyframe at frame 20. We'll label frame 20 as view_thread, as this is where we'll place mcthread on the next layer we're going to build.

3. Let create that layer now. Add a second layer, name it movie clips, and drag it beneath the actions layer. We labeled frame 1 as forum_main, so that's what we'll put on frame 1 of the movie clip layer. Drop mcduplicate onto frame 1 and give it the instance name posts. In order for the posts to appear in the correct area of the screen in the final forum we need to move the movie clip so it's slightly off center. Set x to -181.6 and **y** to −10.9 in the Info Panel for this object.

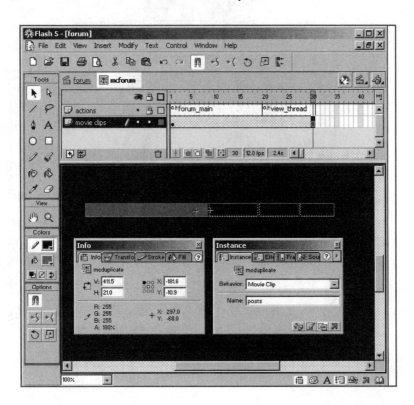

4. Create a blank keyframe at frame 20 of this layer. On this frame we're going to insert mcthread. Drop the movie clip onto the stage, give it the instance name view_thread. Once again we need to be exact with positioning of the movie clip so it displays in the correct place. Set the *x* value of the movie clip to -99 and the y value to 19.1.

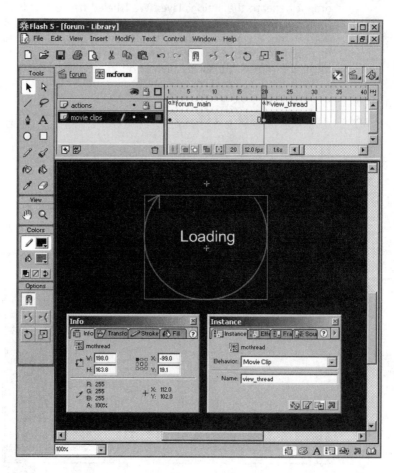

5.   There is one final layer that we need to add to this movie clip: the buttons layer. Create this layer and drag it below the movie clips layer. On this layer we're going to place the up and down buttons that we made in Chapter 2, so drag bnup and bndown from the library. They are going to sit on the left of the posts and thread so once again we need to place them with specific x and y positions. For the up button use x= -232.2, y=-6, and for the down button, x= -232.2, y= 57.6. Now create a keyframe at frame 20. We need to do this because the buttons will move the list of posts up and down while the main forum page is displayed, but move the thread up and down when the thread is displayed. Let's start with the actions for the button instances on frame 1. Select the down button and open the Object Actions panel. Here's the code we need to add:

```
on (release) {
    if (10 +_level0.count >=_level0.thread_count)
{
        _level0.count = _level0.count;
    } else {
        _level0.count = _level0.count+1;
        x = 1;
        while (x<=_level0.thread_count) {

_level0.forum.posts["post"+x].no_replies =
➡_level0["no_replies_"+(_level0.count +x)];
            _level0.forum.posts["post"+x].title =
            ➡_level0["title_"+(_level0.count +x)];

_level0.forum.posts["post"+x].author_name =
➡_level0["author_name_"+(_level0.count +x)];

_level0.forum.posts["post"+x].date_post =
➡_level0["date_post_"+(_level0.count +x)];

_level0.forum.posts["post"+x].time_post =
➡_level0["time_post_"+(_level0.count +x)];
            _level0.forum.posts["post"+x].post_id
= ➡_level0["post_id_"+(_level0.count +x)];

            x = x+1;
        }
    }
}
```

As it's a button we want the `on(release)` command so our actions are triggered when the button is pressed. The button should only be active when we have more than 10 posts to be displayed, otherwise there is nothing to scroll. This is why we need a conditional if statement to see if the button needs to work at all.

```
if (10 +_level0.count >=_level0.thread_count) {
        _level0.count = _level0.count;
    }
```

When we add some code to the main timeline, we'll set the variable count to 0, now bear in mind that the scroll buttons will only work if the count value is altered either upwards or downwards. What the above statement asks us is whether the value of count plus 10 is greater than or equal to the number of posts that the main page is displaying. If it is then we don't need the scroll button to be active as there is nothing to scroll. This is why count is set to equal itself in the second line of the code – we don't want it to do anything.

Let's look at an example to illustrate the theory more clearly. Let's say there are 6 posts to be displayed (thread_count = 6), so the posts don't need to be able to scroll. The posts won't scroll because the left hand side of the equation is equal to 10 (remember the original count value is 0), while the right side is 6. This satisfies our if statement that the left hand side is greater than or equal to the right hand side and so the count value remains unaltered. If the number of posts is equal to 11 (thread_count = 11), we want the posts to scroll. Let's look at the if statement in this scenario. The left hand side will be equal to 10, but the right hand side will be equal to 11, so the if statement is not satisfied and the else statement will run which will make the posts scroll.

Let's look at the else statement now. It starts off by increasing the value of count by 1. Why? Well, we can see if we once again consider an example where there are 11 posts. If there are 11 posts we only need to scroll one record as we can see 10 at a time. By adding 1 to the count value, the next time we click on the button to scroll down further, when the if statement is run the left hand side will be equal to 11, as will the right hand side. The condition is met, the count value stays the same and we don't scroll. The only other line of code before the while statement set a variable x to 1.

```
_level0.count = _level0.count+1;
x = 1;
```

If we now look at the `while` statement we'll see that it repeats itself until the value of x is equal to the `thread_count`. Again you may ask why? If there are 14 posts in our forum (`thread_count` = 14), we will have 10 displayed initially and 4 below them. When we click the down button we want the 11th record to come into view and the first to move out. So, we need to move every record up one, even those that aren't visible. If we didn't move the 12th record up to the 11th position now, it wouldn't be there to display if we click the down button again.

So, each time the while statement runs through it is moving an individual record upwards, and we need to run through it for every record until they have all moved up, hence:

```
while (x<=_level0.thread_count)
```

Our next step is to look at what the while statement actually moves up. Well, the answer is each of the 5 variables that we display for each record, and it's `post_id` value so we can retrieve the correct thread if we want to view it. We'll only examine one of these as they all do the same thing. We'll look at the number of replies, simply because it's the first one:

```
_level0.forum.posts["post"+x].no_replies =
➥ _level0["no_replies_"+(_level0.count +x)];
```

When we place the forum movie clip on the main stage we'll use the instance name of forum. This will allow is to address each textbox in the instance of mcpost by name using dot syntax. For example, if we could link our textfield from the highest level in a more heavy handed way we would say:

```
highestlevel.[mcform(instance)].[mcduplcate(instan
➥ce)].[mcpost(instance)].no_replies
```

Instead we can use the instance names and we end up with:

```
_level0.forum.posts["post"+x].no_replies
```

You can see a definite advantage even if we could use the first of these methods. Because we use ["post"+x] we're back referring to our specific movie clip replicas again (post1, post2, and so on up to post10). So, in the left half of the equation we're referring to a specific textbox in a specific instance of a movie clip. The right hand side sets the value that will go in the box. It makes use of the count value and increases it by 1. Let's take a look at an example to see what the effect of all this is. Let's use the 11th record of the database, the one that will move into view after the button is pressed. When the while thread runs through this record the value of x will be 10 (as this time it will be the 10th record to be displayed). This will mean that the movie clip it's displayed in is post10 (the bottom one of the 10 on display) when we put the value of x into the left hand side of the equation. On the right hand side of the equation (the actual data that will go into the box), we come up with no_replies_11 (count was increased by 1 at the start of the loop and x=10, add the two together and we get 11). This is the exact value that's been loaded into level 0 for this record by main.cfm. The one piece of code that we haven't yet mentioned that helps to achieve this result is the x = x+1 at the end of every loop. If we didn't have this line x would always be 1 and we'd end up with the loop repeating for ever and only producing one record.

Hopefully, we understand the theory behind this button now and can add the code to the Object Actions window.

6. We now need to add the actions for the up button in frame 1, but don't worry as we've covered nearly all of the theory behind it when dissecting the down button. The if statement is slightly different this time:

```
if (_level0.count<=0) {
    _level0.count = 0;
}
```

Of we think about it, the up button can only be functional if the down button has already been used as we start at the top of the records. This means we only want the button to function if the value of count has moved above 0. Hence it remains alter if that is not the case. The only other difference is that the value of count is decreased by one this time rather than increased. This pretty simple to understand: we want all the records to move a place down rather than up this time. Visualize this as the 11th record moving back down to the 11th place from the 10th. Those are the only changes, so we'll add the code now:

```
on (release) {
    if (_level0.count<=0) {
        _level0.count = 0;
    } else {
        _level0.count = _level0.count-1;
        x = 1;
        while (x<=_level0.thread_count) {

_level0.forum.posts["post"+x].no_replies =
➥_level0["no_replies_"+(_level0.count+x)];
            _level0.forum.posts["post"+x].title =
➥_level0["title_"+(_level0.count+x)];

_level0.forum.posts["post"+x].author_name =
➥_level0["author_name_"+(_level0.count+x)];

_level0.forum.posts["post"+x].date_post =
➥_level0["date_post_"+(_level0.count+x)];

_level0.forum.posts["post"+x].time_post =
➥_level0["time_post_"+(_level0.count+x)];
            _level0.forum.posts["post"+x].post_id
    = ➥_level0["post_id_"+(_level0.count+x)];
            x = x+1;
        }
    }
}
```

7. Our next step is to add the code to the button instances in frame 20. This code scrolls the text within a thread, and is thankfully much, much easier! The code for our down button here:

```
on (release) {
    if (_level0.forum.view_thread.body.scroll <
➥_level0.forum.view_thread.body.maxscroll) {
        _level0.forum.view_thread.body.scroll =
➥level0.forum.view_thread.body.scroll +1;
    }
}
```

This code is pretty simple to understand. A textbox automatically has a scroll value and a maxscroll value. These are the amounts that a textbox has scrolled and the amount it can scroll. If there isn't enough text in the box to scroll the maxscroll value will be 0, so the condition of the if statement can never be satisfied and nothing happens when the button is pressed. If we look at the action of the if statement we'll see that the effect of scrolling is to move a line up by 1 by increasing the value of scroll by 1. Let's look at an example to understand this fully. Let's say that there are 3 lines that can be scrolled in our thread. The maxscroll value will be 3. The initial scroll value will be 0. If we view the first extra line the scroll value will increase to 1. By the time we've scrolled to the last line the scroll value will have increased to 3, so we can scroll no more. Simple! Add the code now.

8. Finally for this movie clip we'll add the actions for the up button at frame 20. Once again they're very simple:

```
on (release) {
     if (_level0.forum.view_thread.body.scroll >1)
{
          _level0.forum.view_thread.body.scroll =
➥_level0.forum.view_thread.body.scroll -1;
     }
}
```

This time the process is the reverse with 1 being subtracted from the scroll value each time and the text moving downwards by a line. The condition for the if statement is slightly different in that the button and will only work if there is actually some text to scroll up to!

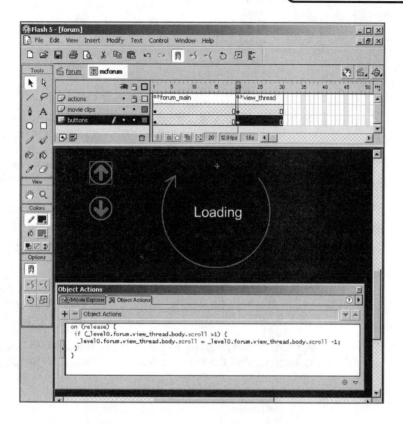

Once we've added this code we've finished the forum movie clip. The last task is to go to the top of our structure and make a few modifications, including adding the forum movie clip.

Back to the timeline

1. Return to the movie's main scene. We'll start by adding an extra 30 frames to each layer, so the movie now finishes at frame 80. Make blank keyframes at frame 51 of the ball guide and mask layers. Both of these have outlived their use by frame 50.

2. We'll deal with the modifications to the actions layer first. Delete the actions on frame 50 and clear the keyframe. Now that we've extended the movie we don't need, or want, it to stop here.

3. Make a new keyframe at frame 50 and label this frame as load. We're going to add code to this frame so open up the Actions panel. You should recognise the function of each of these lines of code:

```
loadVariablesNum ("main.cfm", 0);
done = "no";
count = 0;
reply_count = "0";
thread_count = 0;
```

The first line retrieves all the information that was ready to be sent by main.cfm. The second line sets done to equal no. If you remember back to the variables we primed in main.cfm you'll remember the last one sent set done to yes. So this line makes sure that done is only equal to yes when all the data is loaded. This is useful if we're refreshing the main page, as it will have the value set to yes from previous loads. The next line sets the count value that we used for the down button of the main forum to its default value of 0. The last two lines set the reply_count and thread_count values to 0. This is again useful in clearing values that we used earlier that are no longer applicable. Add this code now.

4. We're going to label a new keyframe at 60 as retry. The only actions we need to add here are a simple play() action. You notice some similarities with the thread movie clip in what we're doing here.

5. On frame 65 we're going to add a check frame as we did in the thread movie clip. Label the frame as load_check and add the following code:

```
// check to see that the variables have been
➥loaded
if (_level0.done == "yes") {
    gotoAndPlay ("start");
} else {
    gotoAndPlay ("retry");
}
```

We should know what all this code is doing by this stage. If all the variables from main.cfm are loaded done will have been set to yes by the output we just mentioned. If not we go back to the retry frame.

6. Finally, we put a stop action on a keyframe at 75, which we'll rather ironically name start. It's the end of the timeline, but also the start of the forum.

7. On frame 75 of the loading movie clip layer we're going to insert a blank keyframe. Onto this frame we'll insert mcforum onto the stage from the library. If you remember some of the dot syntax we've used earlier you'll recall the forum references. Those references refer to this clip so we'll give it the instance name forum now.

8. The final thing to do with this clip is arrange it on the stage. We'll align it to the center of the stage horizontally, but with a y value of 96.4 for its vertical alignment. This y value places the forum messages slightly below our forum heading at the top.

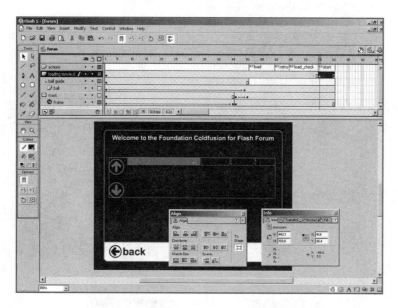

9. Our final task is to add the actions to our back button. Select this on the stage and open up the Object Actions window. We're going to add some really simple actions that clear our reply_count, set done to equal no, and then send us back to frame 51 of the timeline. In plain English, this refreshes our forum, and takes us back to the main page if we're with in thread.

```
on (release) {
    _level0.reply_count = 0;
    _level0.done = "no";
    _root.gotoAndPlay(51);
}
```

Well there you go! We've now finished forum.fla for this chapter and when we test it in a minute we'll have a working forum that let's us view the list of posts and see each individual thread. In the next chapter's case study we'll create the post and reply forms and add them to the forum.

We'll now publish the forum into a SWF file. Make sure it's in the same web server folder as our two modified ColdFusion template and test the SWF in a browser. Remember, we need to use the localhost or remote server address here for it to work. Don't worry if this appears a bit big in your browser as the size will return to normal when we embed it in a ColdFusion template in the next chapter.

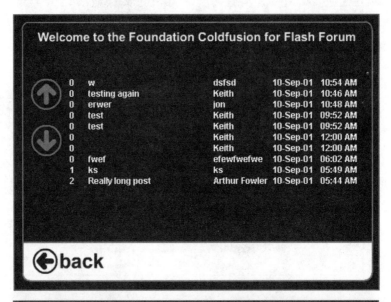

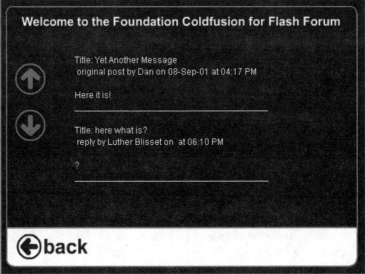

Congratulations! We've gotten through an awful lot in this chapter and now have a working forum. I bet you can't wait until the next chapter's case study now can you!

6 SQL

What We'll Cover in this Chapter

- *More advanced SQL commands including **aggregate** functions*

- *Formatting query results with the GROUP BY function*

- *Using our new knowledge to give our forum more functionality, adding* Next *and* Previous *buttons*

Aggregate functions

We are going to start by looking at aggregate functions, which can be very helpful when we need to manipulate our data. In our forum example, we are only going to use the COUNT function, but it will be beneficial to you as a developer to become familiar with the other aggregate functions available in SQL. As your database applications grow in size and complexity, these aggregate functions will allow you to easily summarize and report on your data.

A very useful SQL command is GROUP BY, and while we will not use GROUP BY in our forum, it is often used in conjunction with aggregate functions and, as such, we'll introduce it here.

Simply put, aggregate functions are used to assist us in summarizing large volumes of data in our databases. In this section, we will be examining the 5 aggregate functions available to us in SQL. The easiest way to explain these functions is to see them at work.

Who gets what?

We are going to create a salaries table in our board data source. Creating a new table will not, in any way, affect our forum application, we will just be using it for practice.

1. Open your database file in Access and create a new table called salaries.

2. Create a new table in Design view and add just two fields: Name and Salary.

3. Set the Name field with the data type Text, and the Salary field as a Currency field.

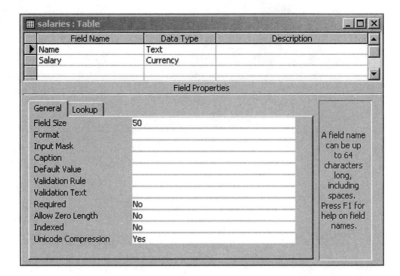

4. Once your table is set up open it in DataSheet View. (Right-click on its title bar and select DataSheet View from the pop-up menu.) Enter the following values:

Name	Salary
Jane Kae	50000
Joe Black	40000
Alex Smith	60000
Susie Mac	65000

Your table should now be set up like this:

Name	Salary
Jane Kae	£50,000.00
Joe Black	£40,000.00
Alex Smith	£60,000.00
Susie Mac	£65,000.00
▶	£0.00

Access has formatted the bare numbers we typed, adding a sterling symbol a comma and a decimal point with two decimal places shown. Your currency settings may be different (a dollar sign $ would be more common) but the formatting Access does here has no bearing on our code, ColdFusion Server will only pass the unformatted data to our CFML.

The definition of the 5 aggregate functions is provided here in a table. Don't worry too much if the definitions are a bit unclear, we'll see each function in action very soon. The first 4 definitions make reference to "NULL" values. We haven't worked with NULL values yet and they tend to be a bit confusing.

> *A NULL value is not the same thing as an empty string and is not equal to anything. For that reason, any field with a value set to NULL is simply skipped over in aggregate calculations.*

Function	Description
AVG(column)	The AVG function computes the average value of a column in a selection. NULL values are ignored.
MAX(column)	The MAX function returns the highest value in a column. NULL values are ignored.
MIN(column)	The MIN function returns the lowest value in a column. NULL values are ignored.
SUM(column)	The SUM function returns the total sum in a column. NULL values are ignored.
COUNT(column)	The COUNT function counts each value found in a column.

To best understand how each of these functions work, let's use our sample data to run a few examples.

For each of the examples, we are going to construct a <cfquery> statement and then a <cfoutput> statement with the result. For our examples, we will use the salaries table that we just set up.

AVG Function

In this example the AVG function adds all the salaries together and then divides that number by the total number of records in the database. That average number is then stored in the variable name sal_avg which we use in our <cfoutput> tag.

1. Add this CFML to a new template called avg.cfm and save it within the web root directory on your server.

```
<cfquery name="sample" datasource="board"
dbtype="ODBC">
SELECT AVG(Salary) AS sal_avg
FROM salaries
</cfquery>

<cfoutput query="sample">
#DollarFormat(sal_avg)#
</cfoutput>
```

2. View avg.cfm in your browser and you'll simply see:

```
$53,750.00
```

SUM Function

In this example the SUM function adds all the salaries together. That total number is then stored in the variable name sal_sum which we use in our <cfoutput> tag.

3. Create a new template, or simply alter the previous one to read.

```
<cfquery name="sample2" datasource="board"
dbtype="ODBC">
SELECT SUM(Salary) AS sal_sum
FROM salaries
</cfquery>

<cfoutput query="sample2">
#DollarFormat(sal_sum)#
</cfoutput>
```

4. And in our browser view we'll see:

```
$215,000.00
```

MIN Function

In this example, the MIN function records the smallest salary figure in a variable called sal_min. This variable is then used in our <cfoutput> statement.

5. The code within our template should now read:

```
<cfquery name="sample3" datasource="board"
dbtype="ODBC">
SELECT MIN(Salary) AS sal_min
FROM salaries
</cfquery>

<cfoutput query="sample3">
#DollarFormat(sal_min)#
</cfoutput>
```

6. Save the template and open it in your browser, the salary of the worst paid employee will now be shown: (he's still on good money though!)

```
$40,000.00
```

MAX Function

As you've probably come to expect by now, in this example, the MAX function records the greatest salary figure in a variable called sal_max. This is the variable that <cfoutput> will show us.

7.   Construct your template like so:

```
<cfquery name="sample4" datasource="board"
dbtype="ODBC">
SELECT MAX(Salary) AS sal_max
FROM salaries
</cfquery>

<cfoutput query="sample4">
#DollarFormat(sal_max)#
</cfoutput>
```

8.   And the richest employees salary will become know to all those viewing the template in a browser:

```
$65,000.00
```

COUNT Function

COUNT does something slightly different, instead of returning data in the same format as the field it's working on, it outputs nothing more than an integer. In this example, the COUNT function records the number of salaries in the database in a variable called sal_count.

9.   The CFML perform this is: (Type it in, go on.)

```
<cfquery name="sample5" datasource="board"
dbtype="ODBC">
SELECT COUNT(Salary) AS sal_count
FROM salaries
</cfquery>


<cfoutput query="sample5">
#sal_count#
</cfoutput>
```

10.   Seeing as there are four salary records in our database table, view the template in your browser and all you'll see is a solitary, lonely, figure 4.

Let's get together, combining functions and GROUP BY

The above examples are very simple, and you might not think that they show the power of these functions. There will be many times when you simply want to know the number of records in a table, but the real interesting stuff comes by combining the functions. Let's do just that.

Group hugging

The GROUP BY function adds even more flexibility to our queries. For this example, we are going to modify our salaries table a little bit.

1. Open up your salaries table in the DataSheet view and add the following:

Name	Salary
Jane Kae	$20,000

    Now in our salaries table, lucky old Jane Kae is receiving two salaries. In our previous examples, we have been using aggregate functions that returned only one row of data. If we want to run a query that returns a value for every value in a column, we need to employ GROUP BY.

2. Create a template with the following query:

    ```
    <cfquery name="sample6" datasource="board"
    dbtype="ODBC">
    SELECT
    Name, Salary
    FROM salaries
    </cfquery>
    ```

3. With this <cfoutput> statement:

    ```
    <cfoutput query="sample6">
    #Name# #DollarFormat(salary)#<br>
    </cfoutput>
    ```

4. Looking through the browser window, we get the following results:

    ```
    Jane Kae $50,000.00
    Joe Black $40,000.00
    Alex Smith $60,000.00
    Susie Mac $65,000.00
    Jane Kae $20,000.00
    ```

Now, what if we wanted to sum Jane's total salaries? Enter the GROUP BY function.

5. We simply change our query to get the desired result:

```
<cfquery name="sample6" datasource="board"
dbtype="ODBC">
SELECT
Name, SUM(Salary) AS total_salary
FROM salaries
GROUP BY Name
</cfquery>
```

6. Remembering of course to alter our <cfoutput> statement accordingly:

```
<cfoutput query="sample6">
#Name# #DollarFormat(total_salary)#<br>
</cfoutput>
```

This template should yield the following:

```
Alex Smith $60,000.00
Jane Kae $70,000.00
Joe Black $40,000.00
Susie Mac $65,000.00
```

> *It is important not to confuse* GROUP BY *with the optional* group *attribute available with* <cfoutput>. *The group attribute allows you to define output groups.   When this attribute is included in your* <cfoutput> *tags, your data will be grouped together so that duplicate rows are not displayed (only the first occurrence appears).* GROUP BY, *on the other hand, is normally used with aggregate functions to give a summarized output of your data.*

Now, let us look at few more advanced examples before moving on. These examples will involve **subqueries** (or **nested queries**).

First off, let's say we wanted to look up the name of the person with the highest salary. To get this info – we are going to need to use a subquery. You can use subqueries in either the SELECT or WHERE portions of your query.

Subqueries can be introduced into your statements in three ways, using the equal sign or by using the IN or EXISTS keywords. We are going to focus only on the equal sign method.

Building nests

Looking again at our `salaries` table, we could use the following query to find out who is making the most money.

1. Create a new template and add this CFML:

    ```
    <cfquery name="sample7" datasource="board"
    dbtype="ODBC">
    SELECT
    Name, Salary
    FROM salaries
    WHERE Salary = (SELECT MAX(Salary) FROM salaries)
    </cfquery>
    ```

    The first portion of our query is a very simple SELECT statement. It searches the database for the name of the person whose salary meets the requirements of the WHERE clause. The subquery portion of our query finds the single highest `salary` value in our `salaries` table ($65,000.00).

2. Here is the `<cfoutput>` statement, add this to your template:

    ```
    Maximum salary example:<br><br>

    <cfoutput query="sample7">
    #Name# #DollarFormat(Salary)#
    </cfoutput>
    ```

    As you might have guessed, this query returns the following result:

But, as we saw before, Jane Kae makes more money than Susie (because of her two salaries). Selecting that salary is a little too complex for us at this stage, but if you're really enjoying delving into SQL why not try it for yourself.

SQL in the forum

In this section of the chapter, we are going to look at how we can control the output and flow of our data with ColdFusion. To best illustrate this, we are going to add an important feature to our forum application; a *next* and *previous* button. We will accomplish this by using different SQL statements as well as attributes in the <cfoutput> tag.

Let's imagine for a second that our forum gets very popular and that we get hundreds of posts. If this were in fact the case, we would certainly not want to display all of these posts on the same page. What can we do to limit the amount of posts that are displayed? We can use the maxrows attribute in our <cfoutput> tag. When we initially built the main.cfm template, we omitted this attribute in all of our <cfoutput> tags. As such, all rows were displayed.

If we go back to that template and change that, we will see very different results.

Open up main.cfm in Studio and change the line of code (and add the comment, no slacking!). You'll notice that the code is identical, save for the <cfoutput> statement.

```
<!-- Output all of the posts and their details
here -->
<!-- limit the results to three per page -->
<cfoutput query="current_posts" maxrows=3>
<tr>
```

Now, if we were to view this template, provided that we have at least 4 rows of data in our post table, we would only see the top 3 posts. If you haven't added many posts to your forum yet, go and do so – or you won't see all this working!

How Many

Now, this works well enough, but what if we wanted to give forum viewers the option to select the number of posts that they want to display. To accomplish this, we are going to create a new template called start.cfm. This will be a very simple template consisting of one form that will allow viewers to select the number of posts to display.

1. Create the new template and add this code:

```
<!-- start.cfm -->

<!-- template that will allow users to select
number of posts to display -->

Welcome to our ColdFusion for Flash forum.
Please select the number of posts you would like
to display.<br><br>

<form action="main.cfm">
<select name="view_rows">
<option value="all" selected>View All</option>
<option value="1">1</option>
<option value="3">3</option>
<option value="5">5</option>
<option value="10">10</option>
</select>

<input type="submit" value="View Forum">
</form>
```

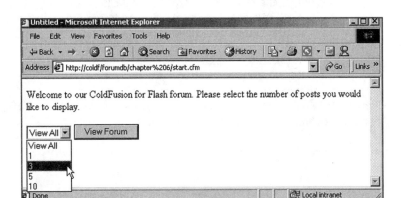

This template sends view_rows to main.cfm, and we'll change
main.cfm to expect it, if we try to access our main.cfm without going
through start.cfm, we'll get an error because view_rows is undefined.

2. So open up main.cfm and, right at the top, add:

```
<cfif IsDefined("view_rows")>
```

3.   And right at the bottom:

```
<cfelse>
<cflocation url="start.cfm">
</cfif>
```

This code will direct our browser back to start.cfm if anyone, or any template, tries to access main.cfm without specifying view_rows.

When the viewer clicks on the submit button, they are taken to the main.cfm template, with view_rows defined. In order for the form to be displayed properly, we will need to make the following changes to the main.cfm template.

In the last example, we saw that by changing our <cfoutput> statement from:

```
<cfoutput query="current_posts">
```
to
```
<cfoutput query="current_posts" maxrows=3>
```

we limited the displayed results to only 3 posts. If the maxrows attribute is left out, all the rows get displayed. In that case, if a viewer makes the choice to View All (the default choice), we need to make sure that this attribute is omitted. This can be accomplished with a simple <cfif> statement.

> *Also, note that we should change the comments at the beginning of the template to reflect the changes that we are making. Doing this will help you track changes made to your applications over time.*

4. Enclose the `<cfoutput>` for the `current_posts` query with our new `<cfif>` and, since we don't want to limit the posts in this instance, remove the `maxrows` attribute :

```
<!-- Output all of the posts and their details
here -->
<!-- limit the results to the number selected. If
the viewer selected all, display them all -->
<cfif view_rows IS "all">
<cfoutput query="current_posts">
<tr>
  <td>
<!-- insert number of replies for that post here -
->
#no_replies#
     </td>
<!-- insert post text here -->
     <td>
#title#
     </td>
     <td>
<a href="mailto:#author_email#">#author_name#</a>
     </td>
     <td>
<!-- Insert Date of post here -->
#DateFormat(date_post)#
     </td>
     <td>
<!-- Insert Date of post here -->
#TimeFormat(time_post)#
     </td>
     <td><a
➥ href="view_thread.cfm?post_id=#post_id#">
➥ View Thread!</a></td>
     </tr>
</cfoutput>

</cfif>
</table>
```

If the user selects to view all posts, the `<cfif>` is true and the `<cfoutput>` without `maxrows` will be run.

Otherwise we need to use our `view_rows` variable to limit the number of posts, the `else` statement is true and the `maxrows` attribute is included. The `view_rows` variable from the `start.cfm` template is used to set `maxrows`.

5. Copy the whole query, from `<cfoutput>` to `</cfoutput>`. Now add a `<cfelse>` and paste a copy of the query within the code as shown:

```
<!--- Output all of the posts and their details
here --->
<!--- limit the results to the number selected. If
the viewer selected all, display them all --->
<cfif view_rows IS "all">
<cfoutput query="current_posts">
<tr>
  <td>
<!--- insert number of replies for that post here
--->
#no_replies#
    </td>
<!--- insert post text here --->
    <td>
#title#
    </td>
    <td>
<a href="mailto:#author_email#">#author_name#</a>
    </td>
    <td>
<!--- Insert Date of post here --->
#DateFormat(date_post)#
    </td>
    <td>
<!--- Insert Date of post here --->
#TimeFormat(time_post)#
    </td>
    <td><a
➥ href="view_thread.cfm?post_id=#post_id#">
➥ View Thread!</a></td>
    </tr>
</cfoutput>

<cfelse>
<!--- if the user wants to limit the number of
posts display those results here --->
<cfoutput query="current_posts"
➥ maxrows=#view_rows#>
<tr>
  <td>
<!--- insert number of replies for that post here
--->
#no_replies#
```

```
      </td>
<!-- insert post text here -->
      <td>
#title#
      </td>
      <td>
<a href="mailto:#author_email#">#author_name#</a>
      </td>
      <td>
<!-- Insert Date of post here -->
#DateFormat(date_post)#
      </td>
      <td>
<!-- Insert Date of post here -->
#TimeFormat(time_post)#
      </td>
      <td><a
➥ href="view_thread.cfm?post_id=#post_id#">
➥ View Thread!</a></td>
      </tr>
</cfoutput>
</cfif>
</table>
```

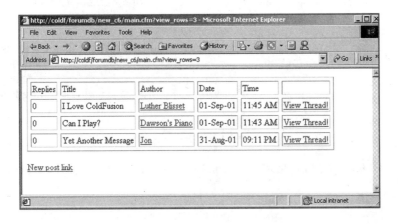

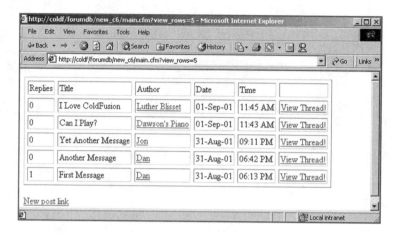

That system works well to limit the number of posts per page, but now we need to give viewers the ability to see the next and/or previous set of posts.

Query variables

Before going further, it is important to point out that every time we use the `<cfquery>` tag, it creates three query variables:

- `query_name.RecordCount` The total number of records returned by the query.

- `query_name.CurrentRow` The current row of the query being processed by `<cfoutput>`.

- `query_name.ColumnList` Returns a comma-delimited list of the query columns.

Let's look at an example of the `RecordCount` variable.

6.   Add the following code to our `main.cfm` template right above our table:

```
<cfoutput>
#current_posts.RecordCount# posts found.  You
chose to display #view_rows# posts.
</cfoutput>
```

This will tell the viewer exactly how many posts are currently in the database, no matter how many they chose to display.

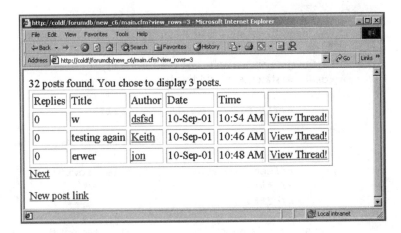

We have already seen and used the maxrows attribute in the <cfoutput> tag earlier in this chapter. The other attribute that we will need to use for our next and previous buttons is the startrow attribute. startrow specifies the row from which to start output.

> Another ColdFusion tag that we will need to use is <cfparam>. This tag allows us to specify default values for parameters that will be used in our template.

7. The first thing that we will need to do is add a <cfparam> tag to the top of our main.cfm template. We will use this tag to specify a default startrow value. This value will be set to one which assures that the most recent post will always be the first displayed.

The tag will look like this:

```
<!-- initialize the start value -->

<cfparam name="start" default="1">
```

That way, if the user has not yet pushed the next button, they will see the first few posts (depending on the number they decide to view per page).

8. On the other hand, if the viewer has already pushed the next button, we now need to define the new starting row, which we will call new_start. To do this, we will add the rows variable (from the start.cfm template) to the start variable. We will accomplish this with the following <cfset> statement, add this below our <cfparam>:

```
<cfif view_rows IS NOT "all">
<cfif start GT 1>
<cfset new_start = #start# + #view_rows#>
<cfelse>
<cfset new_start = 1 + #view_rows#>
</cfif>
</cfif>
```

Surrounding the entire thing is a <cfif> statement that checks whether the rows variable is equal to all. If it is, the <cfset> statements are ignored since the next button will be unnecessary.

The next thing that we will need to do is to add the startrow attribute to the output statement. The startrow value that we will use is the dynamic variable we defined earlier – start.

9. Our second <cfoutput> statement should now look like this:

```
<cfoutput query="current_posts" startrow=#start#
maxrows=#view_rows#>
```

Now, most of the hard stuff is done. All we have to do is finalize the code for the next button. We will be adding this in after our posts table and before the link for a new post.

The first thing that we will need to do is check whether or not a next button is even needed. If there are no more rows to display or the viewer selected to view them all at once, we won't bother with the button. We'll check this with the following <cfif> statements:

```
<cfif rows IS NOT "all">
and
<cfif #new_start# LTE current_posts.RecordCount>
```

If both those <cfif> statements are false, we will need to include our link. The link will be to the same page (main.cfm) except we will be appendingtwo variables to the url; the new_start and rows variable.

10. The completed code will look like this. Add it below our closing `</table>` tag:

```
<cfif view_rows IS NOT "all">
<!-- add next button here -->
<cfoutput>
<!-- do not display the button if no records
remain -->
  <cfif #new_start# LTE current_posts.RecordCount>
  <a
➥ href="main.cfm?start=#new_start#&view_rows=
➥ #view_rows#">Next</A>
  </cfif>
</cfoutput>
</cfif>
```

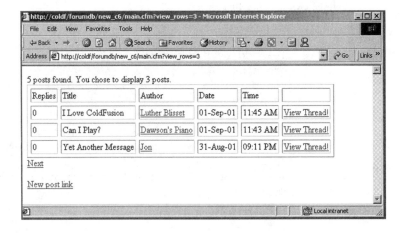

You should now have a working next button for your forum application. Now we need to create a previous button to complete our work.

Adding this button is even easier than the next button. The first thing that we'll need is another `<cfif>` statement. This statement will check to make sure that the start variable is not 1. If it is, we're seeing the first posts, and a previous button is not necessary.

The `<cfif>` statement will look like this:

```
<!-- check to see if a previous button is
necessary -->
<cfif start IS NOT 1>
```

If the `start` variable is not 1, we will include the previous link like this:

```
<a href="main.cfm?start=#Evaluate(start -
➡ view_rows)#&view_rows=#view_rows#">Previous</a>
```

The `#Evaluate(start-view_rows)#` statement will take the current start value and subtract the `view_rows` variable. This will take the viewer back to the previous page.

11. So, add in these lines and the complete code for our Next and Previous links should look like this:

```
<cfif view_rows IS NOT "all">
<!-- add next and previous buttons here -->
<cfoutput>
<!-- check to see if a previous button is
necessary -->
<cfif start IS NOT 1>
<a href="main.cfm?start=#Evaluate(start -
➡ view_rows)#&view_rows=#view_rows#">Previous</a>
</cfif>
<!-- do not display the button if no records
remain -->
  <cfif #new_start# LTE current_posts.RecordCount>
  <a
➡ href="main.cfm?start=#new_start#&view_rows=
➡ #view_rows#">Next</a>
  </cfif>
</cfoutput>
</cfif>
```

12. Just to check that we've got everything in the right place, check your `main.cfm` listing. The complete code listing for `main.cfm` is:

```
<!-- initialize the start value -->

<cfif IsDefined("view_rows")>

<cfparam name="start" default="1">

<cfif view_rows IS NOT "all">
<cfif start GT 1>
<cfset new_start = #start# + #view_rows#>
<cfelse>
<cfset new_start = 1 + #view_rows#>
</cfif>
</cfif>

<!-- query to get current posts for the current
forum -->
<cfquery name="current_posts" datasource="board"
➥ dbtype="ODBC">
SELECT
*
FROM posts
ORDER BY post_id DESC
</cfquery>

<cfoutput>
#current_posts.RecordCount# posts found. You chose
➥ to display #view_rows# posts.
</cfoutput>

<table border="1" cellspacing="6" cellpadding="2">
  <tr>
  <td>Replies</td>
  <td>Title</td>
  <td>Author</td>
  <td>Date</td>
      <td>Time</td>
      <td> </td>
  </tr>
<!-- Output all of the posts and their details
here -->
<!-- limit the results to the number selected. If
the viewer selected all, display them all -->
<cfif view_rows IS "all">
```

```
<cfoutput query="current_posts">
<tr>
  <td>
<!-- insert number of replies for that post here
-->
#no_replies#
    </td>
<!-- insert post text here -->
    <td>
#title#
    </td>
    <td>
<a href="mailto:#author_email#">#author_name#</a>
    </td>
    <td>
<!-- Insert Date of post here -->
#DateFormat(date_post)#
    </td>
    <td>
<!-- Insert Date of post here -->
#TimeFormat(time_post)#
    </td>
    <td><a
    ➥ href="view_thread.cfm?post_id=#post_id#">
    ➥ View Thread!</a></td>
    </tr>
</cfoutput>
<cfelse>
<!-- if the user wants to limit the number of
posts display those results here -->
<cfoutput query="current_posts" startrow=#start#
maxrows=#view_rows#>
<tr>
  <td>
<!-- insert number of replies for that post here
-->
#no_replies#
    </td>
<!-- insert post text here -->
    <td>
#title#
    </td>
    <td>
<a href="mailto:#author_email#">#author_name#</a>
    </td>
    <td>
```

```
<!-- Insert Date of post here -->
#DateFormat(date_post)#
      </td>
      <td>
<!-- Insert Date of post here -->
#TimeFormat(time_post)#
      </td>
      <td><a
  ➥ href="view_thread.cfm?post_id=#post_id#">
  ➥ View Thread!</a></td>
      </tr>
</cfoutput>
</cfif>
</table>

<cfif view_rows IS NOT "all">
<!-- add next and previous buttons here -->
<cfoutput>
<!-- check to see if a previous button is
necessary -->
<cfif start IS NOT 1>
<a href="main.cfm?start=#Evaluate(start -
  ➥ view_rows)#&view_rows=#view_rows#">Previous</a>
</cfif>
<!-- do not display the button if no records
remain -->
  <cfif #new_start# LTE current_posts.RecordCount>
  <a
  ➥ href="main.cfm?start=#new_start#&view_rows=
  ➥ #view_rows#">Next</a>
  </cfif>
</cfoutput>
</cfif>

<p><a href="new_post.cfm">New post link</a></p>

<cfelse>
<cflocation url="start.cfm">
</cfif>
```

Open up our forum in your browser and test out the buttons. The forum is looking better and better already.

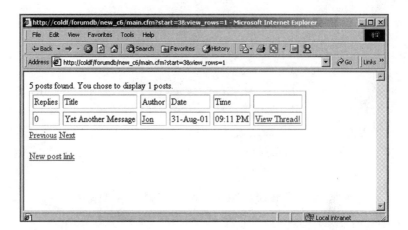

Case study

At the end of the last chapter we had a working forum that could display the list of posts and view any related thread. In this chapter we're going to add the forms that allow us to post to the forum and reply. We'll start by creating the post form first and then add a few modifications to this and save it as the reply form.

Building the post and reply forms

1. Open up a new Flash movie and save it as `post.fla` in our casestudy folder. We want our post form to have a similar appearance to the main forum, so we'll use the same red and black color scheme. We'll set the movie properties the same as for our main movie.

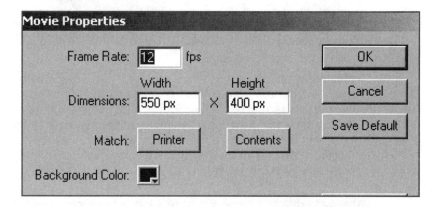

2. When this form is called by the main forum movie it will sit on top of the main forum. Unless we put a background into the movie the form will appear transparent. We're going to make the background a black rectangle with rounded corners in the same fashion as our red frame on the main movie. Name the default layer background, set the corner radius to 10 again, and draw a rectangle with a black fill and no stroke on the stage. Make this 450px by 350px and center it on the stage. Make this layer 5 frames long by inserting a frame at 5.

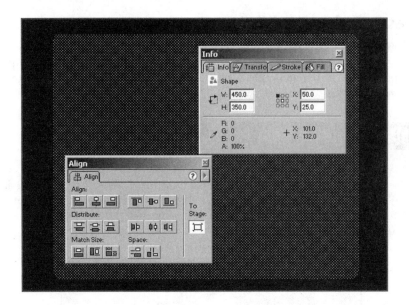

3.   Create a second layer, name it frame, and on this frame we're going to make another red frame. With the corner radius still set at 10, on this layer draw a second rectangle, this time with no fill and the stroke set to 2 and a red color. Match the dimensions of the rectangle on the bottom layer, and center it so the frame sits exactly on top of the background rectangle. When this movie is displayed in the final movie it will have the red frame as its outer edge.

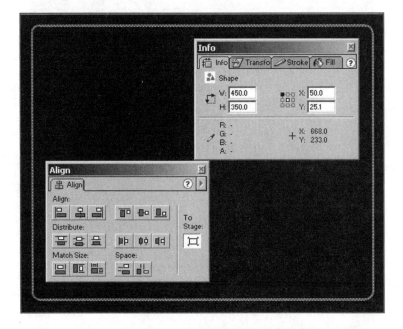

4. We'll now create a third layer, and this one will contain the actions for the movie clip. As with all our other layers that contain actions we'll name it actions. On the keyframe at frame 1 we'll add a `stop()` action. At a new keyframe at frame 5 we'll add the following code:

```
stop ();
_level0.gotoAndPlay(51);
unloadMovieNum (10);
```

The `stop` action needs no explaining to us, and the `gotoAndPlay()` command send the user back to frame 51 of the main forum movie where the forum loading started after our Flash introduction. The last line of the code unloads this movie so that data is not stored the next time we open the post form. When we link to the post form in the main movie we're going to load it to level to, and that is where we unload it from here.

5. That's it for the actions layer and we'll now create the most important layer of this movie, the one that contains the text input boxes. Add this new layer below the actions layer and name it text fields. The font that we're going to use for each of these textfields is Arial, 14pt and black. Let's set this now in the Character panel.

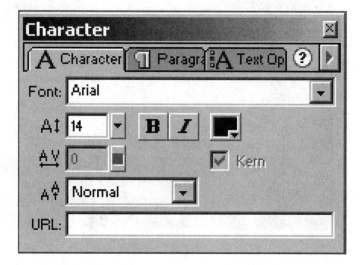

6. There are 4 input boxes in this form: name, e-mail address, title and post. The first three of these will live in identical input boxes, the only difference being that we set the relevant variable for each. Let's look at the first of these, the name box. This field will be where the author of a thread enters their name, and we all know by now that this is referred to as author_name in our database, Flash movie and ColdFusion templates. Click on the stage with the Text Tool and open up the Text Options panel. We want this to be an input field, so select Input Text from the drop-down menu. We only want one line for this input so make sure Single Line is selected. We'll now enter our variable name author_name. I've also checked the Border/Bg box although this makes no real difference with the color scheme we're using. The only thing left to do to complete this box is resize the box. Select the textbox with the Arrow Tool and make it 250 pixels wide. We'll keep the default single line height that the Text Tool created.

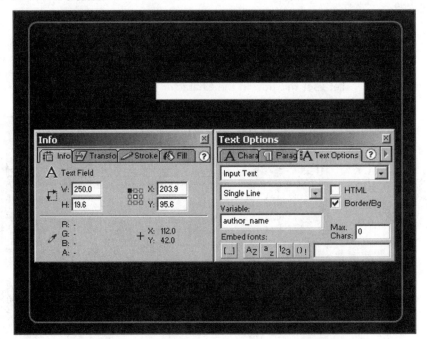

7. We'll now repeat the same process to create the e-mail address and title input boxes. The only difference between each text box will be the variable names, which for these two are author_email and title respectively. Once we've created the three identical textboxes there is only the box for the actual post to create. With the Text Tool draw a text field that look about 5 or 6 times the height of our other fields, mine ended up at 113px, but the exact size isn't vital. This input box wants to be Multiline with Word wrap on as our posts will often be longer than one line. In case you haven't guessed, the variable will be post. The final job for this textbox will be to change the width of the box to 350px using the Info panel.

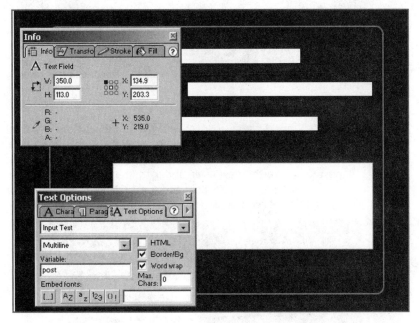

8. Now that we've created all our input boxes we want to arrange them on the stage, and also add labels so the user knows what to enter in each box. I'll leave it up to you to decide exactly how to arrange the boxes on the stage, but I aligned the right edge of each box with each other using the Align panel. This panel also helped me to distribute the boxes evenly. I added my labels with the Arial font set to 14, the color to white and the bold option selected. The next screenshot shows how my stage looked after I finished my arranging and labeling. Be as creative as you like.

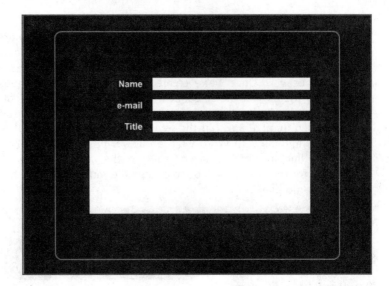

9. There is one final layer to create in this movie clip – the buttons layer. This layer will contain the button to submit the post and also a button to take the user back to the main forum if they change their mind about posting. Make the new layer under the text fields layer. In the Character panel choose Arial, white, bold and size 18. Now at the bottom of the stage, but within the red frame, type send on the right hand size of the stage.

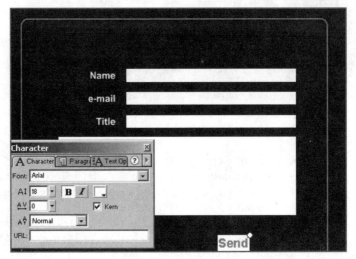

10. Our next step is to select send and convert it to a symbol (Insert>Convert to Symbol). We'll make it a button called bnsend.

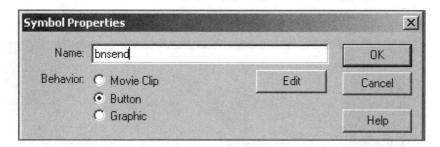

Inside the buttons edit mode create a keyframe over the Hit state. On this frame draw a rectangle over the text. Once again the color of the rectangle doesn't matter as it will be invisible and only serves the purpose of making in whole of the area an active button rather than just the lines of the text.

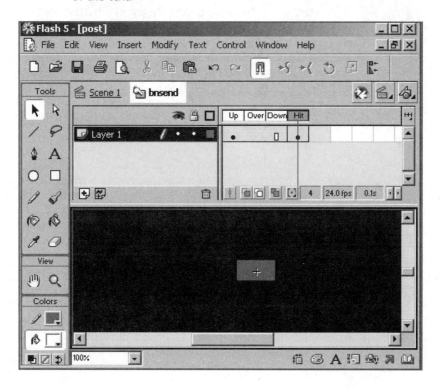

11. We'll create the second button in an identical fashion to the first, but with the text as cancel rather than send, and the button called bncancel. Once we've created the second button the only thing we need to do is add the actions to the two buttons.

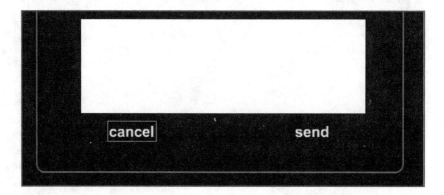

We'll start with the actions for the cancel button. With the button selected open up the Object Actions panel. The actions for this button are very simple. All we need to do is unload the post forms movie clip and that's it. It will close and we'll be back at the main forum. Remember that we're going to load this movie to level 10, so that's the level we need to clear. Here's the code:

```
on (release) {
    unloadMovieNum (10);
}
```

12. Now the actions for the send button. When this button is clicked we want the data to be sent to the database, and we again use the insert_post.cfm template to do this. As with all our variables, they will go via level 0 and we'll use the POST method. The movie is then sent to the unload frame which we added earlier. Add the code to the button now:

```
on (release) {
    loadVariablesNum ("insert_post.cfm", 0,
➡"POST");
    gotoAndPlay ("unload");
}
```

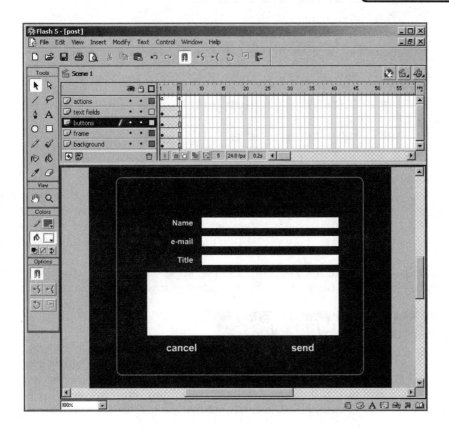

The post movie is now completed and we can now move onto the reply form after we've published the movie into SWF format. As I said earlier these templates are very similar so instead of creating the reply form from scratch we'll just make a copy of the post movie.

13. With your copy of the post movie still open, select the Save As… option and save the file as reply.fla. On frame 1 of actions layer we currently only have a stop action. We'll add one extra line to this frame after the stop action:

```
post_id = _level0.post_id;
```

As we're replying to a specific post we have to make sure the post_id is passed on so the reply is linked to the right post.

14. On the text fields layer we need to change the variable names for each field to the equivalent reply variables. Change the following:

- `author_name` to `reply_name`

- `author_email` to `reply_email`

- `title` to `reply_title`

- `post` to `reply`

Once we've changed the actions for the send button we've finished this movie clip. It really is that simple! And the only thing we need to change in that code is to change the file name from `insert_post.cfm` to `insert_reply.cfm`. Don't forget to publish the file to a SWF format.

So, we've now finished the twin movie clip that act as our post and reply forms. We'll now go back to the main forum movie clip and add the actions to call these forms.

Back on the main stage...

1. Reopen your working copy of `forum.fla`. Go into the edit in place mode for mcforum, making sure you can see where this movie fits into the main movie. On frame 1 of the buttons layer, drag a copy of the post button (bnpost) from the library onto the white area at the bottom of the screen.

2.   We'll now add the code to make this button work. Open up the Object
      Actions panel with the button selected. The actions for this button are as
      simple as:

```
on (release) {
     loadMovieNum ("post.swf", 10);
}
```

This loads our post form into the level 10 position that we mentioned
earlier. We only want the user to be able to post when they are viewing
the main forum page, and reply when they are viewing a thread. So, we'll
put the reply button on frame 20 of this layer.

This time the button actions load the reply.swf movie:

```
on (release) {
        loadMovieNum ("reply.swf", 10);
}
```

That's all we need to do for the forum in Flash!

Finishing off the forum

There are a few things we need to do to finish off our forum. The first thing is to get copies of the `insert_post.cfm` and `insert_reply.cfm` files that we made in Chapter 5 and put these into our `casestudy` folder with the rest of the case study files. These files pass the variables from our Flash movie into the database.

The next thing we need to do is open up our database again. Before we introduced Flash into our forum the time and date values were set by ColdFusion in the `new_post.cfm` and `new_reply.cfm` templates. In our Flash forum we don't need those files because we input the data through our Flash post and reply forms. However, we still need to get the date and time from somewhere and Access lets us record a date and time when the record is created.

Open up your database and select the posts table in the Design View (View>Design View). Select the `date_post` field and look at the parameters that appear at the bottom of the screen. You should see that there is a default value option under the General tab. Click on this field and you'll see a button appears to the right. If we click on this button we'll se that an Expression Builder window opens. If we follow through the options we can set the default value to the date the post is entered into the database.

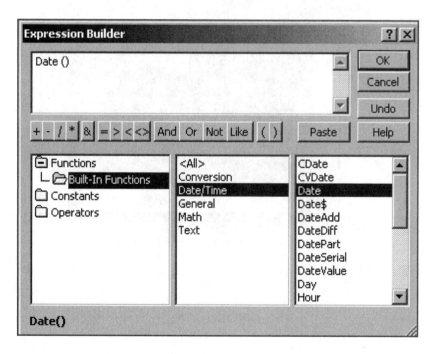

We can do exactly the same with the `time_post` field. The time option is can be found on the same expression builder menu as the date. Once you've set these two default values do the same on the reply table for `date_reply` and `time_reply`.

Our final task is to embed our Flash movie in a ColdFusion template. Open up ColdFusion Studio and save a new template, `index.cfm`, in the casestudy folder. We'll use the default HTML template this time. Enter a title for the forum within the `<title>` tags. We now need to embed the Flash movie in this template. If you're like me you'll want to give your typing fingers a rest by now, so we'll take a shortcut here. Open up your `forum.fla` file and through the Publish Settings publish the file to a HTML document. Next open that HTML document in ColdFusion Studio and cut and paste everything within the `<object>` tags into the `index.cfm <body>` tags. Let's also add some `<center>` tags just within the `<body>` tags to center our movie. The final thing is to add a black background color to the body tag (`<body bgcolor="#000000">`). That's everything done!

If we now open up the `index.cfm` file using the localhost, or remote server address we can admire our fully functioning forum. Make some posts and replies and test everything works! Remember that we can use the back button to refresh the forum at any time, which is useful if the forum is online and people are posting all the time. It's also useful if your server is running a bit slow and your post doesn't appear straight away!

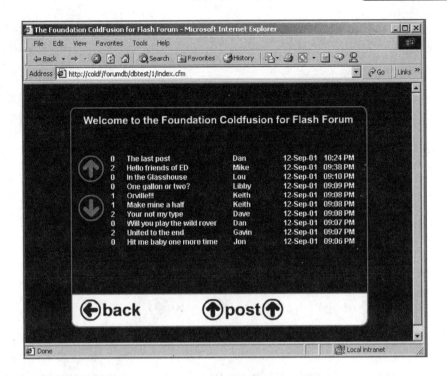

We've now come to the end of the case study in this book, but you'll find many useful features that you may wish to append to this forum in the remaining chapters. For example, why not add a Flash menu from the Component Kit (Chapter 11) onto your forum? Or e-mail postings and validation (Chapters 8 and 9)? It may be a cliché, but the possibilities really are endless.

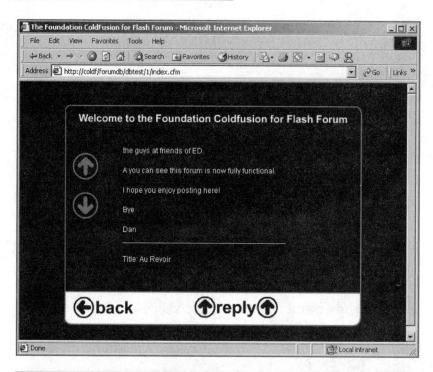

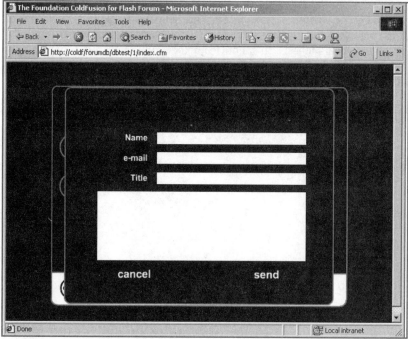

Summary

Before we came into this chapter we had seen CFML and ColdFusion send and retrieve data to and from a data source, but that was it, now we know how to ask for exactly what we want. The beauty of SQL is how the simple functions can be combined and nested to provide us with exact selections, picking the data that is important to us. We've turned our forum from having a very simple interface to a much more functional one, and with only a few lines of CFML - OK it still doesn't look too pretty but that's Flash's area!

Users of our forum can now post whatever they want, and while we don't want to stifle creativity we do want the data to be meaningful. Yes we're talking data validation, and as you'll see in the next chapter there are a number of ways we can do this.

7 Data Validation and Form Handling

What We'll Cover in this Chapter

- *Validating data supplied by the user to prevent errors*

- *Server-side validation, where the validation workload is handled by the server*

- *Client-side validation, where the validation process is run inside the user's browser*

- *Performing validation in both CFML and Flash*

Why validation is important

As web developers, gathering form data is normally very important – and even more important to our clients. It helps us to gather the data that we need to use, rather than the data that our clients might think we want. Unfortunately, web site users are have a horrible habit of not filling out forms correctly. Validation (client- or server-side) allows us to control the data being sent in the forms – it's our way of helping visitors to our site fill out forms properly!

Introduction to client- vs. server-side validation

Whether to use client-side or versus server—side validation is a very popular topic of constant debate. **client-side** validation takes place within the client's web browser – **before** any results are sent to the web server. To achieve this, developers commonly embed JavaScript instructions within the HTML code to validate various input fields. This script is run in the user's browser, and then the data – if valid – is sent to the server.

With an entirely server-side based approach, the data is sent to the server, and then checked for validity. If the data is invalid, then the client will have to resend the entire data package.

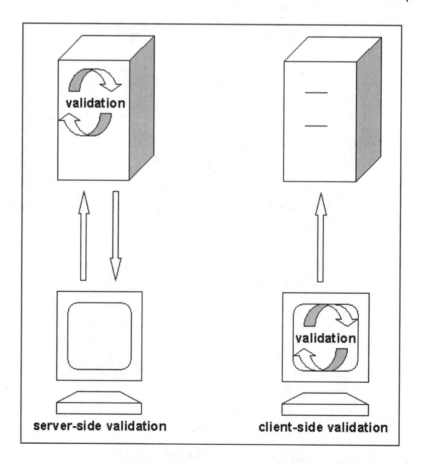

For example, we could add validation code to our new_post.cfm template which would make text entry into the author-name field mandatory. If a visitor tried to submit a blank form, we could issue a message like this:

The advantage of this type of validation is that it saves server resources. The form results do not get to the server for processing until all the criteria specified in the client-side script are met. Furthermore, if a user makes a mistake they can correct it without losing any data. With server-side validation, in contrast, a user will often have to click on the back button to return to the form after an invalid submission, only to find the fields they previously filled out are now blank. This becomes a much bigger problem as your forms become more complex.

Client-side validation is also easier than ever to perform thanks to the many script creation/editing packages that are now available. Macromedia Dreamweaver, for example, has several built-in functions that allow you to build complex JavaScript validation instructions for your forms quickly and easily. ColdFusion also has its own client-side validation that is part of the <cfform> family of tags. We will look at <cfform> later in this chapter.

There are, however, limitations to client-side validation. First of all, it commonly relies on JavaScript or VBScript, which are not supported by all browsers, and their scripting functionality can be turned off completely by the user if they wish. Trying to incorporate support for all possible browser configurations becomes very complex. Secondly, client-side validation does not allow any interaction with a database. Therefore, validating a user name or a password would be impossible with client-side validation.

Server-side validation happens after a form is submitted, and this type of validation offers a much greater level of flexibility to the developer. Server-side validation in ColdFusion is normally handled by writing conditional code with one or more `<cfif>` statements, depending on the level of complexity needed.

With server-side validation, a user would only see an error message after the form has been submitted. This is one of the main drawbacks to this form of validation. On the other hand, it is completely browser-independent, and offers the ability to validate records with database queries.

To illustrate the difference between the two validation approaches, let's go back to our `forum` application and add some validation functionality.

Server-Side validation for our forum

The first thing we'll do is add some server-side validation to our `insert_post.cfm` template. This is the template that processes the form on the `new_post.cfm` page.

> Before and after versions of the templates used in this chapter are available for reference at www.friendsofed.com.

The current code on the `insert_post.cfm` page looks like this:

```
<!-- insert_post.cfm -->

<!-- insert the new post into the db -->

<cfinsert datasource="board" tablename="posts"
dbtype="ODBC">

<!-- tell the user that their post has been
accepted -->

 Thank you, your post has been inserted.

<cfoutput>
<a href="main.cfm">back to main</a>
</p>
</cfoutput>
```

As you can see, this template simply inserts the data into the database – it assumes that the user has filled the form out correctly. To **ensure** that the form has been completed properly, we want to run some validation code before the `<cfinsert>` statement is processed.

The form on the page in question only has three form elements: two input text fields and one text area field.   We're going to start our validation scheme by making it mandatory that the user enter their name in the `author-name` field. We can do this quite easily.

1.   Open up the `insert_post.cfm` page for editing and insert the following code before the `cfinsert` statement:

```
<!-- check to make sure that the author field is not blank -->

<cfif Len(Trim(author_name)) IS 0>
Please be sure to fill out the author field.
<cfabort>
</cfif>
```

Here, we're using two new string manipulation techniques. The `Trim` function returns the entered string with both leading and trailing spaces removed. We do this in case the user sneakily entered a space into the input box. We are looking for characters, not empty spaces.

The Len function simply returns the length of the author_name string. Once we strip out any possible spaces, and provided the length of the author field is not zero, the <cfif> statement is ignored and the <cfinsert> statement is processed. If the <cfif> statement **is** satisfied (i.e. the input field is blank) the user receives the error message text and the <cfabort> tag is processed. The <cfabort> tag halts the processing of the template at the tag location, meaning that the <cfinsert> statement will not be processed.

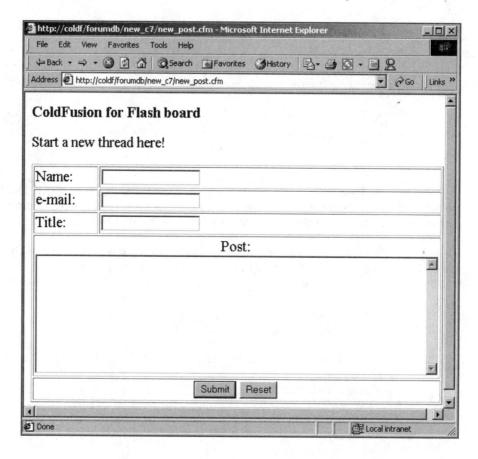

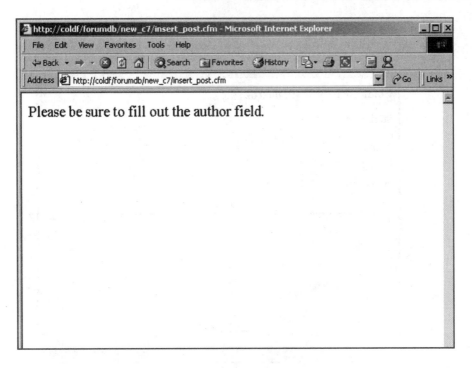

We can implement a similar validation model for the title input field.

2. Insert the following code right after the new cfif statement that validates the author field:

    ```
    <!—- check to make sure that the title field is
    not blank —->

    <cfif Len(Trim(title)) IS 0>
    Please be sure to fill out the post title.
    <cfabort>
    </cfif>
    ```

The template will now first check the author-name field and then move on to the title field. If the user fills out the author-name field and not the title field, the template is once again aborted and the user receives the new error message:

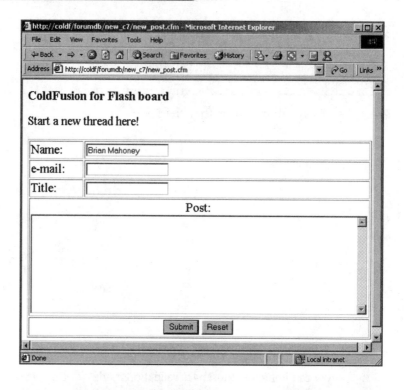

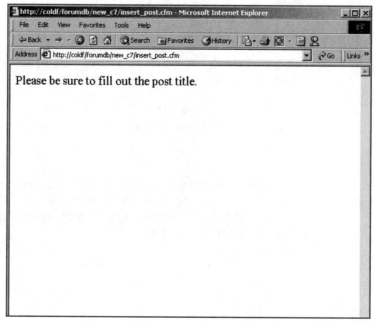

We can use a virtually identical piece of code to validate the post field. Doesn't this user want to say anything?

3.   Below our title validation code, insert this:

```
<!-- check to make sure that the post field is
not blank -->

<cfif Len(Trim(post)) IS 0>
Please be sure to fill out the post text.
<cfabort>
</cfif>
```

4.   Try this out in your browser, fill in the author and a title for the post but leave the actual post field blank. You should get the message:

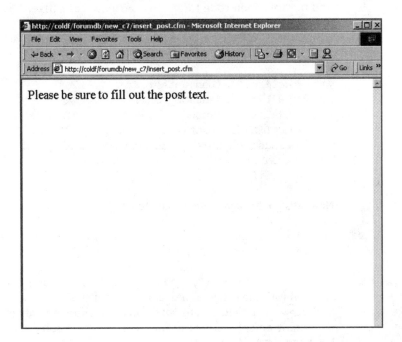

Saving the best for last, we will now validate the author_email field. This time though, we're not only going to check that it is not left blank: we're also going to test for the inclusion of the @ and . symbols in the e-mail address, and for the appropriate text between them. Validating for e-mail addresses is never foolproof – but we'll give it our best shot.

Before looking at the code, we need to introduce a few new list manipulation functions. For this validation scheme to work, we're treating the `author_email` field as a **list**. In ColdFusion lists of any kind are represented as strings.

We'll test that list with the following functions:

- **Len** – the same function we discussed previously

- **Trim** – another function we've already looked at

- **ListLen** – this function will return the **number** of elements in the list

- **ListLast** – returns the **last** element of the list

5. Add this validation code to the `insert_post.cfm` page. After the:

    ```
    <!-- check to make sure that the email address is
    valid -->

    <cfif TRIM(Len(author_email)) LT 1
    OR ListLen(author_email, "@") NEQ 2
    OR ListLen(author_email, ".") LTE 2
    OR LEN(ListLast(author_email, ".")) LT 1>
    Please be sure to provide a valid email address.
    <cfabort>
    </cfif>
    ```

    Now let's go through it line by line to clarify its purpose and functionality.

- `TRIM(Len(author_email)) LT 1` - tests to make sure that the `author_email` field is not blank.

- `ListLen(author_email, ""@"") NEQ 2` - uses the `ListLen` function with the @ sign as a delimiter. The inclusion of the @ sign in the `author_email` field means that there are two elements in the list. If only one element is found in the field, we can assume that the @ sign has been omitted.

- `ListLen(author_email, "".""") LTE 2` - also uses the `ListLen` function, but this time with the "".""" sign as the delimiter. This line checks to make sure that at least one "".""" has been included in the address.

■   LEN(ListLast(author_email, ""."")) LT 1> checks to make sure that the length of the list element after the ""."" – the co, org, com extension – is more than one character in length. For example, the following email address would be rejected: test@test.c, but this next address –test@test.co – would be accepted, since the length of the element after the ""."" is greater than one character.

The issue of e-mail validation is a thorny problem, as even if an address is valid in structure it may not exist! This is why most mailing lists require you to reply to an e-mail set to your subscription address.

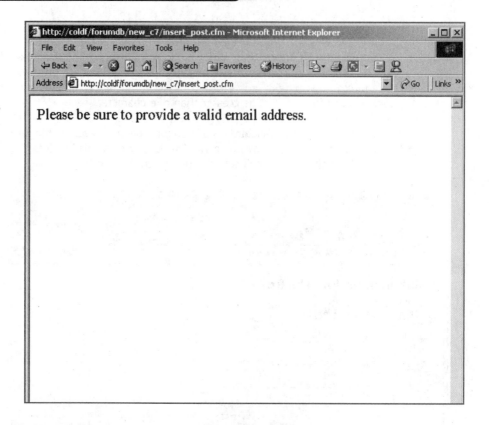

Client-side validation for our forum

These server-side validation routines have added a little more robustness to the quality of the data that the user will provide us with. Now let's take a look at how we could deal with these issues client-side.

There are a number of JavaScript validation scripts around on the Internet that can be configured for your HTML forms. When we validate on the client again, under a client-side validation scenario, the form is not submitted until all elements are correct. Quite often, these scripts are hard to decipher and do not yield consistent results. Luckily CFML contains a way of integrating client-side validation scripts with ease.

Enter `<cfform>`, `<cfform>` allows us to build in several custom controls that are not available in standard HTML forms. `<cfform>` automatically generates the JavaScript necessary to validate our forms. You can use normal HTML input tags within `<cfform>` tags, but to take advantage of the validation options you need to use the following tags, which are specific to `<cfform>`:

- ■ `<cfinput>` – creates a form input element (radio button, text box, or check box) and can validate form input.

- ■ `<cfselect>` – creates a drop down list box.

- ■ `<cfslider>` – creates a slider control.

- ■ `<cftextinput>` – creates a text input box.

- ■ `<cftree>` – creates a tree control. Tree control is a method of organizing data.

- ■ `<cfgrid>` – creates a grid control for displaying tabular data in a ColdFusion form.

- ■ `<cfapplet>` – embeds a registered Java applet in a ColdFusion form. Applets are registered in the ColdFusion Administrator.

The `<cfform>` element we'll concentrate on here is `<cfinput>` . To take advantage of these tags, we will make some modifications to our `new_post.cfm` template.

1. First, change the `<form>` tag to a `<cfform>` tag:

    ```
    <cfform action="""insert_post.cfm""" method="""POST"""
    ➥enctype="""multipart/form-data"""
    ```

2. Next, change your closing `</form>` tag to `</cfform>`.

    You'll immediately see that the tags are almost identical. `<cfform>` also has a few other features not available in the HTML `<form>` tag, they are for controlling the more advanced JavaScript features so we will not go into them here.

    Now that we have our `<cfform>` tag, we are going to change our `<input>` tags for author_name, author_email and title to cfinput tags so that we can take advantage of `<cfform>`'s built-in validation techniques.

    Make those changes now, so that the modified `<input>` tags look like this:

    ```
    <cfinput type="text" name="author_name">
    ```
    ...

    ```
    <cfinput type="text" name="author_email">
    ```
    ...

    ```
    <cfinput type="text" name="title">
    ```

Once again, these tags are almost identical to the standard HTML `<input>` tags.

The `<cfinput>` tag has several attributes though that makes it much more powerful than the standard `<input>` tag and we will be looking at two of them in detail here.

The first performance modifier we'll use is the `required` attribute. `required` has two options, `yes` or `no`. By default, `no` is selected. If we change this attribute to `yes`, the form will not be submitted if the field is left blank.

The other attribute of interest is `validate`. The `validate` attribute can be used to check the validity of the information passed by the form, depending on the criteria that you specify. Valid entries are:

- `date` — –verifies US date entry in the form *mm/dd/yyyy*.

- `eurodate` — verifies valid European date entry in the form *dd/mm/yyyy*.

- `time` — verifies a time entry in the form *hh:mm:ss*.

- `float` — verifies a floating point entry.

- `integer` — verifies an integer entry.

- `telephone` — verifies a telephone entry. Telephone data must be entered as ###-###-####. The hyphen separator (-) can be replaced with a blank. The area code and exchange must begin with a digit between 1 and 9.

- `zipcode` —— (U.S. formats only.) Number can be a 5-digit or 9-digit zip in the form #####-####. The hyphen separator (-) can be replaced with a blank.

- `creditcard` — Blanks and dashes are stripped and the number is verified using the mod10 algorithm.

- `social_security_number` — – number must be entered as ###-##-####. The hyphen separator (-) can be replaced with a blank.

You'll notice that the list does **not** contain an entry for e-mail. As such, we'll continue to use the "'email checker'" that we created in the `insert_post.cfm` template earlier.　It's important to note that there are quite a few **custom tags** available in the **developers exchange** at allaire.com that will add this function to our form – check out:

http://devex.allaire.com/developer/gallery/index.cfm

> Custom tags are complete ColdFusion templates that other developers make available to the ColdFusion community.

The conditional statements we've added to our `insert_post.cfm` template will soon become redundant (the ones used to check if the `author_name`, `author_email` and `title` fields were not blank). We'll simply use the `required` attribute to assure that the field is not blank.

Add the `required` parameters to the `<cfinput>` tags so that they look like this:

```
<cfinput type="text" name="author_name"
➥required="Yes">
...

<cfinput type="text" name="author_email"
➥required="Yes">
...

<cfinput> type="text" name="title" required="Yes">
```

If you view the `new_post.cfm` template in your browser, you should see that the form **looks** identical to the previous one.

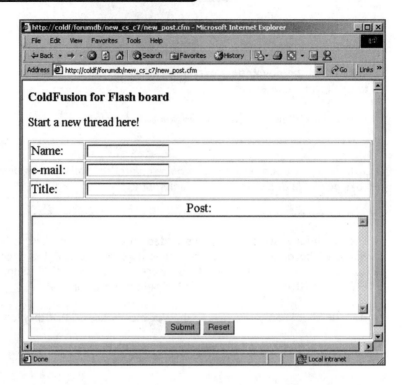

Upon closer inspection of the rendered source code (right click on the page, and click "View Source"), you'll find that a lot of JavaScript has been automatically inserted at the beginning of our document:

```
<script LANGUAGE=JAVASCRIPT TYPE="text/javascript" >
<!--

function _CF_onError(form_object, input_object, object_value, error_message)
        {
        alert(error_message);
        return false;
        }


function _CF_hasValue(obj, obj_type)
        {
        if (obj_type == "TEXT" || obj_type == "PASSWORD")
                {
                if (obj.value.length == 0)
                        return false;
                else
                        return true;
                }
        else if (obj_type == "SELECT")
                {
                for (i=0; i < obj.length; i++)
                        {
                        if (obj.options[i].selected)
                                return true;
                        }
                return false;
                }
        else if (obj_type == "SINGLE_VALUE_RADIO" || obj_type == "SINGLE_VALUE_CHECKBOX")
                {

                if (obj.checked)
                        return true;
                else
                        return false;
                }
```

Furthermore, our `<cfform>` tag has also changed. It now reads like this:

```
<FORM       NAME="""CFForm_1"""        ACTION="""insert_post.cfm"""
➡METHOD=POST   onSubmit="""return   _CF_checkCFForm_1(this)"""
➡ENCTYPE="""multipart/form-data""">
```

Finally, the `<cfinput>` tags were also changed (back to their original state in fact):

```
<INPUT TYPE="""Text"""  NAME="""author""">
```

> *This is because* View Source *shows us the browser scripting delivered by our ColdFusion server, and in this case the CFML tags produce JavaScript as well as HTML.*

Now, if you try to submit the form with a blank field for "author_name", you'll see the following error:

5. We want to customize the generic error message, so we add the "message" attribute to the `<cfinput>` tag for author_name. Changing the code to...

```
➡<cfinput type="""Text"""  name="""author_name"""
➡message="""This field is required"""  required="""Yes"""
```
    would result in the following error message if the user failed to type an entry in this field:

6. Let's change our default messages to something more useful. Change the `<cfinput>` tags to read:

```
<cfinput type="Text" name="author_name"message="An Author's
➥Nameis required" required="Yes">
...
<cfinput type="text" name="author_email" message="An Email
➥Address is required" required="Yes">
...
<cfinput type="text" name="title" message="A Title for the
➥post is required" required="Yes">
```

Much nicer!

As you can see, changing to a `<cfform>` and using `<cfform>` tags, we are now using some client-side validation for our form – the form does not get submitted unless the fields are properly completed.

Combined validation server- and client-side

While this type of validation is convenient and effective, we cannot easily complete our application this way: we're not able to validate the e-mail address with the `<cfinput>` tag, and there is no "required" attribute on the `<textarea>` tag. To address this shortfall, we'll combine server-side and client-side validation.

7.   This will be accomplished by removing the conditional statements of our insert_post.cfm that check for author_name and title, since these are made redundant by the required attribute we've added to the form. The statements used to validate the textarea tag and then to validate for the author's email address are kept. By doing so, we have successfully used a combination of server and client-side validation to ensure that our form is properly filled out.

To keep our forum consistent we should apply these same validation techniques to the insertion of a new reply, for that we'll need to alter two more templates insert_reply.cfm and new_reply.cfm.

8.   Open up new_reply.cfm for editing. In much the same way as we added the <cfform> and <cfinput> tags in new_post.cfm we change the template to read thus:

```
<cfform action="insert_reply.cfm" method="POST"

➡enctype="multipart/form-data">
 <table width="50%" border="1" cellspacing="2"
cellpadding="2">
   <tr>
<!-- insert the post -->
     <cfoutput query="get_post">
        <td colspan="2"><b>Post: </b>#post#<br>
        <b>Author:</b> #author_name#
        </td>
         </cfoutput>
       </tr>
     <tr>
     <td width="16%">Name:</td><td width="84%">
       <cfinput type="text" name="reply_name"
➡message="Your Name is required" required="Yes">
       </td></tr>
     <tr>
     <td width="16%">e-mail:</td><td width="84%">
       <cfinput type="text" name="reply_email"
➡message="An Email Address is required"
➡required="Yes">
       </td></tr>
     <tr>
     <td width="16%">Title:</td>
     <td width="84%">
       <cfinput type="text" name="reply_title"
➡message="A Title for your reply is required"
➡required="Yes">
```

```
            </td>
          </tr>
          <tr>
           <td colspan="2">
            <div align="center">Reply:<br>
             <textarea name="reply" wrap="VIRTUAL"
cols="50"></textarea>
             </div></td></tr>
          <tr>
           <td colspan="2">
            <div align="center">
                    <cfoutput>
            <input type="hidden" name="post_id"
value="#post_id#">
                    <input type="hidden"
➥name="date_reply" value="#DateFormat(Now())#">
                    <input type="hidden"
➥name="time_reply"
value="#CreateODBCTime(Now())#">
                   </cfoutput>
       <input type="submit" value="Submit">
       <input type="reset" value="Reset">
       </div></td></tr>
      </table>
      </cfform>
```

Again we're unable to perform client-side validation for either the e-mail address or the bulky <textarea> of the reply, so we'll do this server-side in insert_reply.cfm.

9. Open up `insert_reply.cfm` in Studio and add two little pieces of code that should seem vaguely familiar:

```
<!-- insert_reply.cfm -->

<!-- check to make sure that the reply field is
not blank -->
<cfif Len(Trim(reply)) IS 0>
Please be sure to fill out the reply text.
<cfabort>
</cfif>

<!-- check to make sure that the email address is
valid -->
<cfif TRIM(Len(reply_email)) LT 1
OR ListLen(reply_email, "@") NEQ 2
OR ListLen(reply_email, ".") LTE 2
OR LEN(ListLast(reply_email, ".")) LT 1>
Please be sure to provide a valid email address.
<cfabort>
</cfif>

<!-- insert the new reply into the db -->

<cfinsert datasource="board" tablename="replies"
➥dbtype="ODBC">
```

And that is it, this completes the data validation we're going to do for our forum at this point. As a brief aside the way we added the validation to the replies input code is a beautiful example of code-reuse in action.

Client-side validation in Flash

To complete this chapter, we're going to look at how we can validate input text fields in a Flash movie. This example will not be part of our forum example, and is simply to illustrate validation techniques available to us in Flash so that we can use them in the forum example later. As such, don't worry about fine-tuning the visual appearance of this file.

Making a required field

First, we'll look at how to make a text field a **required** field, and then we'll wrap things up by checking for a valid e-mail address. This is an important lesson and will certainly help later on when we are sending Flash variables to ColdFusion templates for processing. These validation techniques will help us to control the output from Flash and will eliminate many possible errors in our ColdFusion code.

1. Start by creating a new Flash movie with three layers:

●   actions

●   text fields

●   buttons

2. Then, on the first frame of your actions layer, add the following actions and label the frame "start":

```
stop ();
name = "";
```

3. Next, on the text fields layer, add two input text boxes with the following variable names: email and name.

4. Finally, on the buttons layer, create a simple submit button.

Your stage should now look something like this:

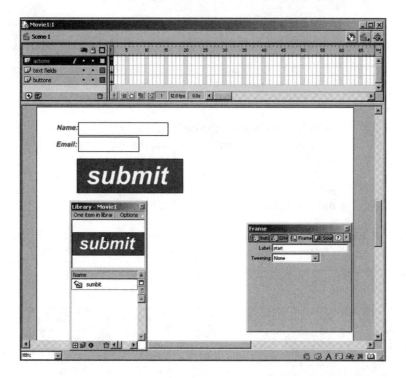

5. Now insert the following code to the object actions on the submit button:

```
on (release) {
    if (name =="") {
        gotoAndStop("bad");
    } else {
        gotoAndStop("good");
    }
}
```

This code checks to see if the variable name is blank or not. If it **is**, the user is sent to the "bad" frame and gets the appropriate error message. Otherwise, the user is sent to the good frame and gets the 'you were successful' message.

6. Insert two more keyframes on the actions layer, and add with a stop action on each one. Label the first additional keyframe bad and the second one good.

7. Now add a back button to each frame, and attach the following actions to the button:

    ```
    on (release) {
        gotoAndStop ("start");
    }
    ```

8. Then, on the frame labelled bad, insert a message on the stage telling the user that they did not fill out the form correctly. I've used the text You Must Enter Your Name!

9. Finally, on the good layer, insert a message telling the user that they **did** enter the information correctly.

10. Publish your SWF Since there's no ColdFusion linkage in this movie you can save it on any machine you like - not just your server.

    Here's what happens if you try it out:

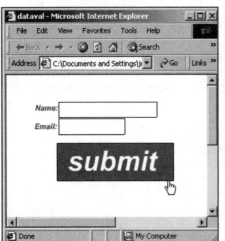 

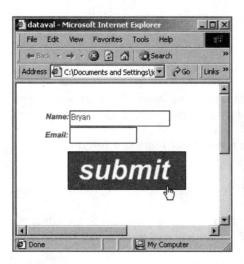 

Let's build on this by making sure that the user enters a valid e-mail address.

Checking for an e-mail address

To accomplish this, we are going to have to develop a conditional statement in Flash that is similar to the one we used in our `insert_post.cfm` template. In fact, our Flash script will be even more compact than our ColdFusion code. It will, however, use three string functions that I will introduce here:

String handling ActionScript

String.Substring
Here's the syntax for this function:

```
myString.substring(from, to);
```

This function will return a string consisting of the characters between the points specified by the `from` and `to` arguments. If no `to` argument is included, the end of the substring will be the **end** of the string.

String.IndexOf
The syntax for this function looks like this:

```
myString.indexOf(value);
```

This function will search the string and return the position of the first occurrence of the specified value. If the value is not found, the function returns -1.

String.LastIndexOf

This function's syntax is very similar to the preceding one:

```
myString.lastIndexOf(substring);
```

This last function searches the string and returns the index of the last occurrence of the substring found within the calling string. If the substring is not found, the method returns -1.

To set up our email validation movie, we're just going to make a few small changes to the Flash movie we used in the previous exercise.

1.   Insert a new blank keyframe on the actions layer, call it bad_email.

2.   In this frame on the text fields layer add a message to the effect of Enter A Valid E-mail Address! (Although you may want to be a bit more polite!)

3.   Add another instance of the back button to the buttons layer on this frame.

4.   And as its Object Actions we'll need exactly the same ActionScript as before:

```
on (release) {
    gotoAndStop ("start");
}
```

Leaving your timeline looking similar to this:

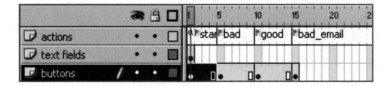

5. Next, we will change the code on the submit button to the following:

```
on (release) {
    if (name == "") {
        gotoAndStop ("bad");
    } else {
        if (email.indexOf("@") != -1 &&

➥email.lastIndexOf(".")>email.indexOf("@") &&

➥length(email.substring(email.LastIndexOf("."))) >
2) {
            gotoAndStop ("good");
        } else {

            gotoAndStop ("bad_email");
        }
    }
}
```

Let's deconstruct this statement:

If the name is present then:

- The first argument in the if statement checks for the occurrence of the @ sign. If the indexOf function returns a value of –1, this indicates that there is no @ symbol present in the string, and the if clause fails.

- The next argument in the if statement checks to see if the last. character comes after the last occurrence of the @ symbol.

- Finally, the last argument makes sure that the length of the substring after the final "." is greater than 1. This makes sure that an email address like test@test.c is not valid.

- If any of these arguments cause the if statement to be untrue then the movie is directed to the bad_email frame.

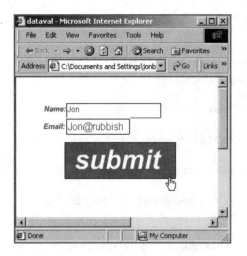

Publish the movie, try it out! You'll find that you now need to input both a name and a valid e-mail address

Summary

In this chapter we've looked at data validation which is a very important part of any dynamic system as the wrong type of input can cause untold errors further along the line. Garbage In, Garbage Out! So our best course of events is to prevent the garbage getting into our systems.

In any environment there are choices to be made about where this validation is best performed. We've looked at both client-side and server-side validation and discussed which is most suited to particular types of tasks. Very broadly speaking:

- Client-side validation is faster and reduces load upon your server.

- Server-side validation can be more complex and can include validations based upon your database. Checking user names and passwords for example.

We these and other issues in mind we added a mixture of both techniques to our ColdFusion forum. Finally we looked at how to implement some client-side validation within a Flash movie.

Validation goes some way to making the interface of a system more transparent to the user. In the next chapter we'll continue to improve this - giving them some help in filling in forms by remembering who they are. Welcome to the beautiful world of client/session management.

8 Client/Session Management

What We'll Cover in this Chapter

- Discuss the Web Application Framework and the tools it contains.

- Try out all of these in our forum project, discovering how they make altering templates easier.

- Discover the practicalities and advantages of using each type of persistent variable.

Until this point, the templates that we've created have not really been connected **directly**: we've passed variables from template to template in URLs and in form elements. With the Web Application Framework, variables can be made available to each template in the application. Furthermore, these variables can **persist** across sessions. What does all of this mean? Persistent variables can, for example, enable a user on your web site to add items to a shopping cart, close their browser, open it up several days later and still have the items residing in the shopping cart. This information may be stored on the user, or client's, machine as well as our server. How we store and manage the data is referred to as client and session management.

Web Application Framework

The Web Application Framework is like crazy glue for developers – in that it provides us with a glue that bonds our entire application together. Without this glue, our templates act independently from one another. Once our templates our bound together, we can more easily control the overall look and feel of our application, we can define and share variables throughout the application and also set up custom error screens to override the default settings from the ColdFusion server.

This chapter will introduce you the following tools that will make up our Web Application Framework:

- The `Application.cfm` template

- The `OnRequestEnd.cfm` template

- Persistent client and session variables

- Cookies

When used together, these tools allow you to more easily develop and manage complex applications.

When referring to the Web Application Framework, there are other functions that are beyond the scope of this chapter. They are; Server variables, Application variables and custom error handling. Information on these functions is readily available in the ColdFusion manuals.

To get a better understanding of the Web Application Framework, we'll look at each of the tools mentioned above and how they can be used in our forum application.

From the top - Application.cfm

The key component to the Web Application Framework is the `Application.cfm` template, typically placed on the root of the web server. Whenever a ColdFusion template is requested on the server, the server searches the page's directory tree for the `Application.cfm` template. If it finds one, that code is included at the beginning of the template that was referenced in the original call to the server.

The `Application.cfm` template is often used to define the following settings and functions:

- Datasource names, so that if changing data sources, each template doesn't have to be altered.

- Application-wide appearance settings style sheets for example, or a title so each template doesn't have to include one.

- Client and Session state management, controlling the:

  - Default variables
  - Application variables

For example, we'll define the `datasource` and `page` title for every page in our message board application.

Global page settings with Application.cfm

It is important to remember the following when using the `Application.cfm` template:

- `Application.cfm` must be spelled with a capital 'A'.

- The ColdFusion server will only include the code of the **first** `Application.cfm` template that it finds. In other words, if the template you're calling resides in a subfolder on the root and there is no `Application.cfm` template in that folder, it will search up to root. If, however, there is an `Application.cfm` template in the subfolder, then the code from that one will be included and any `Application.cfm` template found in any parent directories will be ignored.

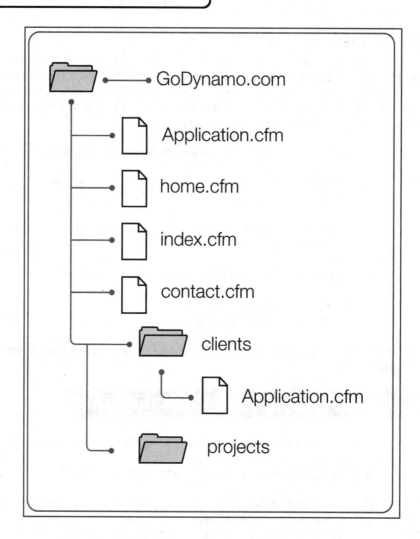

With a file structure set up as in this diagram, CFML templates stored in the clients directory would include only the Application.cfm within clients, while templates in the projects directory would include the Application.cfm in the goDynamo.com web root - as would templates stored in the root directory.

- The code found in Application.cfm is included just as if you had manually inserted a <cfinclude> at the top of each of your individual.cfm templates.

1. Open a new template in Studio, and build this code:

    ```
    <!-- Application.cfm -->
    <!-- use this template to define default
    ➥variables and dsn's -->
    <!-- set the datsource name here -->

    <cfset datasource="board">

    <!-- set a default page title -->

    <cfset title="ColdFusion for Flash Forum">

    <!-- Leave a welcome message -->

    <h2>Welcome to our ColdFusion for Flash
    ➥Forum!</h2>
    <br>
    ```

    The first `<cfset>` statement sets our `datasource` name. This `datasource` variable will be available to all templates using this particular `Application.cfm`.

    The second statement sets a variable called `title`, which we'll use to add a page title to each individual page. The last part of the template adds a welcome message to the top of each page.

2. Save this file as `Application.cfm` on the root of your web server without making changes to any other template.

3. Open up your . in the browser, after choosing the number of posts – it should now look like this:

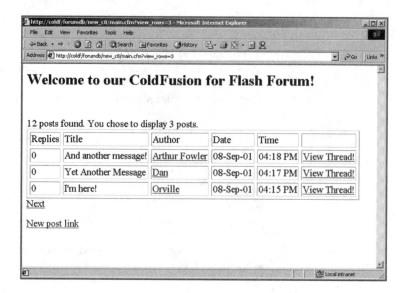

At the top of our page, we see the message that we added at the bottom of our
Application.cfm template. If we click on Next or choose to view one of the
threads, we'll see that the message remains there at the top of the page:

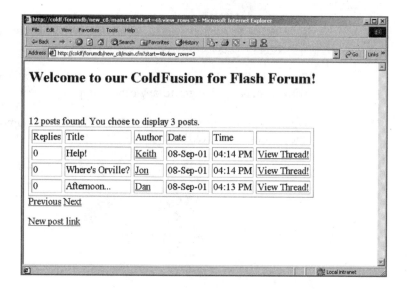

Working with Application.cfm variables

The first variable that we set – the `datasource` variable – is also available for us to use in any of our ColdFusion templates. Why is this useful? Well, let's imagine that our data source for the message board had to change. To implement this without the Web Application Framework, we would have to open up each of one of our templates and manually change each individual reference to the current datasource name, `board`. If, however, we used the Web Application Framework properly, we could simply change the `data source` variable in our `Application.cfm` template and the changes would be made globally.

In order to use the `datasource` variable in our templates, we will have to make certain changes to our templates. Look at the following `<cfquery>` as an example:

```
<!-- query to get current posts for the current
➡forum -->

<cfquery name="current_posts" datasource="board"
➡dbtype="ODBC">
SELECT
*
FROM posts
ORDER BY post_id DESC
</cfquery>
```

We would need to change this (and all the other templates in our application that make reference the datasource) to the following under our Application framework:

```
<!-- query to get current posts for the current
➡forum -->

<cfquery name="current_posts"
➡datasource="#datasource#" dbtype="ODBC">
SELECT
*
FROM posts
ORDER BY post_id DESC
</cfquery>
```

The only thing that changes is the `datasource` argument. Instead of providing each `<cfquery>` with the actual datasource name, our `Application.cfm` template takes care of this for us. To alter all of the queries at this late stage would be very time consuming. For best practice though, you should use these types of variables from the start.

Finally, we'll look at how we can use our `title` variable that we also defined in the `Application.cfm` template.

4. We will need to add the following code to all of our templates, go and do this now.

```
<!-- include the default page title here -->
<cfoutput>
<title>#title#</title>
</cfoutput>
```

What is the advantage of defining page titles or data source names this way? Well, imagine that your application grows from just a few templates to many, many templates. Changing the page titles or datasources in 30 or 40 templates can be time consuming and tedious. With the Web Application Framework however, changes can be made quickly and easily. The browser tile bar now shows the same information regardless of which template we're viewing.

ColdFusion for Flash Forum - Microsoft Internet Explorer

This is an excellent example of how we can control the look and feel of our application with the framework. The Application.cfm template works great for inserting code right before the beginning of each template, but the Web Application Framework would not be complete without the ability to include code at the bottom across the entire scope of our application. The ability to do so would further enhance our control over the look and feel of our applications. Enter the OnRequestEnd.cfm template.

At the end - OnRequestEnd.cfm

The OnRequestEnd.cfm is a separate template that can be used to add application-wide data to the bottom of our templates. For instance, if we wanted to include a copyright notice and a web site link at the bottom of each of our pages, we could quickly accomplish this with OnRequestEnd.cfm.

Using OnRequestEnd.cfm

This is just what we'll do.

1. Open a new template in Studio and add the following code:

    ```
    <!-- OnRequestEnd.cfm -->
    <!-- insert a horizontal line and a copyright
    ➥notice -->

    <hr>
    <div align="center">copyright <a
    ➥href="http://www.friendsofed.com"
    ➥target="_blank">friends of ED</a> 2001</div>
    ```

This code inserts a horizontal bar at the bottom of each page with a copyright notice and a link to a web site. Each of our templates will now have this information that can quickly be updated.

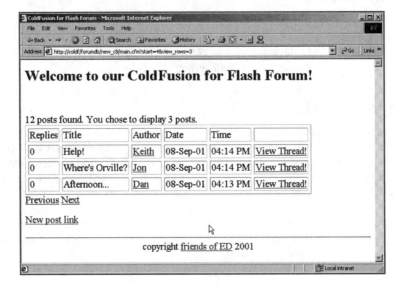

Another common use for the `Application.cfm` template is to define an application, which allows control of persistent variables.

Defining an application with Application.cfm

ColdFusion allow us to create three types of variables that can be maintained separately for each visitor: cookies, client variables and session variables.

Cookies

Cookies are used to store simple data on a client's machine. They are often used to remember things like preferences, names, or e-mail addresses. Cookies can only be used to store simple values (like strings) and have a very limited storage capacity. Furthermore, cookies carry a negative connotation with many web users and can be easily turned off at the browser level.

Cookies are not native to ColdFusion, developers using other languages can use them - it's up to you whether you decide this is an advantage. Finally, cookies can expire at the end of a user's session, or they can persist indefinitely (or at least until the user deletes them from memory).

Client variables

Client variables are similar to cookies, except that the information is stored in a datasource on the server and not on the client's machine. Client variables can persist for long periods of time and they have a much larger storage capacity than cookies. On the down side, client variables can also only hold simple values.

Session variables

Session variables are also stored on the server – but this time in the server's RAM so they do not persist if the server restarts. As such, they are designed with temporary data in mind (shopping cart information is a great example). Session variables can be used to store simple **and** complex data types (structures, arrays etc.) and can also be used without setting cookies (although, once again, a bit more work is required for the developer).

You define an application in ColdFusion using the `<cfapplication>` tag. This tag is generally used to enable certain types of persistent variables that will be available to all the templates in our application.

The syntax for the tag is as follows:

```
<CFAPPLICATION NAME="Name"
    CLIENTMANAGEMENT="Yes/No"
    CLIENTSTORAGE="Storage Type"
    SETCLIENTCOOKIES="Yes/No"
    SESSIONMANAGEMENT="Yes/No"
    SESSIONTIMEOUT=#CreateTimeSpan(days, hours,
➥minutes, seconds)#
    APPLICATIONTIMEOUT=#CreateTimeSpan(days,
➥hours, minutes, seconds)#
    SETDOMAINCOOKIES="Yes/No"
>
```

Let's now look at how the arguments are important to us:

- **Name** – this is where we provide a name for our application. The name can be anything you choose and can be no longer than 64 characters long. You should choose a unique name for each application. This argument is required.

- **ClientManagement** – if yes is selected for this argument, Client Management is enabled. The default for this argument is no.

- **ClientStorage** – if Client Management is enabled, this option allows us to select where we would like to store our client variables. The default option for this argument is the server's registry. The other options that we have are to store the variables in a cookie or in a special database that we set up using the Administrator. If we choose to use the database option, we must provide it's datasource name here.

- **SetClientCookies** – the default value here is yes. When client variables are enabled, ColdFusion automatically creates two cookies (cfid and cftoken), which are used to properly track client variables for each browser. If no is selected, these values, cfid and cftoken, will need to be passed in the URL from template to template in our application.

- **SessionManagement** – the default here is no. Selecting yes will enable the use of session variables.

- **SessionTimeOut** – this argument is optional and it allows us to use the CreateTimeSpan function to specify the number of days, hours, mins, secs that our session variables will persist. If no argument is provided here, the default value you have set in the Administrator will be used.

Let's us look at the Client Variables page in ColdFusion administrator.

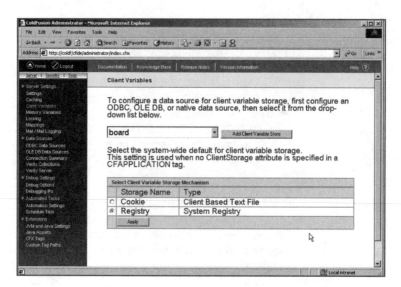

The first thing that to notice is the Client Variable Storage option. With this, we can select a registered DSN and set it up to store our client variables. If you choose to save client variables in a datasource, ColdFusion will automatically create two new tables in the database that you select: cdata and cglobal. The next option allows us to specify where our client variables will be stored by default. Don't alter this, as in our example we'll store them in the server's registry.

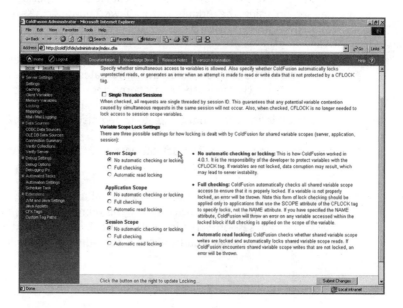

Let's move on to the Memory Variables page. This is where we can set most of the default values for our persistent variables. We set our default timeout values for application and session variables. The default timeout value will be used if we do not specify a timeout in the <cfapplication> tag. The maximum timeout value will be used instead of the value specified in the <cfapplication> tag if its value is larger than the maximum value listed here.

We will now go through an example of each of these variables. We are going to use them to remember the name and e-mail addresses of user's visiting our forum application.

Cookies in the forum

The first variable type that we will look at will be cookies.

1. To begin, we are going to change our Application.cfm template to look like this:

```
<!-- Application.cfm -->

<!-- use this template to define default
➡variables and dsn's -->

<!-- set the datasource name here -->

<cfset datasource="board">

<!-- set up the default values for our cookies --
➡>

<cfparam name="COOKIE.name" default="">
<cfparam name="COOKIE.email" default="">

<!-- set a default page title -->

<cfset title="ColdFusion for Flash Forum">

<!-- Leave a welcome message -->

<h2>Welcome to our ColdFusion for Flash
➡Forum!</h2>
```

You'll notice that we added two <cfparam> tags to set up default values for our two cookies, name and email. We will be using these cookies to remember a user's name and e-mail address that they use in posts and replies.

2. Now, we are going to have to change our new_post.cfm template to include these cookies.

Open it up in Studio and make the following changes:

...

```
<!-- insert a new post into the current question -->


   <p><b>ColdFusion for Flash board</b></p>
   <p>Start a new thread here!</p>
   <cfoutput>
   <cfform action="insert_post.cfm"method="POST"
➥enctype="multipart/form-data">
    <table width="50%" border="1" cellspacing="2" cellpadding="2">
    <tr>
   <td width="16%">Name:</td>
   <td width="84%">
      <cfinput type="Text" name="author_name" value="#COOKIE.name#"
➥message="An Author's Name is required" required="Yes">
    </td>
   </tr>
   <tr>
   <td width="16%">e-mail:</td>
   <td width="84%">
      <cfinput type="text" name="author_email" value="#COOKIE.email#"
➥message="An Email Address is required" required="Yes">
    </td>
   </tr>
   <tr>
   <td width="16%">Title:</td>
   <td width="84%">
    <cfinput type="text" name="title" message="A Title for the post is
➥required" required="Yes">
    </td>
   </tr>
   <tr>
   <td colspan="2">
    <div align="center">Post:<br>
   <textarea name="post" wrap="VIRTUAL" cols="70" rows="10"></textarea>
    </div>
   </td>
   </tr>
   <tr>
   <td colspan="2">
    <div align="center">
```

```
      <input type="submit" value="Submit">
      <input type="reset" value="Reset">
    </div>
   </td>
  </tr>
 </table>
<input type="hidden" name="no_replies" value="0">
<input type="hidden" name="date_post" value="#DateFormat(Now())#">
<input type="hidden" name="time_post" value="#CreateODBCTime(Now())#">

</cfform>
</cfoutput>
```

Once again, we did not have to change much with this template. Firstly you'll notice that the entire <cfform> is contained within <cfoutput> tags. This is so that we can properly reference our two cookies. Next, we changed our <cfinput> tags for author_name and author_email to the following:

```
<cfinput type="Text" name="author_name"
➥value="#COOKIE.name#" message="An Author's Name
➥is required" required="Yes">

<cfinput type="text" name="author_email"
➥value="#COOKIE.email#" message="An Email
➥Address is required" required="Yes">
```

If this is a user's first time using the new_post.cfm template, the values for our cookies will be blank (as defined in our Application.cfm template). We now need to modify our insert_post.cfm template to update these cookies whenever a user submits the form.

3. To accomplish this, we will make the following changes to our insert_post.cfm template. Open it up and below the <cfinsert> statement, type the following code:

```
...
<!-- insert the new post into the db -->

<cfinsert datasource="board" tablename="posts"
➥dbtype="ODBC">

<!-- reset the COOKIE values for the name and
➥email address -->
<cfoutput>
<cfset COOKIE.name=#form.author_name#>
<cfset COOKIE.email=#form.author_email#>
</cfoutput>
<!-- tell the user that their post has been
➥accepted -->
  Thank you, your post has been inserted.
<cfoutput>
<a href="main.cfm">back to main</a>
</p>
</cfoutput>
```

At the bottom of our code listing, we update the value of the cookies for the author's name and e-mail address with the values that were submitted in the form. Now, when a user creates a new thread, their cookies will be updated. The next time that they click on the new post link, the author and e-mail fields will automatically fill out for them.

For example, if I create a new post like the following:

And submit it, the next time that I click on the new post link, the name and e-mail fields are automatically filled out.

To take our example one step further, we are also going to make changes to our reply templates to make sure that the information is automatically filled out there as well.

4. The `new_reply.cfm` template has to be altered in the same manner as `new_post.cfm` was:

```
<!-- insert the post -->
  <cfoutput query="get_post">
    <td colspan="2"><b>Post: </b>#post#<br>
    <b>Author:</b> #author_name#
    </td>
    </cfoutput>
    <cfoutput>
    </tr>
  <tr>
    <td width="16%">Name:</td><td width="84%">
      <cfinput type="text" name="reply_name"
➥value="#COOKIE.name#" message="Your Name is
```

```
➥required" required="Yes">
   </td></tr>
  <tr>
   <td width="16%">e-mail:</td><td width="84%">
    <cfinput type="text" name="reply_email"
➥value="#COOKIE.email#" message="An Email
➥Address is required" required="Yes">
   </td></tr>
  <tr>
   <td width="16%">Title:</td>
   <td width="84%">
    <cfinput type="text" name="reply_title"
➥message="A Title for your reply is required"
➥required="Yes">
   </td>
  </tr>
  <tr>
   <td colspan="2">
    <div align="center">Reply:<br>
     <textarea name="reply" wrap="VIRTUAL"
➥cols="50"></textarea>
    </div></td></tr>
  <tr>
   <td colspan="2">
    <div align="center">
            <input type="hidden" name="post_id"
➥value="#post_id#">
               <input type="hidden"
➥name="date_reply" value="#DateFormat(Now())#">
               <input type="hidden"
➥name="time_reply"
➥value="#CreateODBCTime(Now())#">

    <input type="submit" value="Submit">
    <input type="reset" value="Reset">
   </div></td></tr>
    </cfoutput>
  </table>
</cfform>
```

*Beware when adding the <cfoutput> tags around your form that you
don't nest any other <cfoutput> tags - ColdFusion will not allow this.
You may need to delete those already around the ##ed variables.*

This way, if the author has recently started a new post and now wants to reply to some other threads, he will not need to fill out his name or email address. On the other hand, if the user goes directly to the new_reply.cfm template without submitting a new post, these fields will be blank. If the user posts a reply and then a new post his information will not appear.

5. In order to set the same cookies if the user fills out a reply, we will need to change our insert_reply.cfm template to contain `<cfset>` tags to set the cookies :

```
<!-- insert_reply.cfm -->
...

<!-- insert the new reply into the db -->

<cfinsert datasource="board" tablename="replies"
➥dbtype="ODBC">

<!-- update the number of replies in the posts
➥table -->
<cfquery name="get_replies" datasource="board"
➥dbtype="ODBC">
SELECT
COUNT(reply_id) AS no_replies
FROM
replies
WHERE post_id = #post_id#
</cfquery>
<cfoutput query="get_replies">
<cfquery datasource="board" dbtype="ODBC">
UPDATE posts
SET no_replies = '#no_replies#'
WHERE post_id = #post_id#
</cfquery>
</cfoutput>

<!-- reset the cookie values for the name and
➥email address -->
<cfoutput>
<cfset COOKIE.name=#form.reply_name#>
<cfset COOKIE.email=#form.reply_email#>
</cfoutput>

<!-- send user back to thread -->
```

```
<cfoutput>
<cflocation
➥url="view_thread.cfm?post_id=#post_id#"
➥addtoken="No">
</cfoutput>
```

This way, whether the user fills out a post or a reply, their coordinates get saved in the cookies and the author only has to fill out the information once.

If we were to close our browser, re-open it and click on the new post link, we'd see that our information has been lost - go and try this out. If we wanted those variables to persist, we could set our cookies with the <cfcookie> tag – which will give us even more flexibility.

Don't you forget about me - <cfcookie>

The <cfcookie> tag allows us to add the optional argument expires. The argument can be set three ways:

- NOW - which would essentially delete the cookie

- NEVER – which sets the expiration date way into the future so that the cookie essentially never expires

- MM/DD/YY – we could also provide a certain date value where the cookie would expire.

Armed with this new information, we can change our <cfset> statements to the corresponding <cfcookie> statements:

6. Open insert_post.cfm and change the <cfset> statements:

```
<cfoutput>
<cfcookie name="name" value="#form.author_name#"
➥expires="NEVER">
<cfcookie name="email" value="#form.author_email#"
➥expires="NEVER">
</cfoutput>
```

7. We do have to change insert_reply.cfm as well:

```
<cfoutput>
<cfcookie COOKIE.name=#form.author_name#
➥expires="NEVER">
<cfcookie COOKIE.email=#form.author_email#
➥expires="NEVER">
</cfoutput>
```

By setting the expires argument to NEVER, we can now close our browser, re-open it and our values have persisted (provided that we enter at least one post or reply).

If the user's browser has cookies disabled, the code as it stands will not work,

Client Variables in the forum

Client variables work in very much the same way as cookies do, the main difference being that client variables are stored on the server.

The first thing that we need to do before using client variables in our example is to enable Client Management in our Application.cfm template. If we try to set client variables without first enabling Client management, we will get an error.

1. Add this code to our Application.cfm template - so it now looks like this:

```
<!-- Application.cfm -->

<!-- use this template to define default
➥variables and dsn's -->

<!-- set the datsource name here -->

<cfset datasource="board">

<!-- enable Client Management -->

<cfapplication name="forum" clientmanagement="Yes"
➥Âsetclientcookies="Yes">
```

In this code listing, we see the <cfapplication> tag. The name of our application is forum and we have enabled client variables.

2. Now we will change all of our COOKIE prefixes to CLIENT prefixes.

```
<!-- set up the default values for our client
➥variables -->

<cfparam name="CLIENT.name" default="">
<cfparam name="CLIENT.email" default="">

<!-- set a default page title -->

<cfset title="ColdFusion for Flash Forum">

<!-- Leave a welcome message -->

<h2>Welcome to our ColdFusion for Flash
➥Forum!</h2>
```

3. We now have to go ahead and change the prefixes in our other templates. Our insert_post.cfm template will now have the following code at the bottom to handle the variables:

```
<!-- reset the client values for the name and
➥email address -->
<cfoutput>
<cfset CLIENT.name=#form.author_name#>
<cfset CLIENT.email=#form.author_email#>
</cfoutput>
```

Note how client variables use <cfset> and cannot take the expires attribute.

4.   In new_post.cfm all that needs to be altered is the word COOKIE replaced by the word CLIENT.

```
<cfinput type="Text" name="author_name"
➥value="#CLIENT.name#" message="An Author's Name
➥is required" required="Yes">
  </td>
  </tr>
  <tr>
  <td width="16%">e-mail:</td>
  <td width="84%">
    <cfinput type="text" name="author_email"
➥value="#CLIENT.email#" message="An Email Address
➥is required" required="Yes">
```

5.   We must also be sure to replace the COOKIE prefixes in the other two templates (new_reply.cfm and insert_reply.cfm) in the same way. Go and do this now.

Now, if we create either a new post or a new reply, the client variables (name and email) are saved on the server. These variables are therefore available if you close your browser and re-open it – much like our cookies but they'll never expire.

Session variables in the forum

Session variables are the last variable type that we will look at. Like client variables, session variables also reside on the server – but they only persist for a user's session (the length of the session can be defined in the <cfapplication> tag or in the Administrator).

Sessions also differ from cookies and client variables in that they can be used to store complex data like structures and arrays. ColdFusion uses the same CFID and CFTOKEN cookies to track session variables whenever session management has been enabled.

1. To enable session variables, we need to change the code in our
    `Application.cfm` template to the following:

    ```
    <!-- Application.cfm -->

    <!-- use this template to define default
    ➡variables and dsn's -->

    <!-- set the datsource name here -->

    <cfset datasource="board">

    <!-- enable SESSION Management -->

    <cfapplication name="forum"
    ➡sessionmanagement="Yes" ➡setclientcookies="Yes">

    <!-- set up the default values for our SESSION
    ➡variables -->

    <cfparam name="SESSION.name" default="">
    <cfparam name="SESSION.email" default="">

    <!-- set a default page title -->

    <cfset title="ColdFusion for Flash Forum">

    <!-- Leave a welcome message -->

    <h2>Welcome to our ColdFusion for Flash
    ➡Forum!</h2>
    ```

    This time, we chose to enable session management. We then went
    ahead and changed the CLIENT prefixes in the <cfparam> tags to
    SESSION. We must also change all other all CLIENT prefixes to SESSION
    in the rest of our templates.

2. Change the appropriate part of insert_post.cfm:

```
...
<!--- reset the SESSION values for the name and
➡email address --->
<cfoutput>
<cfset SESSION.name=#form.author_name#>
<cfset SESSION.email=#form.author_email#>
</cfoutput>
...
```

3. And insert_reply.cfm:

```
...
<!--- reset the SESSION values for the name and
➡email address --->
<cfoutput>
<cfset SESSION.name=#form.reply_name#>
<cfset SESSION.email=#form.reply_email#>
</cfoutput>
...
```

4. And new_post.cfm:

```
...
<cfinput type="Text" name="author_name"
➡value="#SESSION.name#" message="An Author's Name
➡is required" required="Yes">
   </td>
  </tr>
  <tr>
   <td width="16%">e-mail:</td>
   <td width="84%">
     <cfinput type="text" name="author_email"
➡value="#SESSION.email#" message="An Email
➡Address is required" required="Yes">
   </td>
```

...

5. And finally new_reply.cfm:

```
...
<td width="16%">Name:</td><td width="84%">
  <cfinput type="text" name="reply_name"
➥value="#SESSION.name#" message="Your Name is
➥required" required="Yes">
  </td></tr>
<tr>
  <td width="16%">e-mail:</td><td width="84%">
    <cfinput type="text" name="reply_email"
➥value="#SESSION.email#" message="An Email
➥Address is required" required="Yes">
  </td></tr>
...
```

If you load up the main.cfm template and insert a new post or new reply, the next time that you go to do so, your name and e-mail address have been remembered for you. Also, since our default timeout period is set to 20 minutes, we can even close our browser and re-open it within 20 minutes and the information will still be there. It can be difficult to see this in operation without actually trying it twenty minutes apart - how about reading through the rest of the chapter then going back to check?

If we want to set up our own timeout number that is less or more than the default one, we can use the sessiontimeout argument in our <cfapplication> tag. Security conscious applications, online banking for example, often have shorter logon sessions allowed.

For example, if we wanted our session variables to expire after 5 minutes of inactivity, we could change our <cfapplication> tag to the following:

```
<cfapplication name="forum"
➥sessionmanagement="Yes" setclientcookies="No"
➥sessiontimeout="#CreateTimeSpan(0,0,5,0)#">
```

The sessiontimeout argument looks for a ColdFusion time span value to indicate the number of days, hours, minutes and seconds. You create this value using the CreateTimeSpan function.

Locking Variables

These client and session persistent variables we have been using are considered **Shared Scope Variables**. They are so named because they are stored in the ColdFusion server's RAM and it is shared by all of the threads used by ColdFusion Server to run requests. ColdFusion is a multithreaded application – it can process multiple page requests at the same time.

These multiple requests can come from different users or the same user. Web pages with multiple frames, a user clicking the reload button several times in succession or a user working with multiple browser windows can cause these multiple requests. Each one of these threads will be competing to access (either reading or writing) the same variables at the same time. This competition often leads to memory corruption – and this can make the ColdFusion server unstable – at times requiring a restart.

> *Locking these variables alleviates this problem by only allowing one thread to access the shared scope variable at a time, with the other requests waiting in line.*

The <cflock> tag can be implemented as *exclusive* or as *read-only*. Exclusive is used when we need to write to a session variable and excludes all other threads access to that variable until the request has been fulfilled. If another template is being accessed at the same time, it will stop when it reaches the <cflock> tag and will only start again once the variable has been released – and the requests that have been waiting in line will have access to the session variables on a first come first served basis.

Read-only locks will allow multiple threads to access the session variables at the same time – but they will be unable to write to the variable. Furthermore, an exclusive lock cannot be achieved while another thread is reading from the variable.

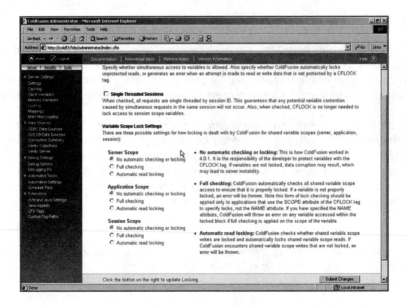

Memory corruption is much less likely to occur when we are using session variables and if we don't want to have to include <cflock> tags around all of our session variables, it is a good idea to enable the Single-Threaded Sessions option in the ColdFusion Administrator. Enabling this option eliminates the need to use <cflock> when reading and writing to session variables as it forces individual browser sessions to use only one thread at a time,

Enabling this option and making sure that no there is no checking or automatic locking on the session scope will ensure the proper functioning of your board application with session variables.

Summary

In conclusion, we saw that the three variable types worked pretty much the same way in our examples. Which one should you choose then? It all depends. Cookies are often the easiest to implement, work well with other programming languages and can persist between sessions, but users can turn cookies off. Client variables (as well as session variables) can be used even if cookies have been disabled, and also can persist between sessions. On the other hand, client variables cannot be used to store complex data like arrays or structures (unless you use WDDX which is beyond the scope of this chapter). Finally, session variables can easily handle complex data types, but sessions generally do not persist very long. Also, session variables need to be locked to prevent problems with the server.

What you will probably find is that as your applications become increasing complex, you'll have to use a combination of all of these variable types to achieve the desired results. For example, in a storefront application, client variables could be used to remember clientID's and other information that is likely to persist across many sessions, while session variables could store shopping cart information in arrays for individual sessions!

We've spent most of this chapter adding new posts to our forum, gathering e-mail addresses as we went, but rather than simply redisplaying them for other users to click on wouldn't it be useful to use them with CFML? To allow our application to send e-mails? Well that's exactly what we'll do in the next chapter.

9 E-mail with ColdFusion

What we'll cover in this chapter

- *How to send e-mail with ColdFusion.*

- *We will look at the tags necessary to accomplish this,*

- *Work with some examples*

- *And conclude with an example that sends e-mail from a Flash movie*

E-mail is often an important component of a web application, whether it's a basic auto-reply application that confirms that you've posted comments to a forum, or a shopping cart application that will log the types of purchases you are making and keep you updated, vie e-mail when similar products become available.

ColdFusion Administrator e-mail setup

Before we can begin sending e-mail through a ColdFusion application ColdFusion Server 5 will need to be configured, to do this, we need to configure our ColdFusion. At the end of this short exercise any mails sent via the ColdFusion server will be managed by the settings entered below. If accessing the server via a network make sure that your systems administrator has given you sufficient access rights.

1. Open up your ColdFusion Administrator in a browser

2. Click on the Mail/Mail Logging link under the Server Settings header, this will bring up the mail server connection settings screen below:

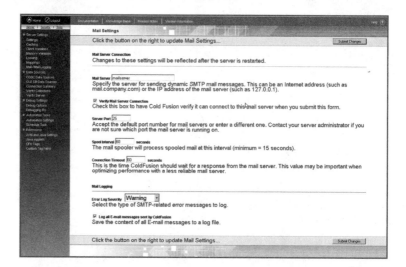

3. In the Mail Server box, you need to provide ColdFusion with a valid e-mail server (either the servers name or its IP address). For testing purposes, you could set this value to the one that you specify as your SMTP server in your normal e-mail program. If you are still having trouble obtaining this information, contact your ISP or network administrator.

4. The next setting is for the Server Port. This value will probably already be set to 25 (the default port used for the mail server) and you should only change this value if you know that your server operates on a different port, again check with your ISP or network administrator if in doubt

5. The Spool Interval option allows you to control how often ColdFusion spools e-mail to the mail server. The default value is 60 seconds, which is a reasonable interval. If, however, you expected a high volume of mail to pass through the ColdFusion application it would be sensible to reduce the spool interval to avoid a build up of unsent mail.

6. Connection timeout is used to specify how long the ColdFusion server should try and connect to the mail server. If the server doesn't respond in the indicated time, ColdFusion will display an error.

7. Once you have set up all the variables, click verify and if ColdFusion connects properly, you'll see the following screen:

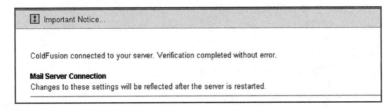

If you get this screen...

..... it may be for one of these reasons:

- No network connection exists

- The TCP/IP protocol isn't installed on the ColdFusion Server PC

- The spelling of the mail server name is incorrect

- The IP address, if used, is wrong

- The ColdFusion Server PC has insufficient access right to the mail server

These are our default mail settings and, as you will see later on, we can overwrite these settings with our <cfmail> tag. For instance, if you want to send a message using a different mail server, you could specify that in the tag.

Now that our server is properly set up, we are going to look at the <cfmail> tag and how it is used to send simple messages.

Using the <cfmail> tag

The <cfmail> tag makes it easy to send e-mail from within your ColdFusion templates. <cfmail> needs only three attributes, to, from and subject, to send your message. Furthermore, you are free to use any ColdFusion variables and functions between the <cfmail> tags (with # signs of course, but with no <cfoutput> blocks – they are not necessary).

Here is the complete syntax for the tag:

```
<cfmail TO="recipient"
    FROM="sender"
    CC="copy_to"
    BCC="blind_copy_to"
    SUBJECT="msg_subject"
    TYPE="msg_type"
    MAXROWS="max_msgs"
    MIMEATTACH="path"
    QUERY="query_name"
    GROUP="query_column"
    GROUPCASESENSITIVE="yes/no"
    STARTROW="query_row"
    SERVER="servername"
    PORT="port_ID"
    MAILERID="headerid"
    TIMEOUT="seconds">
</cfmail>
```

We will be using the following attributes in our examples:

To: the To field is a required field and must contain an e-mail address. You can manually enter the e-mail address, myname@mailserver.com or multiple e-mail addresses separated by commas (with no spaces). You can also dynamically assign the e-mail address with a variable that contains the address info (**#FORM.author_email#** for example). Finally, you could use the name of a column returned in a query that contains the e-mail address. In the last case, a message will be sent to each record that is returned in the query.

From: the `From` field is also required and must contain the sender's e-mail address. Once again, this could be a static value like `info@goDynamo.com` or a dynamic variable that contains the address information.

CC: the `CC` (carbon copy) field is an optional field where additional e-mail addresses can be specified. These addresses will receive a copy of the e-mail sent.

BCC: the `BCC` field is also optional and is identical in every way to the `CC` field except that additional recipients are not listed in the message header.

Subject: the `Subject` field is the only other required field. This is the subject of the e-mail and can be either static or dynamic (such as **#FORM.subject#**).

Type: the `type` field allows you to indicate whether the e-mail will be sent with HTML formatting or as plain text. E-mails with HTML formatting can include hyperlinks, fonts, images etc. If however, the recipient can't display HTML e-mails, the message won't display properly. The default format is plain text.

Maxrows: the `maxrows` attribute can be used when you are using a `<cfquery>` in conjunction with `<cfmail>` and it allows you to specify how many messages to send. It works the same way that the `maxrows` attribute works with `<cfoutput>`

Query: this optional field allows you to specify the name of a `<cfquery>` from which you want to include data from in your `<cfmail>` tag. You can use this option to send messages to multiple recipients found in the query or to send results of the query to a single recipient.

Group: this optional field works the same way as the **GROUP** attribute, in allowing us to specify a column to group on, and only send one message. For example, if we wanted to send an e-mail to every person who had ever started a post on our message board, we would want to **GROUP** using the `author_email` field. This way, if a user had started many posts and their e-mail address appears numerous times in the database, they would only get the e-mail once. Without specifying the **GROUP** attribute, the user would receive an e-mail for each post he had made.

GroupCaseSensitive: a Boolean attribute that indicates whether the **GROUP** attribute should be case sensitive when grouping the output results. The default value is **Yes**

The server, port and timeout attributes allow us to overwrite the default options that we set up earlier in ColdFusion Administrator.

CFMAIL in action

Everyone loves getting mail! So, let's start by setting up a template that does just that, sends us an e-mail!

Type the code below into ColdFusion Studio or another text editor and save it in a folder in the c:\intepub\wwwroot directory, on the web as email_me.cfm

```
<!doctype HTML PUBLIC "-//W3C//DTD HTML 4.0
➥Transitional//EN">
<html>
<head>
    <title>
        Untitled
    </title>
</head>
    <body>    <!-- email_me.cfm -->

        <!-- ColdFusion template that will send us an e-
➥mail -->

        <!-- insert the cfmail tag here -->
        <cfmail to="keiths@friendsofed.com"
➥from="reader@friendsofed.com" subject="I'm sending myself
➥an e-mail">
                I am sending myself an e-mail
        This will be a plain text e-mail

        </cfmail>
        <!-- insert a message to confirm that our message
➥has been sent -->

    Success, you should get your email shortly
    </body>
</html
```

If you call the **email_me.cfm** template you will see the success message as displayed below, if your template is processed properly.

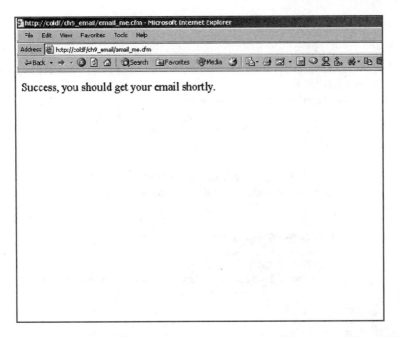

The message that we are sending ourselves is contained within the `<cfmail>` tags. The first message that we send ourselves is plain text so the white space that we include (i.e. the line break in this case) is preserved when we receive the e-mail.

The e-mail arrived like this:

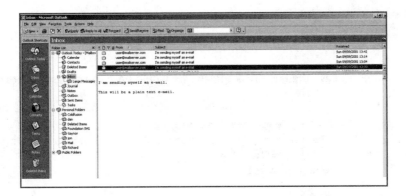

Now, if we were to change the `<cfmail>` tag to the following:

```
<cfmail to="reader@mailserver.com"
➥from="sender@mailserver.com" subject="I'm sending myself an
➥e-mail" type="html">
I am sending myself an e-mail.

This will be a HTML email.
</cfmail>
```

We have now added the **type** attribute to the tag, and have indicated that this will be HTML e-mail. With HTML formatting, the white space is stripped out and the e-mail arrives like this:

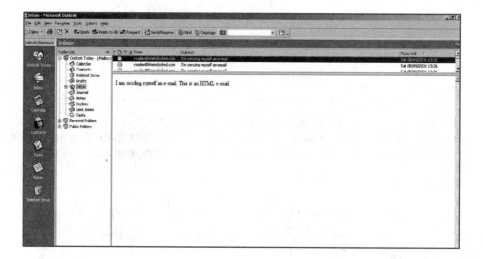

If we wanted to have the line break remain, we would have to change our `<cfmail>` tag once again:

```
<cfmail to="reader@mailserver.com"
➥from="sender@mailserver.com" subject="I'm sending myself an
➥e-mail" type="html">
I am sending myself an e-mail.
<br>
This will be an HTML e-mail with a line break.
</cfmail>
```

This time, we have inserted a `<br>` tag for the line break. With HTML formatting, you could also include links, tables, pictures and other elements to your e-mail. This is especially helpful when formatting is a major issue.

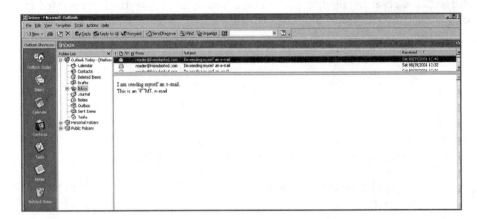

In the preceding example we used static variables in the `<cfmail>` tag. What if we wanted to assign these variables dynamically? Let's say for example that we wanted to send each user in the forum an e-mail when they start a new thread.

The **new_post.cfm** template that we set up earlier had the following input fields:

- `author_name`
- `author_email`
- `post`
- `title`

We could use the `author_email` field for our To attribute in `<cfmail>` and we could use the author and post fields in the actual body of the e-mail.

To accomplish this, we will need to modify our `insert_post.cfm` template. That template already validates for a proper e-mail address, so using `<cfmail>` is a logical extension.

When using dynamic variables with `<cfmail>`, we don't need to use the `<cfmail>` blocks. Any variables located between the `<cfmail> ></cfmail>` tag is treated as if they were between `<cfoutput>` tags.

`<cfmail>` is great for sending personalized e-mails to recipients. If we wanted to send each user that starts a new thread an e-mail, we could use the code in this listing:

```
<!-- insert_post.cfm -->
<!-- include the default page title here -->
  <cfoutput>
      <title>
          #title#
      </title>
  </cfoutput>
  <!-- check to make sure that the post field is not blank
➥-->
  <cfif Len(Trim(post)) IS 0> Please be sure to fill out
➥the post text.
      <cfabort>
  </cfif>
  <!-- check to make sure that the email address is valid -
➥-->
  <cfif TRIM(Len(author_email)) LT 1
OR ListLen(author_email, "@") NEQ 2
OR ListLen(author_email, ".") LTE 1
OR LEN(ListLast(author_email, ".")) LT 2>  Please be sure to
➥provide a valid email address.
      <cfabort>
  </cfif>
  <!-- insert the new post into the db -->
    <cfinsert datasource="board" tablename="posts"
➥dbtype="ODBC">
<!-- reset the COOKIE values for the name and email address
➥-->
  <cfoutput>
              <cfset SESSION.name=#form.author_name#>
        <cfset SESSION.email=#form.author_email#>
  </cfoutput>
  <cfmail to="#FORM.author_email#" from="forum@goDynamo.com"
➥subject="Your recent post">
        Hello #FORM.author_name#,

        you recently posted the following on our message
➥board:

        #FORM.post#
```

```
</cfmail>
<!--- tell the user that their post has been accepted --->
 Thank you, your post has been inserted.
<cfoutput>
<a href="main.cfm">
back to main
</a></p>
</cfoutput>
```

The first part of the insert_post.cfm template is exactly the same as what we saw before. But, after the <cfinsert> statement, we have added the following <cfmail> tag:

```
<cfmail to="#FORM.author_email#" from="sender@mailserver.com
➥" subject="Your recent post">
Hello #FORM.author_name#,

you recently posted the following on our message board:

#FORM.post#
</cfmail>
```

This tag sends an e-mail, in plain-text form, to the author of the post.
In the body of the message, we address the author by name (or the name that he/she entered in the form) and we allow the author to see exactly what they posted.

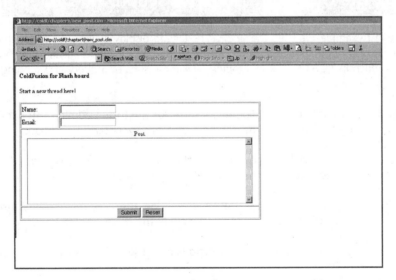

Try it out for yourself, and you should get something similar to this:

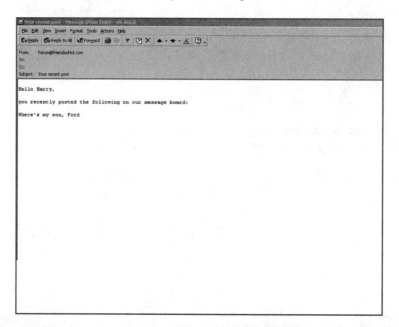

Using the QUERY attribute to send Data-Driven mail

In the last example, we used the <cfmail> tags to display dynamic variables that we would normally display using <cfoutput> tags. In this example we will again show how <cfmail> is very much like CFOUTPUT, by looping over the results of a query and sending multiple e-mails.

To illustrate this, we are going to build a form for the forum administrator that will allow him to e-mail each person in the database who has ever started a thread.

1. We will start by building the email_form.cfm template. We will need to include three form fields in the template.

sender_email: this field will be used as the From attribute in the <cfmail> tag and should include the sender's email address

email_subject: this field will be used in the Subject attribute

email_body: this text area field will be included between the <cfmail> tags and will appear as the body of the message.

2. Here is the code listing for email_form.cfm:

```
<!-- email_form.cfm -->

<!-- form that will allow forum administrator to email list
➡of thread starters -->
<form action="send_email.cfm" method="post">
  <table>
    <tr>
      <td colspan="2"><b>Use this form to email all thread
➡starters in the Database:</b></td>
    </tr>
    <tr>
      <td>Please specify the sender's email address:</td>
      <td>
        <input type="text" name="sender_email" size="30">
      </td>
    </tr>
    <tr>
      <td>Please enter the subject:</td>
      <td>
        <input type="text" name="email_subject" size="30">
      </td>
    </tr>
    <tr>
      <td colspan="2">Enter the body of the message
➡here:<br>
        <textarea cols="50" rows="10" name="email_body"
➡wrap="VIRTUAL"></textarea>
      </td>
    </tr>
    <tr>
      <td colspan="2">
        <div align="center">
          <input type="submit" value="Send Email!">
        </div>
      </td>
    </tr>
  </table>
</form>
```

Your form should look like this:

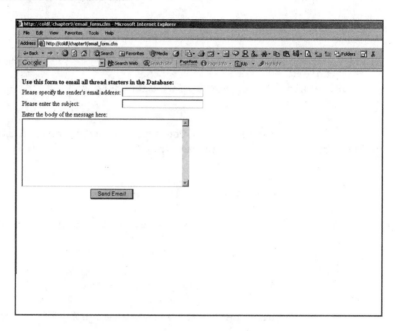

In the `<form>` tag, we listed the `send_email.cfm` template in the action attribute. This is the template that we will now build to send out all of our e-mails.

Here is the listing for `send_email.cfm` create the template like so:

```
<!-- send_email.cfm -->

<!-- this template will process the email_form.cfm template
-->

<!-- run a query to get a list of names and email address
➥from the posts table in our database -->
  <cfquery name="get_email" datasource="board"
➥dbtype="ODBC">
        SELECT
        author_name, author_email
        FROM posts
  </cfquery>
  <!-- send ONE email to each email address that we find in
➥the database -->
  <<cfmail> query="get_email" group="author_email"
➥to="#author_email#" from="#FORM.sender_email#"
➥subject="#FORM.email_subject#" groupcasesensitive="no">
```

```
        Hello #author_name#,

        #email_body#

        Thank you,

        The Forum Team
    </<cfmail>>
    <!-- Tell the forum administrator that the emails have
➡been sent -->

    You successfully sent the following message to the forum
➡community:<br>
    <cfoutput>
            #FORM.email_body#
    </cfoutput>
```

The `<cfquery>` tag retrieves the names and e-mail addresses of the people in the posts table.

Our `<CFMAIL>` tag now includes a few extra attributes. The `query` attribute tells it which query to use (`get_email` in this case). Also, we have the group and `groupcasesensitive` attributes as well. So, our `<CFMAIL>` tag is going to send one e-mail to each e-mail address that it finds in the posts table. We set the `groupcasesensitive` attribute to `no` so if a user had left two posts with e-mail addresses like me@flashforum.com and ME@FlashForum.com , that person would only receive one e-mail from our template.

The body of the e-mail addresses the person by the name that they originally entered and then delivers them the message that the forum administrator chose to include in the form.

If the forum administrator wanted to send an e-mail notifying the users about maintenance to the forum's servers they might use the form like this:

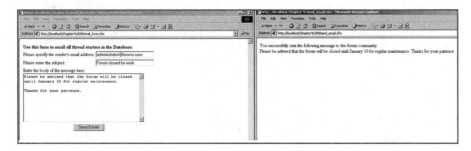

And just like that, we sent a personalized e-mail to every address in our list, almost as easily as if we'd sent one message. We could have sent a few hundred or even a few thousand.

Using <cfmail> to send e-mail from Flash

In our final example, we will build a Flash form that we will use to send e-mail using <CFMAIL>. Once the e-mail has been sent, we will send a message back to the Flash movie confirming delivery.

Building the Flash movie

In the this exercise we will:

- Create a Flash movie to handle the sending of e-mails

- Set up the variables needed to pass information to and from our movie

We will start our example with the Flash Form.

1. Start with a blank Flash movie that is 300 x 300 pixels.

2. Create three layers; actions, text fields and buttons

3. On the text fields layer, we need to create five single line input fields and one multiline text field. The variable names for these fields are, sender_name, sender_email, recipient_name, recipient_email subject and message where the message variable is for the multiline input field.

4. On the buttons layer, we need to create a send button.

5. Finally, add the following actions to the first frame of your actions layer:

```
stop ();
loaded = "no";
```

Your stage should be set up like this:

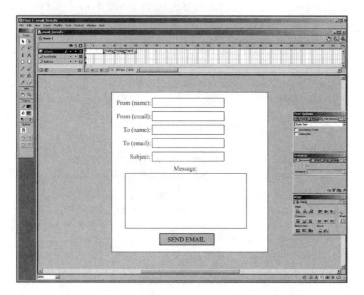

Now that we know what our variable names are, we will create the ColdFusion template that will process the e-mail. This template will be called flash_email.cfm and will perform two operations. First of all, it will contain a <CFMAIL> tag that will send an e-mail to the recipient specified in our Flash movie. Once the e-mail has been sent, the template will send a message back to our Flash movie confirming that the e-mail was sent.

Whenever we send variables back to Flash, we must be very careful about white space, as Flash can't interpret it and your movie will crash. A good practice is to use the <cfsetting> tag to enable ColdFusion output only. What that means is that the only thing that will be displayed is content that is between <cfoutput> tags. Also, any data that we send to Flash should be URL-encoded and we will use the ColdFusion function **UrlEncodedFormat** to handle this for us.

Flash expects to receive name – variable pairs, (e.g. loaded=no) when we send it data, so that is how we will set up our data. These name variable pairs will be separated by the & character. It is also a good idea to insert one of the & characters at the beginning and end of our string of data.

6. Finally, we will add a final name – variable pair once all the other data has been outputted to let our Flash movie know that we are finished loading variables. In this case, we will use the following:

```
loaded=yes
```

That way, if the `loaded` variable isn't equal to `yes` in our Flash movie, we know that the variables are not yet loaded.

7. On the sent keyframe add a `stop` action.

8. Also on the sent keyframe, add a dynamic text field with the variable name `confirmation`. Finally, add a back button and assign the following action to it:

```
on (release) {
    gotoAndPlay (1);
}
```

Before changing anything else, make sure that your stage resembles this:

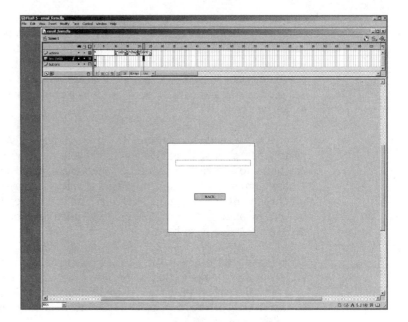

9. Now, go back to the first frame and insert the following actions on the send email button:

```
// send the variables to the ColdFusion template for
➥processing.
on (release) {
    loadVariablesNum ("flash_email.cfm", 0, "POST");
    gotoAndPlay ("retry");
}
```

This is where all action is. Make sure that you choose to send the variables using POST. Sending the variables using POST allows ColdFusion to treat them like form variables. If we sent the variables using GET, we would not be able to reference the variables in our ColdFusion template with the #form# prefix.

When you press the send button, the variables in our Flash movie are sent to the flash_email.cfm template, that we'll create in a moment, and the e-mail is sent. We are then taken the retry frame where we will assign the following actions:

```
// this frame will allow the movie to loop until the
➥variables have been properly loaded
play ();
```

10. Now, the final piece of the puzzle is the actions on the check frame. We need a conditional statement to check whether the *loaded* variable from our ColdFusion template is now equal to yes. If it is, we know that the <CFMAIL> template has been processed and that the confirmation variable has been loaded. Otherwise, we need to go back to the retry frame and wait a bit longer. You might also want to put a small message on the retry frame telling users the message is being sent.

Here is the conditional statement that we'll use on the check keyframe:

```
// check to see if the confirmation variable has been
➥properly loaded
if (loaded == "yes") {
    gotoAndPlay ("sent");
} else {
    gotoAndPlay ("retry");
}
```

Once on the sent keyframe, the confirmation variable gets loaded into our dynamic text field and the user knows his message has been sent.

11. Save your Flash movie and publish it as email_form.swf insert it onto a new HTML page and we are ready to test.

12. Next type in the code below and save it with your other .cfm files as flash_email.cfm:

```
<!-- flash_email.cfm -->

<!-- template to send email from flash form -->

<!-- we don't want any whitespace when sending variables
➡back to flash so use cfsetting -->
    <cfsetting enablecfoutputonly="Yes">
<!-- send the email here -->
  <<cfmail> to="#FORM.recipient_email#"
➡from="#FORM.sender_email#" subject="#FORM.subject#">
        Hello #FORM.recipient_name#,

        #FORM.message#

        From,

        #FORM.sender_name#
  </<cfmail>>
    <!-- use a CFSET statement to create confirmation
➡variable -->
    <cfset confirmation="Your email has been sent">
<!-- output these variables back to flash -->
  <cfoutput>

&confirmation=#URLEncodedFormat(confirmation)#&loaded=yes&
  </cfoutput>
```

The <CFMAIL> statement should be very familiar. After that, we use <cfset> to create a variable called confirmation that we will then URL encode and send back to our Flash movie.

With our template now set up, we have to make the final changes to our Flash movie. On the actions layer, we are going to insert three new keyframes called retry, check and sent respectively.

Here is the final product:

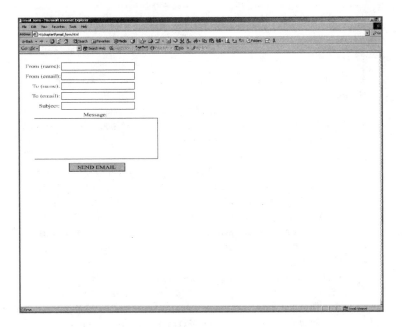

There is only one problem with our application. <cfmail> has three required attributes, To, From and Subject. If a user omits those in the Flash form, the <cfmail> tag will fail and the confirmation will never be sent. As a result, our Flash Movie will loop indefinitely between our retry and check frames.

We need to add just a bit more functionality to our application before it is complete.

The From and Subject attributes are not as important as the To attribute. Therefore, we can use the <cfparam> tag in ColdFusion to specify default values for these. We can't, however, specify a default value for the To. We, therefore, need to send a different confirmation statement to Flash if this variable is omitted.

Let's take another look at the revised flash_email.cfm template.

```
<!-- flash_email.cfm -->

<!-- template to send email from flash form -->

<!-- we don't want any whitespace when sending variables
➥back to flash so use cfsetting -->
    <cfsetting enablecfoutputonly="Yes">
<!-- set default values for the <CFMAIL> tag -->
    <cfparam name="FORM.sender_email"
➥default="none@yourserver.com">
    <cfparam name="FORM.recipient_name" default="">
    <cfparam name="FORM.sender_name" default="">
    <cfparam name="FORM.message" default="">
    <cfparam name="FORM.subject" default="None">
    <cfparam name="FORM.recipient_email" default="">
<!-- if the recipient email had been specified, send the
➥email here -->
  <cfif recipient_email IS NOT "">
        <<cfmail> to="#FORM.recipient_email#"
➥from="#FORM.sender_email#" subject="#FORM.subject#">
                Hello #FORM.recipient_name#,


#FORM.message#


From,


#FORM.sender_name#
        </<cfmail>>
        <!-- use a CFSET statement to create confirmation
➥variable -->
      <cfset confirmation="Your e-mail has been sent">
<!-- output these variables back to flash -->
        <cfoutput>

&confirmation=#URLEncodedFormat(confirmation)#&loaded=yes&
        </cfoutput>
        <!-- if the recipient_email field was left blank,
➥send an error message back -->
  <cfelse>
            <cfset confirmation="Your e-mail not been sent.
```

```
                    ➡Please be sure to include a valid e-mail address
➡.">
<!-- output these variables back to flash -->
            <cfoutput>

&confirmation=#URLEncodedFormat(confirmation)#&loaded=yes&
            </cfoutput>
        </cfif>
```

This time, we establish default values for all of the variables used in our template. Then we use a `<cfif>` statement that checks for a blank `recipient_email` variable. If this variable is blank, the `<cfmail>` tag doesn't get processed and an error message gets sent to Flash allowing the user to go back and correct the problem.

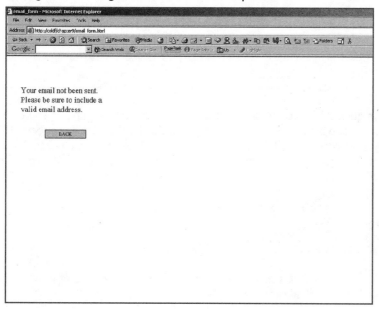

If the user does specify the recipient's e-mail address, the code is processed as before and the confirmation is sent.

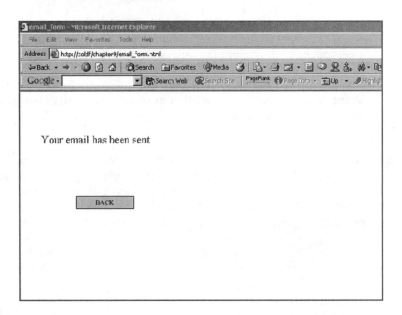

There is quite a bit happening in the flash_email.cfm template, so be sure to go over the entire code block, and be sure that you understand before moving on. This application gives you a great foundation in getting Flash to successfully work with ColdFusion. If you understand what is happening here, you will be realizing what some of the other possibilities are.

Summary

In this chapter we've:

- Set up ColdFusion server to allow the sending of e-mails via a ColdFusion application.

- Built a web application that will send e-mails based on e-mail address entered into a ColdFusion form

- Built and connected a Flash movie to our application

In the next chapter we'll be looking at the Verity searching application for ColdFusion, discussing it's uses, and giving it a basic Flash front end

10 Verity Searching

What We'll Cover in this Chapter

- *The Verity K2 server - a search package bundled with ColdFusion*

- *Creating and indexing a Verity Collection*

- *Using the Verity Wizard to write your CFML code*

- *Performing a full text search*

- *Kicking this all off from Flash.*

What Verity can do for you

Up to this point we've learnt an awful lot about ColdFusion, and how it's used to dynamically manipulate data stored in our data sources. But if you consider contemporary web sites, while databases are a key element for the storage of data, data on web sites can come in many different formats, spreadsheets, word processor documents, presentation software files and text files. Powerful as it is SQL cannot search anything but database files, we need something a more specialised to work with all our various different file formats. That's where Verity comes in.

> *Verity provides* **full-text searching**, *it analyses documents and creates a* **Collection** *which is a special database containing pointers to any indexed data that you specify.*

When you create a collection you specify a directory and the types of files within it that are able to be searched. Verity then builds an index which is a map of your searchable files, containing descriptions the files and their contents. It can later be reindexed, repaired or deleted just as databases can be.

Verity is able to index a wide variety of file formats, here's a quick list, full version support information is included in the ColdFusion help documentation.

Word Processing	**Spreadsheets**
Applix Words	Applix Spreadsheets
Lotus AmiPro	Corel QuattroPro
Lotus Word Pro	Lotus 1-2-3
Microsoft RTF	Microsoft Excel
Microsoft Word	Microsoft Works spreadsheet
Microsoft Works	
Microsoft Write	**Presentation Graphics**
Adobe Acrobat PDF	Corel Presentations
Text files	Lotus Freelance
(HTML, CFML included)	Microsoft PowerPoint
Unicode	
WordPerfect	
XyWrite	

Before we start searching these files we have to create the Verity Collection. The normal process of creating and using a Verity Collection is a two-step process. Firstly, creating the Collection and then creating the search interface to access and view the collection's data. This we'll carry out by creating a collection in ColdFusion Administrator and then creating a search front end using ColdFusion Studio and Flash.

Let's quickly discuss the folder structure that we need to be in place before working with Verity.

We can only have one **root directory** for each web site, but the files Verity indexes do not necessarily have to be within this. As long as the files can be accessed by the server they can be indexed by Verity - but remember that to be viewed by Web users they will need to be within your web root directory.

Creating a Verity Collection

We shall be using ColdFusion Administrator to create our Collection, so without further ado fire up this program on your machine and we'll get to work.

1.   In ColdFusion Administrator, select the Verity Collections link. This shows you the available Verity Collections on your machine.

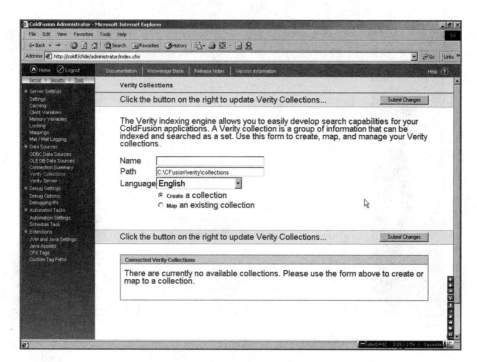

By default you will have no Verity Collections available.

2.   All that has to be done to create a Collection is to enter a name. Let's call ours ProjectCF.

The input box marked Path shows the location within which the Collections will be stored, Administrator will create a new directory for each. We're going to accept the default path C:\CFusion\verity\collections.

If you have the International Search Pack installed, you can select a other than English, for use with your Collection. It can be purchased online from the official site www.allaire.com/store. *Leave it as English for the purposes of this exercise.*

3. Select the Create a collection radio button and click Submit Changes.

After clicking submit, the collection shall be created and ready for use. One thing we haven't done yet though, is fill it with any data!

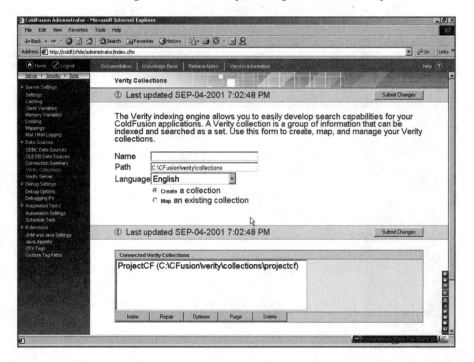

We're going to create two folders, your exact web structure or web server model may differ, but we'll create two folders within our own particular web root directories.

4. Create a new folder in your web root, call it VerityDocs. Ours is on the C: drive of our server machine (C:\InetPub\WWWRoot\VerityDocs)

This folder VerityDocs, is where the documents that to be indexed are to be held.

5. Copy some files to VerityDocs now, use any files you have to hand providing they are in one of Verity's supported formats. The number and type don't matter too much - just make sure that they have some content worth searching!

In my VerityDocs I have placed a mixture of Word Documents (.doc extension), HTML files, and Adobe Acrobat Files (.pdf extensions). By the way if you'd like to use an Acrobat file and don't have one sample chapters of all friends of ED books in PDF format are available for download from www.friendsofed.com.

6. The second folder to create is one called VerityProject, again with your web root. (C:\InetPub\WWWRoot\VerityProject in our case.)

Later on we shall be using ColdFusion Studio to create CFML templates to search and administer our collection, this folder shall hold the templates that Studio creates as we'll as our eventual Flash movie.

Index and search with CFML

Now that we have created our blank verity collection we shall open up ColdFusion Studio and continue the process of populating our Collection and creating our search interface.

1. Open Studio go to File > New, and from the CFML tag, select Verity Wizard.

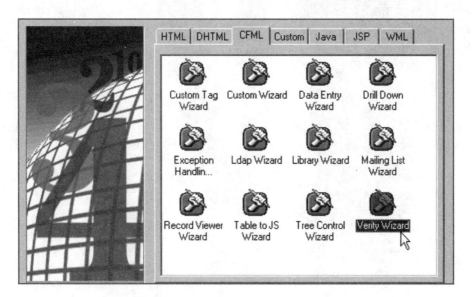

Clicking on OK kicks off the Wizard section of this Studio function. Before we run through the Wizard, lets consider what it'll create.

The bare minimum requirements for a Verity search system, to work with our Collection, are:

- A search page - for the user to input their search criteria.

- A results page - to display the results of a search.

- Administration pages - those that index our Collection and provide the user linkage to indexed files.

Fortunately, ColdFusion creates all three of these for us.

We're off to see the Wizard

In the first page of the Wizard, we are asked for the name of the Verity application and the location for the application's template files to be placed. The Wizard generates them.

2. Call the project MyVerityProject, and use the VerityProject folder that was created earlier.

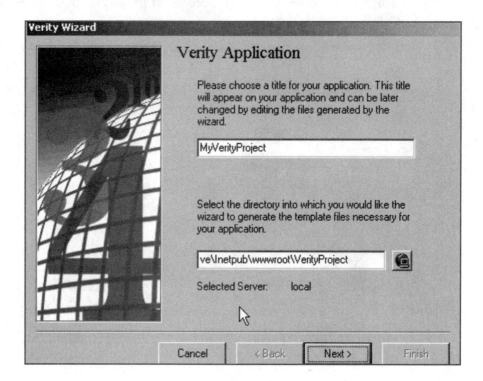

The second wizard screen asks you to offer a name for an existing collection, and the language that shall be used by your collection.

3. We configured these values earlier in ColdFusion Administrator when we created our collection, enter `ProjectCF` for the name of the collection and set the language to english.

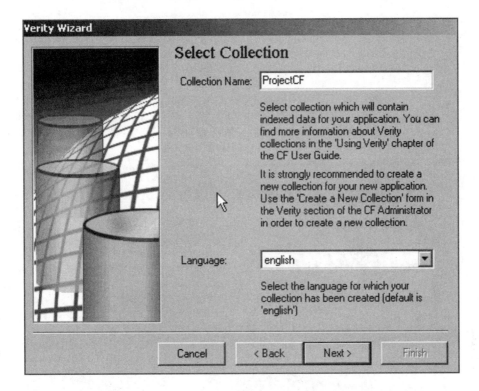

The next screen contains information about the indexing settings for our Collection.

Firstly we have the Directory Path. This is where we enter the directory of the directory of the files that we will be searching The path required is the path of the `VerityDocs` folder - from the point of view of the server. My directory is `C:\InetPub\WWWRoot\VerityDocs`.

4. Enter your own path in the box.

> *Beware of using the .browsing tool if you are running Studio on a different machine from Server. Getting this path correct is essential.*

5. The Recursively index subdirectories checkbox is where we can set whether we want to index sub-directories within the main index directory. Leave the box checked - as is the default setting.

In the File Extensions input box you would enter the applicable file extensions of the documents that exist in your index. Verity will only index files that have the extensions listed here, any others will be ignored.

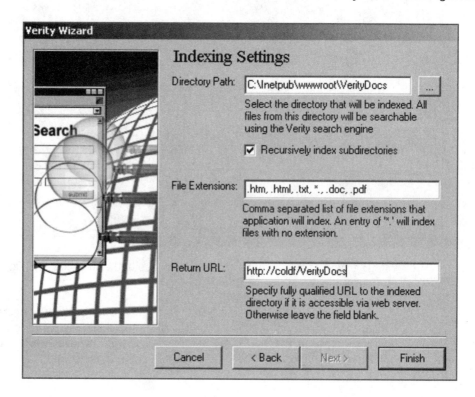

6. Add .doc and .pdf to the File Extensions box as we've files with these extensions within VertiyDocs.

> *The information in the* Return URL *input box is used to create links to the files that our searches return. As such the information will be different from server to server and dependant upon whether you are conduction development on a remote or local host. If you are unaware of this information you will have to consult your web server documentation or System's Administrator.*

7. Fill in your own Return URL box and click Finish.

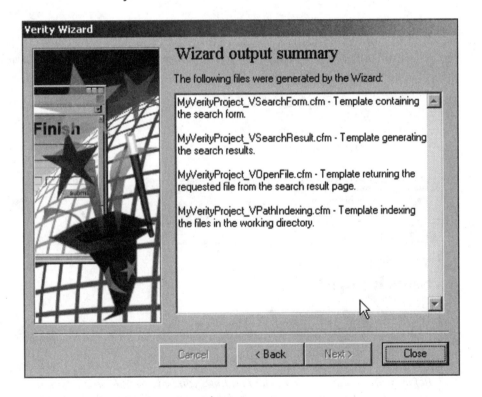

When the Wizard is complete, the resulting output is a list of the files that have been created.

As you can see we have a search form called `MyVerityProject_VsearchForm.cfm`. A page which will contain the results of our search called, `MyVerityProject_VsearchResult.cfm`, a page where we can open the file that the search has returned `MyVerityProject_VopenFile.cfm`. Finally, we have `MyVerityProject_VPathIndexing.cfm` which indexes our files in our working directory.

All of these files will be contained within our `VerityProject` directory.

8.   Click on Close.

CFML search

Now our Verity project is almost complete. Lets look at the whole search application in action.

1.   Open up `MyVerityProject_VsearchForm.cfm`. in a browser. Its URL will be:

http://*YOURSERVER*/VerityProject/MyVerityProject_VsearchForm.cfm

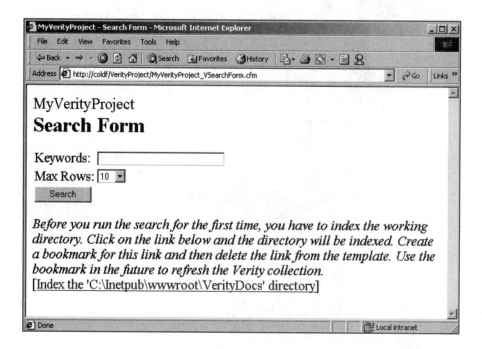

Before we can run the search form for the first time, we have to index our working directory which is done by clicking the hyperlink which offers to Index the C:\Inetpub\wwwroot\VerityDocs directory.

2.   After you click on the link the directory will be indexed and, if everything is OK, you should see the following message:

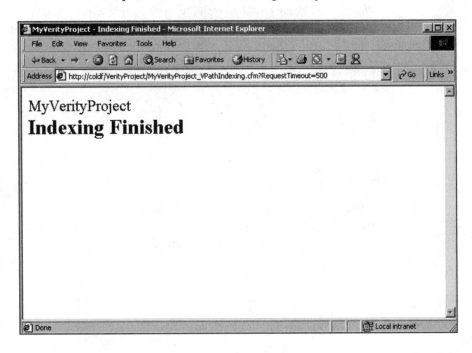

It's possible that you may get a ColdFusion error screen at this point. If you do don't worry; here are two possible causes:

Some of the information entered into the Wizard was incorrect - there's nothing to do in this case but try again. Start from the beginning of the exercise and rebuild with the Wizard, you can use the same filenames and directories as the new ones will simply overwrite the old.

Your Development Mappings are set up incorrectly - select Debug > Development Mappings in Studio (or press ALT+M) *and check that your* Studio, Server, *and* Browser *paths are correct. Allaire have a very clear help article at:* www.allaire.com/Handlers/index.cfm?ID=6355

3. Once you see the Indexing Finished message, reload our search form, click on the browser's Back button.

4. Let's try a search. Type a word which you think should yield results, and press Search.

In this case I have searched with the word Flash, as my working directory contains a number of documents about Flash. It seems fairly safe that the search will return a few hits with this keyword.

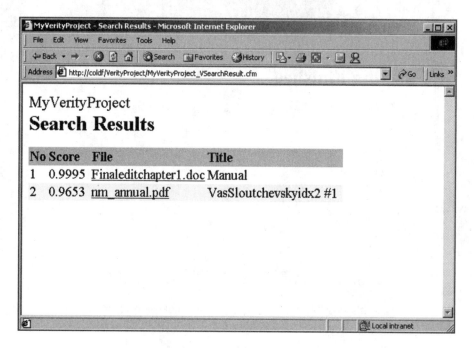

As you can see from this screenshot we have got two results back from our search. Each result contains a hyperlink to open the document, clicking on each hyperlink downloads the file and opens the results up in a browser window.

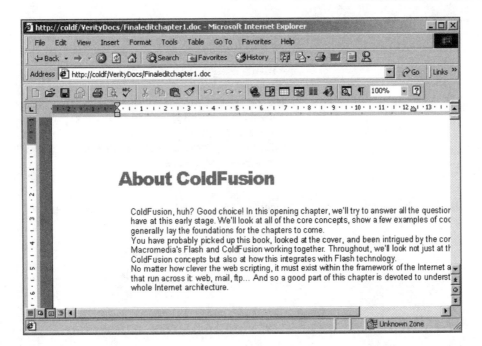

As you can see, with no handcoding and simple Studio wizardry, Verity K2 provides ColdFusion developers with an extremely easy to use and powerful search engine.

Looking at the code within the search form

Before we embark on creating a search application with Flash, we'll take a look at the code within the search code that the Studio wizard created.

Looking at the code that Studio generates is a valuable exercise as it provides information on the CF code needed to invoke our collection. Looking at the `MyVerityProject_VSearchResult.cfm` template, we can see the code that is required to invoke the search within our Verity index.

In the first three lines, we set location of the directory of the verity index:

```
<!-- template settings -->
<cfset SearchDirectory =
➥"C:\Inetpub\wwwroot\VerityDocs">
<cfset SearchCollection = "ProjectCF">
<cfset UseURLPath = "YES">
```

Next within the `<cfsearch>` tags the CFML sets the requirements for the search, its structure is very similar to queries that we've constructed ourselves.

```
<!-- retrieve requested files -->
<cfsearch
    name = "GetResults"
    collection = "#SearchCollection#"
    criteria = "#Form.Criteria#"
    maxRows = "#Evaluate(Form.MaxRows + 1)#"
    startRow = "#Form.StartRow#"
>
```

Much of the remaining code is concerned with the HTML layout of the template:

```
<html><head>
    <title>MyVerityProject - Search
➡Results</title>
</head><body bgcolor="ffffff">

<font size="+1">MyVerityProject</font> <br>
<font size="+2"><b>Search Results</b></font>

<p>

<!-- no files found for specified criteria? -->
<cfif GetResults.RecordCount is 0>
    <b>No files found for specified criteria</b>

<!-- ... else at least one file found -->
<cfelse>

    <table cellspacing=0 cellpadding=2>

    <!-- table header -->
    <tr bgcolor="cccccc">
        <td><b>No</b></td>
        <td><b>Score</b></td>
        <td><b>File</b></td>
        <td><B>Title</b></td>
    </tr>

    <cfoutput query="GetResults"
➡maxRows="#Form.MaxRows#">
    <tr bgcolor="#IIf(CurrentRow Mod 2,
➡DE('ffffff'), DE('ffffcf'))#">
```

```
                <!-- current row information -->
                <td>#Evaluate(Form.StartRow +
➡CurrentRow - 1)#</td>

                <!-- score -->
                <td>#Score# </td>

                <!-- file name with the link
➡returning the file -->
                <td>
                        <cfif UseURLPath> <!-- URL
➡parameter from cfsearch contains URL path info
➡-->
                                <cfset href =
➡Replace(URL, " ", "%20", "ALL")>
                        <cfelse>          <!-- ... else
➡use OpenFile to return the file -->
                                <cfset href =
➡"MyApplication_VOpenFile.cfm?serverFilePath=#URL
➡EncodedFormat(Key)#">
                        </cfif>
                        <a
➡href="#href#">#GetFileFromPath(Key)#</a>
                </td>

                <!-- title for HTML files -->
                <td>#Title# </td>

        </tr>
        </cfoutput>

        </table>
```

This section adds a More button if there are more results than we want to display on one page, it then reloads the template with a new StartRow parameter.

```
        <!-- CFSEARCH tried to retrieve one more
➥file than the number specified in the
➥Form.MaxRows parameter. If number of retrieved
➥files is greater than MaxRows we know that there
➥is at least one file left. The following Xform
➥contains only one button which reloads this
➥template with the new StartRow parameter. -->

    <cfif GetResults.RecordCount gt
➥Form.MaxRows>
            <form
➥action="MyVerityProject_VSearchResult.cfm"
➥method="post">
            <cfoutput>
                    <input type="hidden"
➥name="Criteria" value="#Replace(Form.Criteria,
➥"""", "'", "ALL")#">
                    <input type="hidden"
➥name="MaxRows" value="#Form.MaxRows#">
                    <input type="hidden"
➥name="StartRow"
➥value="#Evaluate(Form.StartRow +
➥Form.MaxRows)#">
                    <input type="submit" value="
➥More ...    ">
            </cfoutput>
            </form>
    </cfif>

</cfif>

</body></html>
```

We will only have to modify this template slightly for our Flash project, but we're jumping ahead of ourselves a little here, we've got some Flash to build.

Flash Search Application

In this section we shall construct a Flash form to search our verity collection and display the results within an HTML page. It is possible to display the results purely in a Flash movie and we will in our case study, but first we'll step into this as simply as possible.

Flash movie design

In our movie we will have two scenes, one which shall act as a welcome screen for the movie and provide a link to index our collection, and the second which shall have a search page.

1. To start, create a Flash movie with two layers `actions` and `buttons and text`.

2. Add two blank keyframes on the `actions` layer, label them `Scene 1` and `Scene 2`

3. Add a `stop` action to each frame.

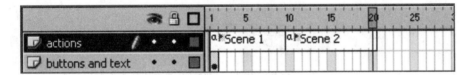

   Your timeline should look something like this.

4. On the `buttons and text` layer in the first frame of `Scene 1` add two buttons and enough text to explain to the user that one will initiate an index of our Verity Collection and the other will take us to a search page.

5. One button shall be used to start an index of our collection. To configure this, add an action to the button. On release it will perform a getURL to the MyVerityProject_VPathIndexing.cfm template.

```
on (release) {
getURL
("MyVerityProject_VPathIndexing.cfm?RequestTimeout
➥=500", "blank");
}
```

Clicking on this button will present the user with a browser window providing information that the index has been completed.

6. To finish off the work with our first scene add the following action to the button which shall act as a link to the search page.

```
on (release) {
    gotoAndPlay ("Scene 2", 1);
}
```

This has the effect of moving the application onto the next scene where we can begin the construction of our search interface.

7. On our search page, place 2 input text boxes. The first called criteria will hold the value to be searched, the next value called maxrows will host the Maximum amount of rows to be output by the results of the search on the Verity collection.

8. Add some explanatory text to make the user aware of what values to input where.

9. Add two buttons to the page, one is to process the search and move the variables into the ColdFusion template that will execute the search on the collection. The other button will be used simply to transfer the user back to scene one.

    Make it as intricate as you like.

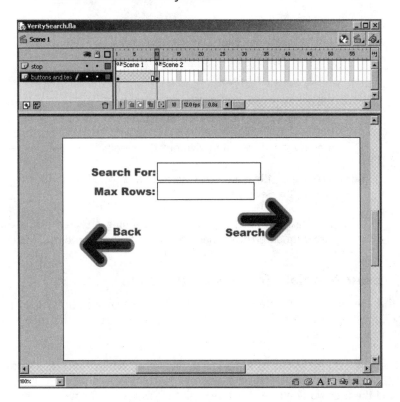

10. We'll act on the Back button first, to send the user back to Scene 1. To do this add the following action to the button:

```
on (release) {
    gotoAndPlay ("Scene 1", 1);
}
```

If new information is added to the Verity Collection it will need to be indexed again, so we will need access to Scene 1 and the indexing button. In most applications indexing would happen transparently, controlled by your code, but it's helpful to us to be able to see everything that goes on.

The Search button will start a search of the Collection based on the user's criteria and maximum rows.

11. Add the ActionScript to make this work to the object actions of the button:

```
on (release, keyPress "<Enter>") {
    getURL ("MyVerityProject_VSearchResult.cfm",
➥"_blank", "POST");
}
```

What this is saying is that on the release of the mouse button over the search button or on the user hitting the RETURN key, post the variables into the MyVerityProject_VsearchResult.cfm template which will process the search, and give out the results in a new browser window.

12. Save the file as VeritySearch.fla and publish it into our VerityProject folder.

The Flash movie is all set up, but running a search at the moment will throw up an error we need to do some work on our CFML code.

Changing our template for Flash interaction

Now that the work is completed on the Flash interface that shall provide a front end to a Verity Collection, we'll have to change the VSearchResult.cfm file which is the script that searches our collection.

The Form.StartRow variable is not accessible from within our Flash form, we could simply remove all of the references to it from our template, but that is little more than a hack and the user wouldn't be able to see all the results. We'll have to alter the template to keep all of our functionality.

1. Open the file `MyVerityProject_VSearchResult.cfm` for editing in Studio.

   Since the template calls itself in the event of finding more results than can be displayed upon one page. The user clicks on the More button and `MyVerityProject_VSearchResult.cfm` calls itself passing a new `StartRow` figure. When Flash calls the template it does so without `StartRow` being defined.

2. We need to add a `<cfif>` tag decision, giving the current `<cfsearch>` if `Form.StartRow` is defined and another if it isn't. Changing this portion of the template to read:

```
<!-- template settings -->
<cfset SearchDirectory =
➥"C:\Inetpub\wwwroot\VerityDocs">
<cfset SearchCollection = "ProjectCf">
<cfset UseURLPath = "YES">

<cfif isdefined("Form.StartRow")>
<!-- retrieve requested files -->
<cfsearch
    name = "GetResults"
    collection = "#SearchCollection#"
    criteria = "#Form.Criteria#"
    maxRows = "#Evaluate(Form.MaxRows + 1)#"
    startRow = "#Form.StartRow#"
>

<cfelse>
<cfsearch
    name = "GetResults"
    collection = "#SearchCollection#"
    criteria = "#Form.Criteria#"
    maxRows = "#Evaluate(Form.MaxRows + 1)#"
    startRow = 1
>
</cfif>
```

Our new `<cfsearch>` tag sets `startRow` as 1, since when the Flash movie calls our template it will always be when the user has seen no results.

`Form.startRow` is used in other parts of the template as well. We can't set this particular variable from within the template, so we need to replace all later references to it with a variable that we *can* set.

3. Make these changes now. Replace all instances of #Form.StartRow# outside our <cfif> and <cfsearch> tags with startRow. Leaving this portion of the template like so:

```
<html><head>
    <title>MyVerityProject - Search
➥Results</title>
</head><body bgcolor="ffffff">

<font size="+1">MyVerityProject</font> <br>
<font size="+2"><b>Search Results</b></font>

<p>

<!-- no files found for specified criteria? -->
<cfif GetResults.RecordCount is 0>
    <b>No files found for specified criteria</b>

<!-- ... else at least one file found -->
<cfelse>

    <table cellspacing=0 cellpadding=2>

    <!-- table header -->
    <tr bgcolor="cccccc">
            <td><b>No</b></td>
            <td><b>Score</b></td>
            <td><b>File</b></td>
            <td><b>Title</b></td>
    </tr>

    <cfoutput query="GetResults"
➥maxRows="#Form.MaxRows#">
    <tr bgcolor="#IIf(CurrentRow Mod 2,
DE('ffffff'), DE('ffffcf'))#">

            <!-- current row information -->
            <td>#Evaluate(startRow + CurrentRow - 1)#</td>

            <!-- score -->
            <td>#Score# </td>

            <!-- file name with the link
➥returning the file -->
            <td>
                    <cfif UseURLPath> <!-- URL
```

```
➡parameter from cfsearch contains URL path info
➡-->
                           <cfset href =
➡Replace(URL, " ", "%20", "ALL")>
                        <cfelse> <!-- ... else use
➡OpenFile to return the file -->
                           <cfset href =
➡"MyApplication_VOpenFile.cfm?serverFilePath=#URL
➡EncodedFormat(Key)#">
                        </cfif>
                        <a
➡href="#href#">#GetFileFromPath(Key)#</A>
             </td>

             <!-- title for HTML files -->
             <td>#Title# </td>

    </tr>
    </cfoutput>

    </table>

      <!-- CFSEARCH tried to retrieve one more
➡file than the number specified in the
➡Form.MaxRows parameter. If number of retrieved
➡files is greater than MaxRows we know that there
➡is at least one file left. The following form
➡contains only one button which reloads this
➡template with the new StartRow parameter. -->

    <cfif GetResults.RecordCount gt
➡Form.MaxRows>
             <form
➡action="MyVerityProject_VSearchResult.cfm"
➡method="post">
             <cfoutput>
                  <input type="hidden"
➡name="Criteria" value="#Replace(Form.Criteria,
➡"""", "'", "ALL")#">
                  <input type="hidden"
➡name="MaxRows" value="#Form.MaxRows#">
    <input type="hidden" name="StartRow" value="#Evaluate(StartRow
➡+ Form.MaxRows)#">
                  <input type="submit" value="
➡More ...    ">
             </cfoutput>
```

```
            </form>
        </cfif>

    </cfif>

    </body></html>
```

We now need to go back inside our new decision structure and set the two possible values for startRow. Adding these <cfset> tags:

```
<cfif isdefined("Form.StartRow")>
<!-- retrieve requested files -->
<cfsearch
    name = "GetResults"
    collection = "#SearchCollection#"
    criteria = "#Form.Criteria#"
    maxRows = "#Evaluate(Form.MaxRows + 1)#"
    startRow = "#Form.StartRow#"
>
<cfset startRow=#Form.StartRow#>

<cfelse>
<cfsearch
    name = "GetResults"
    collection = "#SearchCollection#"
    criteria = "#Form.Criteria#"
    maxRows = "#Evaluate(Form.MaxRows + 1)#"
    startRow = 1
>
<cfset startRow=1>
</cfif>
```

5.   And that's it. Save our amended template.

Open VeritySearch.html in your browser and you should be able to launch a search of your Verity Collection from the Flash movie.

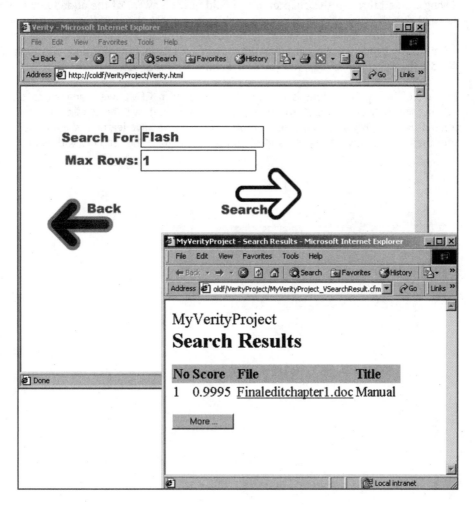

Summary

Having worked through this chapter you should now be aware of the added power Verity K2 can bring to your projects, full text searching on collections of data organized in a wide variety of formats. While SQL allows powerful search facilities on databases and comma-delimited text files, Verity can allow your users to search for information contained in Word documents PowerPoint files or even Adobe Acrobat files.

The use of Verity Collections is made extremely easy in CFML, we managed to create a working search system without ever having to dirty our hands with any coding. The templates created by the Verity Wizard are very simple CFML and we have learnt enough to be able to alter these for our own purposes, and of course to integrate the searches with Flash.

11 Flash Component Kit

What We'll Cover in this Chapter

- *Installing the Flash Component Kit for ColdFusion*

- *How the Kit components are constructed with custom tags*

- *Customizing the sample components for our own projects*

Macromedia, in their efforts to make integration between Flash and ColdFusion more transparent to the developer, released the Flash Component Kit for ColdFusion as a free download. Its intent is to make Flash connection more easily understood by the ColdFusion community and even though most of us are coming in from the other angle we'll find the Kit extremely useful - it's the connectivity we're interested in after all.

What exactly is the Flash Component Kit?

The Flash Component Kit is really just a Macromedia supported set of Flash movies and CFML **custom tags** that have been produced to manipulate and interact with them. These movies use the ActionScript `loadVariables` function and interact with CFML in much the same way we have learnt to do in this book. The Kit is intended to serve two main functions; to allow the ColdFusion developer to easily add some Flash functionality to their site, but also to help developers who use both tools understand the best way to interact the two - creating their own apps.

Custom Tags

We touched on the use of custom tags very briefly back in Chapter 7 and, while creating them for ourselves is a complex process, an area for you to study further if you wish, understanding how they work is very useful to us.

Most custom tags are created within CFML itself as separate templates that can be reused in new projects. They are often distributed across the net (for free mostly) and, in fact, they are responsible for the development of the increasing sense of community felt by ColdFusion developers. Many make use of outside technologies such as JavaScript or DHTML code and most interestingly of all to us Flash. Allaire have a large repository of custom tags for download at http://devex.allaire.com/developer/gallery/customtags.cfm.

In many cases custom tags are called from within CFML by prefixing the name of the custom tag template with <cf_ . This, referred to as **simple syntax**, means that calling a custom tag with a template `mytag.cfm` takes the form `<cf_mytag>`. If the template requires attributes passed to it these are included within the <> angle braces .

When a custom tag is called in this manner ColdFusion first looks in the same directory as the current template. If it is not found there the Server checks its custom tags directories, by default this only refers to `C:\CFusion\CustomTags`, but more can be added in the appropriate section of the Administrator.

As we'll discover soon, we'll have to install some of the Component Kit's, erm, components here.

Limitations of the Component Kit

So all this bonus functionality sounds too good to be true. It isn't, but there is a proviso - at the moment not all components work with all browser versions. The cascading menu runs on Microsoft Internet Explorer on Windows only, due to it using browser specific features, for the others it may depend which browser version the user is running. We'll discuss these problems in depth as we look at each part of the kit.

Hopefully this will be remedied through its developer community. The developer community is a worldwide group of people all adopting the Kit, sharing their findings, components and generally anything related which people would find useful. The good thing is that anyone can join the community by simply submitting their findings to the Developer Forum Area which is at:

http://forums.allaire.com/coldfusion/categories.cfm?catid=106

This is a dedicated support forum for the Kit.

Installing the Kit

You will first have to download the Kit from the Macromedia web site. It is quite compact in its zipped state at 412Kb.

1. Point your browser to the following site and download the Component Kit: www.macromedia.com/software/coldfusion/downloads/

   There is no installation file, so to install the kit you will have to manually decompress the files and place them within the appropriate directories.

   When you unzip the file you will find the following files and directories:

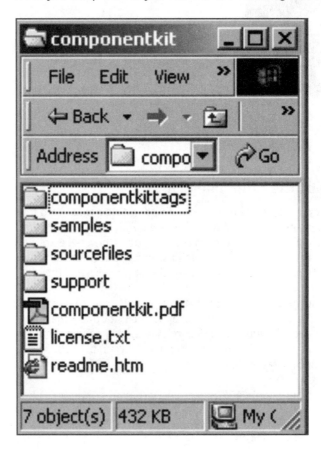

Directory structure

Depending on your server and what parts of the Kit particularly interest you, these files and folders have to be distributed around your system in differing ways. The folder `componentkittags` needs to reside within an Administrator assigned custom tag directory.

2.   For ease of use copy the `componentkittags` directory to the `C:\Cfusion\CustomTags` directory on your sever.

Apart from the custom tags the rest of the Kit is best placed with a web accessible directory within the server file structure. Although you may later, after further ColdFusion experience, decide that other structures fulfill your needs more fully for the remainder of the chapter we'll assume that you've done the following:

3.   Copied the whole `componentkit` folder to your web root directory on your server.

4.   Deleted the, now duplicate, `componentkittags` folder within this.

As we saw in Chapter 8 the `Application.cfm` template contains CFML to be automatically included at the head of every file. The sample applications within the Component Kit require these lines to be present within their particular `Application.cfm`.

```
<cfset
➥ request.uitoolkitcfpath="/componentkit/support/">
<cfset
➥ request.uitoolkitsupportpath="/componentkit/
➥ support/">
```

By default the `componentkit/samples` folder contains an `Application.cfm` template with code to this effect, but this will mean that any templates that reside within this directory won't automatically include CFML from any `Application.cfm` you already have higher in the directory structure. If this is crucial to your projects you must remove this file and add the two lines above to *your* `Application.cfm` template.

What do I get?

The Kit comes with four sample applications: a calendar, a calculator and two menu systems, one horizontal and one cascading. I think it's about time we actually looked at what the components can do. The samples directory contains the four components, placed into an application setting. To begin, open a browser and enter the URL to the `samples` directory. On your machine this will be the URL of your server plus `componentkit/samples/index.htm`

You will get a screen like so:

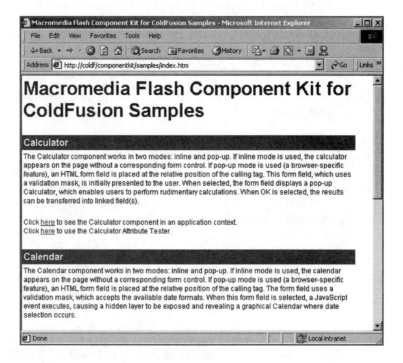

Here you will find descriptions of the components and links to working examples. Scroll down the page and spend some time reading the descriptions and viewing the examples to get a feel for the Kit's real potential.

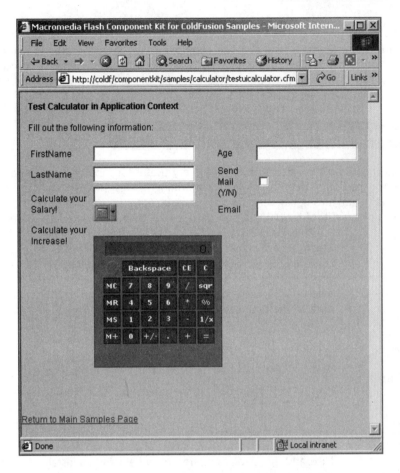

These components utilize many files, Flash movies yes, but if you take a look with the support directory you'll see a directory of JavaScript files and a directory containing more CFML templates and even a couple of GIFs.

Let's take a brief overview of all four components, and then dive head-first into customizing one of them: the cascading menu system.

The calculator

The calculator is a **dual-mode** component, which means that it can either be embedded inside a HTML or CFML page or made to pop-up via a button. It has all the functions you would expect from a simple calculator. It can interact with page elements by either accepting or sending numbers. The pop-up mode works on Mac systems only in IE5, but in both IE and Netscape on a Windows system. In Windows 98, however, the ESC key will no longer function as the C (clear) button.

The calendar

Similarly, the calendar is a dual-mode component, it allows the user to navigate by day, month, or even year. The calendar can also interact with page elements by accepting and sending dates. The pop-up mode of the calendar will only work with IE and Netscape on Windows and with Netscape and IE5 on a Macintosh system.

Form integration with the calendar

The calendar and the calculator are both very useful for inputting data to a CFML form, providing the user with an easy way of confirming figures that may have to be calculated. Here we'll run through a very simple example, without using any of the customizing features of the Kit, of including a pop-up calendar to input a date into a form.

1. Open a new blank template in Studio and save it as `cal.cfm` in the `...\componentkit\samples\calendar\` folder.

2. Insert a `<cfform>` opening tag with the name `calTest` which will pass data to the template `showdate.cfm`:

   ```
   <cfform name="calcTest" action="showdate.cfm">
   ```

3. Add the text `Input a Date:` within `<cfoutput>` tags:

   ```
   <cfoutput>
   Input a Date:
   </cfoutput>
   ```

4. Next add the CFML to insert a form field and an instance of our calendar:

   ```
   <cf_uicalendar
           ➥FormField="date"
           ➥Popup="yes"
           ➥Dateformat="date"
           ➥>
   ```

   The attributes within the `<cf_uicalendar>` custom tag set the name of the form field to which the date selected will be assigned, force it to use pop-up mode, and set the display format of the date (`eurodate` being `DD/MM/YYYY`, date being `MM/DD/YYYY`). There are a wealth of optional customization attributes available. Check the PDF file within the `componentkit` directory for a full explanation.

5. Add a carriage return, a Submit button and close the `<cfform>`:

```
<br>
<input type="submit" value="Submit">
</cfform>
```

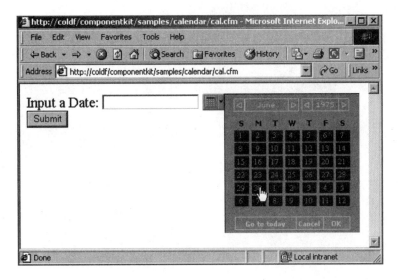

You can save and view `cal.cfm` in a browser now, and see how the calendar interacts with the form input field it creates. But before we can click on submit we have to create the `showdate.cfm` template that the `<cfform>` will send the date to.

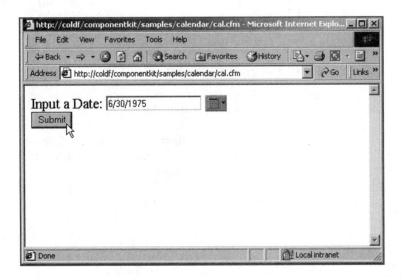

6. Save `cal.cfm` and open a blank new template. Add the following simple `<cfoutput>` tag pair:

```
<cfoutput>
The date you've input is #date#
</cfoutput>
```

7. Save the template as `showdate.cfm` in the same directory as `cal.cfm` and open up `cal.cfm` in your browser.

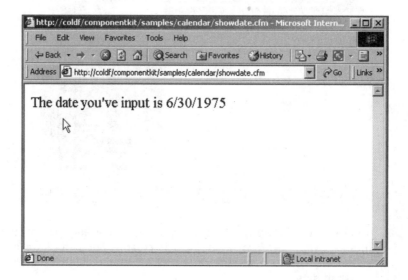

We've created a very simple form that uses the calendar to input a date value. The Kit components can be far more heavily customized though, as we'll see in a moment.

The Internet Explorer cascading menu

This is the component that we'll use to discuss in depth. It is the Kit component that is most available for customization and will give us the greatest insight. As it uses Microsoft Internet Explorer functionality it will only work on Windows systems within the IE browser. It is unfortunate that it will not function on other systems, and would be a problem if we were going to use it on a site that had to be accessible to all. However, if we can fully understand this component then the others should seem like child's play.

The horizontal menu

This is a multi-browser replacement for the cascading menu. It is much more restrictive in its use.

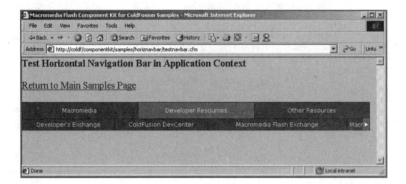

By viewing the examples you can see for yourself what each of the components are capable of, but understanding the implementation of a component is what we will discuss now by talking in depth about the Internet Explorer cascading menu component.

Customizing the cascading menu

The cascading menu is what can be described as a hierarchical, database driven, menu. It gives the functionality of accessing sections of a site without having to click on a menu item, reloading the page, to be then able to get to its submenu navigation. If you click on the menu sample you can see for yourself how easy navigation can become for sites with many areas or levels. We're going to create a site now.

Our menu on our site will have four top level options each with links dropping off them like so:

Flash	*ColdFusion*	*Flash & CF*	*Miscellaneous*
Flash Magazine	CF-Developer	FlashCFM	friendsofED
Flash Kit	CF Comet	Macromedia	freshfoot
Flash Planet			Amazon
Help 4 Flash			

Now we have the basic site structure let's start getting our hands dirty with the component files. The two main ColdFusion tags we'll use are `<cf_uicascadingmenu>` and `<cf_uicascadingmenuitem>`.

To set the look of the menu we will use `<cf_uicascadingmenu>`.

1. Open a new blank ColdFusion template, save it as `menu.cfm` in the `...componentkit/samples/cascadingmenu` directory.

2. Add this tag pair to the template:

    ```
    <cf_uicascadingmenu width="800" scale="1"
    ➥ elasticity="50">

    </cf_uicascadingmenu>
    ```

    What this has done is created an empty shell for us to add the menu items. The width, scale and elasticity attributes control the look and feel of the menu.

3. Within this tag pair we need to add `<cf_uicascadingmenuitem>` tags to populate the menu with options and headings. Add the following tags:

    ```
    <cf_uicascadingmenuitem
            ➥id="1"
            ➥parentid=""
            ➥name="Flash">

        <cf_uicascadingmenuitem
            ➥id="2"
            ➥parentid=""
            ➥name="ColdFusion">

        <cf_uicascadingmenuitem
            ➥id="3"
            ➥parentid=""
            ➥name="Flash & ColdFusion">

        <cf_uicascadingmenuitem
            ➥id="4"
            ➥parentid=""
            ➥name="Misc.">
    ```

Each menu item has to be assigned a unique id number and a name to display. As they are top level items and they do not have a parentid to reference them. Viewing the file from the server address in a browser should produce a very basic, boring looking menu.

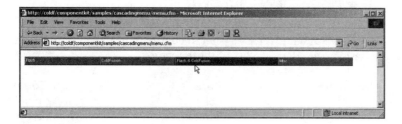

Pointing at an item will cause the menu to shift shape, although there are no sub-menus, neither will clicking on them produce anything. Let's address the second issue first. Adding href and target attributes to our menu item tags will allow them to be used as links.

4.   Add these attributes to our first and second menu items:

```
<cf_uicascadingmenuitem
        ➥id="1"
        ➥parentid=""
        ➥name="Flash"
        ➥href="http://www.macromedia.com"
        ➥target="new"
        ➥>

<cf_uicascadingmenuitem
        ➥id="2"
        ➥parentid=""
        ➥name="ColdFusion"
        ➥href="http://www.allaire.com"
        ➥target="new"
        ➥>
```

Setting the target attribute to new forces the linked site to open in a new browser window, keeping *our* site open to the user as well.

It's still looking a little dull so I think we need to give it some color. You may be wondering how we'll manage to change colors. This is achieved using a style template called stFormatting.cfm. This is a hard coded template which stores all appearance properties of the Flash movie in a ColdFusion structure, allowing us to change them. This file is then included before the Flash movie gets loaded and the appearance details are implemented.

With stFormatting.cfm you can control most details of the appearance of the Flash movie. Here is a list of those features:

Attribute	Data	type To set:
bgcolor	Color	Background color
bgtrans	Boolean	Transparency on/off
bdrstate	Boolean	Border on/off
bdrcolor	Color	Border color
btncolor	Color	Button background color
btnbdrcolor	Color	Button border color
btntxtcolor	Color	Button text color
btntxthicolor	Color	Button text highlight color
btnhicolor	Color	Button highlight color
btnbdrhicolor	Color	Button border highlight color
txtcolor	Color	Text Color
txtfont	Font Name	Name of font
rdonly	Boolean	Read only component. Will not accept data entry
Submitcontrols	Boolean	Components will include ok and cancel buttons

All colors must be entered in hex (##) format otherwise the component will return an error. When entering hex colors with a leading pound symbol (#) when you are within a <cfoutput>, ColdFusion server will return an error as it will try and evaluate the color but complain due to there being no closing #.

You may want to use black which is #000000 but the site will error due to no trailing #. To get round this you have to have two leading # symbols, like so: ##000000. The server and component both accept this fine.

5. Open a new, blank template in the same directory as our menu.cfm, and save it as StFormatting.cfm.

6. Add the following CFML:

```
<cfset stFormatting = structNew()>
<cfset stFormatting.bgcolor = "##494949">
<cfset stFormatting.bgtrans = 1>
<cfset stFormatting.btntrans = 50>
<cfset stFormatting.bdrstate = 1>
<cfset stFormatting.bdrcolor = "##000000">
<cfset stFormatting.btncolor = "##666666">
<cfset stFormatting.btnbdrcolor = "">
<cfset stFormatting.btntxtcolor = "">
<cfset stFormatting.btntxthicolor = "##000000">
<cfset stFormatting.btnhicolor = "##cac62b">
<cfset stFormatting.btnbdrhicolor = "">
<cfset stFormatting.txtcolor = "">
<cfset stFormatting.txtfont = "Arial">
<cfset stFormatting.rdonly = "">
<cfset stFormatting.submitcontrols = 0>
```

7. Include it at the top of your menu.cfm template like so:

```
<cfinclude template="stFormatting.cfm">
```

8. Now you have the new format available you will now need to tell the menu to use the new changes. To do this you will need to change the main tag to use another attribute like so:

```
<cf_uicascadingmenu width="500" scale="1" elasticity="50"
➥ stFormatting = "#stFormatting#">
```

9. To set our new color scheme off, add the HTML <body> tag with a bgcolor like so:

```
<cfinclude template="stFormatting.cfm">

<body bgcolor="#666666">

<cf_uicascadingmenu width="500" scale="1"
➥ elasticity="50" stFormatting = "#stFormatting#">

        <cf_uicascadingmenuitem
                ➥id="1"
                ➥parentid=""
                ➥name="Flash"
                ➥href="http://www.macromedia.com"
                ➥target="new"
                ➥>

        <cf_uicascadingmenuitem
                ➥id="2"
                ➥parentid=""
                ➥name="ColdFusion"
                ➥href="http://www.allaire.com"
                ➥target="new"
                ➥>

        <cf_uicascadingmenuitem
                ➥id="3"
                ➥parentid=""
                ➥name="Flash & ColdFusion">

        <cf_uicascadingmenuitem
                ➥id="4"
                ➥parentid=""
                ➥name="Misc.">

</cf_uicascadingmenu>
</body>
```

10. Save all the templates and refresh the browser and you will see the changed menu.

Play around with the formatting and tag attributes to see for yourself the flexibility of the component.

We now need to add the sub-menus. To do this we need to add more `<cf_uicascadingmenuitem>` tags. This time we need to give them a `parentid`. By doing this we force them to appear as sub-menu items. Each menu item still needs to have a unique `id` number, which means that these will have to start at 5.

11. Add this code beneath our first menu item tag:

```
<cf_uicascadingmenuitem
      ➡id="5"
      ➡parentid="1"
      ➡name="Flash Magazine"
      ➡href="http://
      ➡ www.flashmagazine.com"
      ➡target="_blank">
```

Since the first menu item has a `parentid` of 1, this will create an ID link between the two and thus place our link to Flash Magazine under the Flash section.

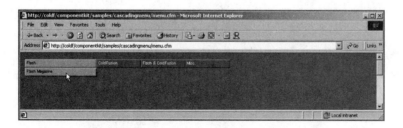

Now we must do the same to all the other links to complete our menu.

12. Change menu.cfm to look like this:

```
<cfinclude template="stFormatting.cfm">

<body bgcolor="#666666">

<cf_uicascadingmenu width="500" scale="1"
elasticity="50" stFormatting = "#stFormatting#">

        <cf_uicascadingmenuitem
            ➥id="1"
            ➥parentid=""
            ➥name="Flash"
            ➥href="http://www.macromedia.com"
            ➥target="new"
            ➥>
                    <cf_uicascadingmenuitem
                    ➥id="5"
                    ➥parentid="1"
                    ➥name="Flash Magazine"
                    ➥href="http://
                    ➥ www.flashmagazine.com"
                    ➥target="_blank">
                    <cf_uicascadingmenuitem
                    ➥id="6"
                    ➥parentid="1"
                    ➥name="Flash Kit"
                    href="http://www.flashkit.com"
                    ➥target="_blank">
                    <cf_uicascadingmenuitem
                    ➥id="7"
                    ➥parentid="1"
                    ➥name="Flash Planet"
                    ➥href="http://
                    ➥ www.flashplanet.com"
                    ➥target="_blank">
                    <cf_uicascadingmenuitem
                    ➥id="8"
                    ➥parentid="1"
                    ➥name="Help 4 Flash"
                    ➥href="http://
                    ➥ www.help4flash.com"
                    ➥target="_blank">
```

```
<cf_uicascadingmenuitem
    ➥id="2"
    ➥parentid=""
    ➥name="ColdFusion"
    ➥href="http://www.allaire.com"
    ➥target="new"
    ➥>
            ➥<cf_uicascadingmenuitem
            ➥id="9"
            ➥parentid="2"
            ➥name="CF-Developer"
            ➥href="http://
            ➥ www.cfdeveloper.co.uk"
            ➥target="_blank">
            <cf_uicascadingmenuitem
            ➥id="10"
            ➥parentid="2"
            ➥name="CF Comet"
            ➥href="http://www.cfcomet.com"
            ➥target="_blank">

<cf_uicascadingmenuitem
    ➥id="3"
    ➥parentid=""
    ➥name="Flash & ColdFusion"
    ➥>
            <cf_uicascadingmenuitem
            ➥id="11"
            ➥parentid="3"
            ➥name="FlashCFM"
            href="http://www.flashcfm.com"
            ➥target="_blank">
            <cf_uicascadingmenuitem
            ➥id="12"
            ➥parentid="3"
            ➥name="Macromedia"
            ➥href="http://
            ➥ www.macromedia.com"
            ➥target="_blank">

<cf_uicascadingmenuitem
    ➥id="4"
    ➥parentid=""
    ➥name="Misc.">
            <cf_uicascadingmenuitem
            ➥id="13"
```

```
➥parentid="4"
➥name="friendsofED"
➥href="http://
➥ www.friendsofed.com"
➥target="_blank">
<cf_uicascadingmenuitem
➥id="14"
➥parentid="4"
➥name="freshfroot"
➥href="http://
➥ www.freshfroot.com"
➥target="_blank">
<cf_uicascadingmenuitem
➥id="13"
➥parentid="4"
➥name="Amazon"
➥href="http://www.amazon.com
➥ /exec/obidos/ASIN/
➥ 1903450403/flashcfm-20/002-
➥ 6658370-0149619"
➥target="_blank">

</cf_uicascadingmenu>
</body>
```

That's our menu complete. Try it out, feel free to change all or any of the tag attributes to create the menu of your choice.

Creating your own components

Having integrated Flash and ColdFusion throughout the book, we've now looked at the creation of custom tags and how they're used. Should have whet your appetite to create your own Flash Component Kit style components. Here is some advice to note before you rush off.

- Keep control of your data - keep the data that needs to be passed between ColdFusion and Flash to a minimum. Test both parts with correct data and add enough data validation to make sure that the chances of error are reduced.

- Test your CFML and Flash separately - make sure both components are robust before combining them. Throughout the book we've ensured our CFML code functions correctly before adding the Flash interface and connectivity.

- Test your CFML and Flash together - after combining the two re-test all parts of the code and re-check all functionality. Nothing annoys a user more than a sudden failure.

Summary

In this chapter we've investigated the Flash Component Kit and hopefully it'll have helped you, as a Flash designer, to see further possibilities of using ColdFusion and Flash together in your own projects. We've investigated the use of CFML custom tags that are as good a basis as any for your continuing development as a ColdFusion programmer.

It's been tough in places hasn't it? But having worked through this entire book you'll have learnt a new language, CFML, and discovered the huge potential of Flash web sites that use dynamic data - updated by our ColdFusion server.

We've created a message board with a completely Flash based front end, with all the added user appreciation and functionality that that brings. We've also added email facilities, and a menu of resource links - ready for seamless integration into a totally Flash site!

Most importantly you will have realized that presenting data on Web does not mean the site has to be utilitarian in its appearance. Adding Flash will take it to another level, enabling you to create web sites that have stunning impact.

Hopefully you're chomping at the bit, itching to get started using all this power - and that's where we'll leave you.

Data presentation can be dull if you want it to be, but then who wants a dull website? The message of this book is take your data, add ColdFusion, and Flash it!

Appendix

CFML Tags Used In This Book

This appendix contains an alphabetical list of CFML tags that have been used in this book, each with a brief description. It's by no means an exhaustive list of CFML, nor does it attempt to provide syntax, it's intent is simply to provide a quick reference to use when looking over CFML code. For further information on specific tags you should use ColdFusion Studio's online help (or, of course, the appropriate section of this book!)

▶

cfapplet

Used to embed Java applets within a `<cfform>`. These applets must have been previously registered with CF Administrator.

cfapplication

Defines an application, these are often used to store persistent variables that are to be available to all the templates we're using. It defines the application name and sets a number of options, it is most likely to be used with an `Application.cfm` file.

cfcookie

Sets-up cookie variables, which unlike normal `<cfset>` variables can be set to expire, at a specific time, now or never.

cfform

Used to build an input form, unlike the HTML tag `<form>`, `<cfform>` is able to perform client-side input validation (when used with the appropriate tags).

cfgrid

When used within a `<cfform>`, `<cfgrid>` sets up a grid control for the collection and display of data. This tag offers a myriad of control attributes, from pixel widths of columns to setting the maximum number of displayed rows. By default the grid produced is populated with data from a `<cfquery>`.

cfgridrow

Can be used with `<cfgrid>` to define a grid row. Using this tag row data may be defined as something other than a `<cfquery>` result, for example a calculation performed on the templates' own variables.

cfgridupdate

Directly updates an ODBC data source, using grid data that may have been changed by the user.

cfheader

Is used to generate custom HTTP headers. It is often used in the form `<cfheader name="Expires" value="#Now()#">` to force a client's browser to purge it's cache of a requested file, to order a *refresh* in other words.

cfif cfelseif cfelse

The basic decision making constructs in CFML.

cfinclude

Instructs ColdFusion to include the specified CFML template at this point in the current template. If the named template isn't in our current directory, directories specified within CF Administrator are searched. Beware, however, that files referenced by the included template may now not be visible (due to relative paths used in URLs).

cfinput

The most common <cfform> tag, as it is used to create radio buttons and checkboxes as well as simple text entry boxes.

cfinsert

Used to insert records into an ODBC data source. In it's basic form it simply supplies the name of the data source and the name of the table into which the data is to be inserted, but there are other options which give advanced control.

cflocation

Simply directs the browser to a specified URL.

cflock

Used to handle multiple requests for the same data, which can cause errors if one template reads data while it is being written to by another. Requests to access the data are queued and executed in the order which they were received.

cfloop

CFML's loop tag which can be used as an index loop, a conditional loop, or more specifically with a query or list. Index loops start from one specified value, incrementing by a 'step' until another value is reached (often known as a *for* loop). Conditional loops *repeat until* the condition is satisfied.

cfmail

Sends an email message from within CFML. It can use variables or the results of a query to populate the email, allowing you to include them within the message text, dynamically creating tailored messages.

cfoutput

Used to display the result of a query, or other operation.

cfparam

Is used to test for the existence, and data type, of a variable. A default value can be specified, to create the variable if it doesn't already exist.

cfquery

The <cfquery> tag encloses SQL statements, which are passed to the specified data source.

cfscript

> This tag encloses a set of CFScript statements. CFScript uses ColdFusion functions, expressions and operators, but has a syntax designed for those more comfortable with JavaScript or similar. Flash developers experienced in ActionScript may find this useful.

cfsearch

> The `<cfsearch>` tag is used to search against data that is indexed in Verity collections. The Verity collections must have been created and populated prior to the search.

cfselect

> When used from within a `<cfform>`, `<cfselect>` produces a drop-down list-box.

cfset

> Used to define a variable, with a name and a value or expression.

cfsetting

> Controls a variety ColdFusion settings, but Flash developers with recurrently use it to prevent white space when passing data (using `<cfsetting enableCFoutputOnly="Yes">`).

cfslider

> Creates a slider control element within a `<cfform>`, these are often used for volume controls or similar. There are a multitude of options that can control the look and feel of the slider.

cftextinput

> Places a single-line text entry box in a `<cfform>`, unlike a HTML text entry box there are a wealth of client-side validation options.

cftree

> Another `<cfform>` tag that creates a tree control element. Tree structures are a way of structuring database information.

cfupdate

> Used to update records, or rows, within a database data source.

Index

The index is arranged hierarchically, in alphabetical order, with symbols preceding the letter A. Many second-level entries also occur as first-level entries. This is to ensure that users will find the information they require however they choose to search for it.

DESIGNER TO DESIGNER™

The New Masters Series – Advanced – *Showing it*

Where can you find out what inspires the top designers? Where can you learn the secrets of their design techniques? New Masters is the ultimate showcase for graphics pioneers from around the world, where they write about what influences their design and teach the cutting-edge effects that have made them famous.

The Studio Series – Intermediate – *Doing it*

The essence of the studio is the collective – a gathering of independent designers who try out ideas and explore techniques in finer detail. Each book in the studio series assumes that the reader has learned the fundamentals of the topic area. They want to grow their skills with particular tools to a higher level, while at the same time absorbing the hard-won creative experience of a group of design experts.

The Foundation Series – Starting out – *Learning it*

Every web designer benefits from a strong foundation to firmly establish their understanding of a new technology or tool. The friends of ED foundation series deconstructs a subject into step by step lessons – stand alone design recipes that build together into a complete model project. Practical, intuitive – a must-have resource.

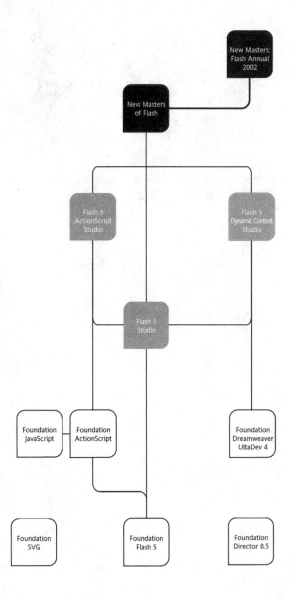

freshfroot
motion web mindfood

oo

stripes

seams & f

warhol

seven day itch

freshfroot is where friends of ED fertilise the designer mind. It's a visual search engine, a daily creative resource and a hard-to-kick addiction. Everyday the froot pickers, along with a select band of celebrity guest editors, search through the web's good, bad and ugly to bring you the diamonds – categorised, critiqued and instantly searchable. freshfroot rejects the usual search engine criteria in favour of daily themes that pull together stylistically similar works and images to provide the rock solid creative resource to complement the technical resource on offer in our books.

freshfroot is the place where Mike Cina, James Paterson, Golan Levin, Mumbleboy, Brendan Dawes and many other new and future masters go to share their inspirations and be inspired. It's the place everyone goes when they need fresh ideas fast. Submit your own found or created masterpieces, spout your opinions and share ideas in the discussion forum. Get involved, be inspired and escape the mediocre.

my froot

my froot

sheet

archive

a‑z   a-z

23   date

?   keyword

search for: inspiration

james pate

forward

hybrid   revolution

urban

playground

brendan dawes

Be inspired.

freshfroot#1 created by ross mawd
simian superstar, new master, friend and froot editor. we love you

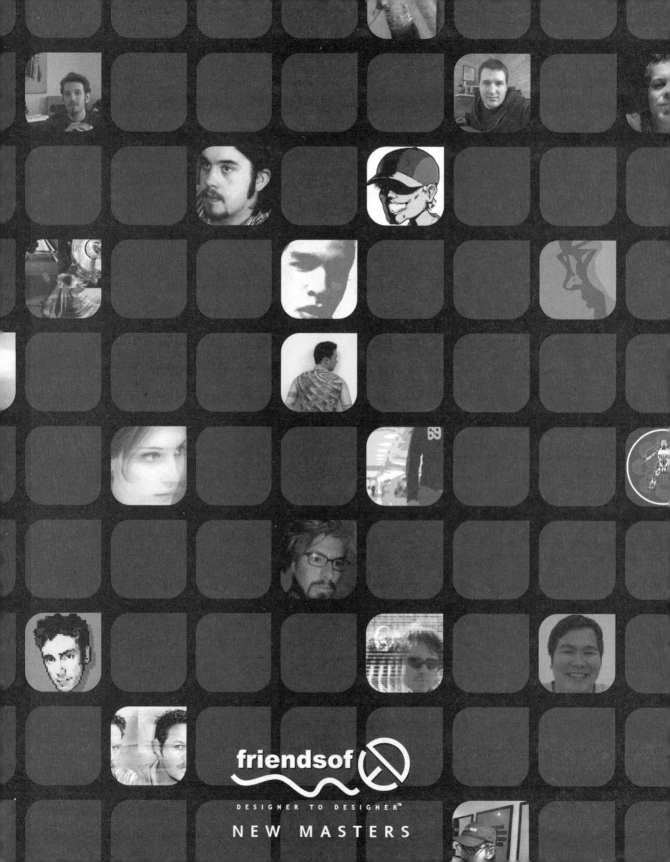

NEW MASTERS OF PHOTOSH

GET SERIOUS.
OUT NOW

friendsof

DESIGNER TO DESIGNER™

NEW MASTERS